MEMORIES

JULIAN HUXLEY, 1965
Photo by Janet Stone

SIR JULIAN _Sorrell_ HUXLEY

Memories

London
GEORGE ALLEN AND UNWIN LTD
RUSKIN HOUSE   MUSEUM STREET

FIRST PUBLISHED IN 1970

© *George Allen & Unwin Ltd, 1970*
ISBN 0 04 925006 X

PRINTED IN GREAT BRITAIN
in 13 on 14 pt Bembo
BY W & J MACKAY & CO LTD
CHATHAM, KENT

Preface

Sitting here at my desk, between the tall windows of the library of our late Regency house close to the open spaces of Hampstead Heath, I am wondering how to introduce this book, which I began nearly four years ago, when I was seventy-nine. John Collier's portrait of my Huxley grandfather presides over the mantelpiece, his eyes gravely probing the scene of my literary labours three-quarters of a century since I saw him in the flesh, yet one which, in many ways, he continues to affect. My books surround me, reminders of my many-sided professional career, as well as curios and works of art from all over the world, collected on my travels. This room has been my workshop as a writer for the last twenty-five years: it has become, like a well-worn suit of clothes, a part of myself.

I was born with great advantages, genetic and cultural – but there were disadvantages too. I inherited my Arnold grandfather's instability of temperament, as well as my Huxley grandfather's determination and dedication to scientific truth. These conflicting elements, added to my own particular character, proved sometimes difficult to cope with and made me prone to so-called breakdowns. I was inwardly timid, but liked getting my own way; unsure of myself, I was often afflicted by a sense of guilt in not living up to my parents' expectations. These certainly spurred me on to whatever success I may have achieved in life, and fed my ambition. Meanwhile my enjoyment of nature and natural beauty, coupled with a sense of poetic wonder, provided a refuge from my own restlessness.

For, looking back, I seem to have been possessed by a demon, driving me into every sort of activity, and impatient to finish anything I had begun: an impatience which, I fear, may have pressed annoyingly those of my colleagues who preferred a more systematic approach. I have been accused of dissipating my energies in too many directions, yet it was assuredly this diversity of interests which made me what I am, and incidentally prepared me for my work at UNESCO, which I shall deal with in a second volume.

I am deeply grateful to my many friends, both for their affection and their loyalty, proved on many occasions, and for the wide range of subjects they helped me to understand and enjoy.

To Aldous, friend as well as brother, I must pay special tribute.

Conversation with him was a delight, a sharpening of wits with a familiar and companionable mind, which his prodigious knowledge made stimulating and fruitful. He was seven years my junior, which meant that in childhood and youth we were too far apart to share many interests. Later, in our young manhood, we found each other and I soon learnt to admire his penetrating wit and omnivorous reading. If he was sometimes withdrawn and seemingly remote, it could be that he was revolving some new problem in his mind, or simply because he was stranded in some far depth of thought, passive and silent. He was infinitely gentle and undemanding, especially in the last years of his life.

Last but not least, I pay tribute to my dear wife, Juliette, who, in spite of initial difficulties, made her home in a foreign country; always supported me against carping critics, though fair enough to see their point; accompanied me on many of my travels, adding her own personal awareness to enrich our experience; enlarged our circle of friends; bore patiently with my humours and faithfully tended me through my periodic bouts of depression; and finally has been of the greatest help in the writing of these memoirs, with her clear memory and zeal in ferreting out details of our joint history. Most important of all, her love has helped me to acquire inner peace and understanding, and has given me a refuge through our fifty years of married life.

In conclusion, I feel privileged to have been able to participate in so many interesting activities. In this era of over-specialization, there are too few polymaths about, and one reason for embarking on these memoirs is to show that embracing inquisitiveness and widespread curiosity can bring their own rewards.

If I am to be remembered, I hope it will not be primarily for my specialized scientific work, but as a generalist; one to whom, enlarging Terence's words, nothing human, and nothing in external nature, was alien.

Julian Huxley.

Contents

Illustrations

CHAPTER I

My Parents and Early Years

My father was on the top of a horse-bus, watching the festivities for Queen Victoria's Jubilee on the night of June 22, 1887, when I was born in the house of my Aunt Mary, my mother's elder sister, at the corner of Chapel Street and Grosvenor Place.

My parents met at Oxford about 1880, while he was still an undergraduate at Balliol, and she one of the first batch of girl undergraduates at Somerville College. They fell in love almost at once, but had to wait several years to be able to marry. He worked as an assistant to Professor Sedgwick at St Andrews before he could qualify as a Classical Master at Charterhouse; the pay was pretty low, but just enough to live on.

My father was a kindly man, full of almost boyish fun. His special gift was teaching, which he did in a way all his life, even as Editor of the *Cornhill Magazine* and Reader for the publishers, Smith and Elder, for he would never return a manuscript without carefully annotating and correcting it, so that the writer of a rejected article or book felt encouraged rather than dejected.

He took his position as T. H. Huxley's eldest surviving son very seriously; he wrote the Life of his father with great loyalty and reverence and, as I and my brothers grew up, encouraged us to live up to T.H.H.'s achievements.

T.H.H. was indeed remarkable, a rebel Victorian, pro-Darwin and anti-clerical, who coined the word *agnostic* to describe his own religious position, as one not prepared to accept orthodox or indeed any dogmatic views on the origin and destiny of man in the absence of scientific evidence. He preferred to remain a free-thinker in Hume's sense, refusing to accept the existence of an all-powerful and omniscient God, religious miracles or personal immortality, until they were properly validated. He rejected the term *atheist* for the same reason; the non-existence of God could not be scientifically proved.

Like Darwin, he owed much of his success to his experiences on a voyage – in his case, as surgeon-naturalist aboard H.M.S. *Rattlesnake*, which was surveying the east coast of Australia. This cruise not only led him to his future wife, who was staying in Sydney, but introduced him to Australia and Melanesian aborigines (so kindling a life-long interest in social anthropology). It also introduced him to many strange forms of invertebrate life, like Portuguese men-of-war and phosphorescent chains of social sea-squirts, floating in the tropical waters. His studies of these creatures, especially his demonstration that the two-layered construction of jellyfish and polyps was comparable to the two-layered stage of the early mammalian embryo, earned him a Fellowship of the Royal Society at the early age of 25.

He had a remarkable artistic gift, though without any professional training. It is revealed in his anatomical drawings, almost as delicate as Leonardo da Vinci's, and in his pencil sketches and water-colours of the scenery and the savages he saw during the voyage.[1]

He used this gift all his life, illustrating many of his letters to his family with comic drawings.

He enjoyed good literature, both German and English, and developed a masterly style of his own; he was a great writer as well as an outstanding scientist.

He was also, in the true sense of the word, a puritan. He often called on the famous writer, George Eliot, whom he greatly admired, yet never allowed his wife to accompany him, for George Eliot was 'living in sin' with a man who was not her legal husband.

---

[1] For his journey and some of his drawings and paintings, see T. H. Huxley's *Diary of the Voyage of H.M.S. Rattlesnake*, miraculously discovered among a jumble of bills and papers after his wife's death, and published, edited by myself, by Chatto and Windus in 1935.

After his return and the many years of struggle for a remunerative position, which came only long after his recognition as a notable scientist, he achieved a brilliant career, which has been much written about. But he also suffered from depressive breakdowns, at least two of which are mentioned in his letters.

His portraits reveal the stern expression of his 'public face', and hide the adorable 'Pater' he was to his family, enjoying fun and jokes. He had three sons and five daughters and, as head of the family, delighted in being as far removed from his public self as possible. Whenever his travels broke the warm continuity of their home life he kept in touch with his wife and the children by letters.

He was certainly a great example to me, and his life and writings influenced my own thinking in many fields.

My father Leonard was T.H.H.'s second son. He enjoyed life – whether at work or play, gardening or on the tennis court, skating, rambling or climbing mountains, botanizing, listening to music or entertaining his friends. Though he had great sorrows in his life, which affected him deeply, I never knew him depressed or illtempered. He was not, in this, a typical Huxley, nor was his brother Harry, the surgeon. It seems as if the Huxley genes skipped a generation to assert their particular characteristics, which are perhaps best defined as temperamental, in his grandchildren.

There was plenty of temperament on my mother's side too. She was the second daughter of Tom Arnold, second son of Dr Thomas Arnold of Rugby. Tom, a brilliant man who had taken a First in Greats at Oxford, became discontented with smug Victorian England, and decided to try farming in New Zealand.[1] This was not a success, for he had nothing of the horny-handed pioneer in his make-up. However, Governor Sorell, of Tasmania, hearing that there was a handsome Oxford-educated young man available in the neighbouring colony, invited him to become Inspector of Schools for Tasmania. He soon met Governor Sorell's daughter, Julia, a great beauty, but given to fits of temper. (She was painted by the artist-poisoner Wainwright, who was then expiating his

---

[1] Thinly disguised, he was the main figure in his friend Arthur Clough's curious poem in English hexameters, 'The Bothie of Tober-na-Vuoilich'.

crimes in the Governor's prison. The painting is a sugary Victorian work, clearly not a good likeness, but evidence of her elegant good looks; I donated it to the Tasmanian Museum years ago, when it was making a collection illustrating the colony's early years.)

There is a tantalizing notebook of Tom Arnold's courtship of Julia Sorell, mentioning the dates of his many visits at the Governor's mansion, with a succinct account of his expenditure, mostly on pairs of white gloves! His good looks and fresh intelligence soon won the girl's heart, and they were married at Hobart, the colony's capital. It was there that their first child was born, my Aunt Mary, who later became Mrs Humphry Ward. Though nominally a member of the Anglican church, at one time he had openly declared his sympathy with the revolutionary movements on the continent, and with secularist systems of education. But he lacked toughness and needed an authority as firm as that of his rigidly disciplinarian but much-loved father. He began to doubt his free-thinking views. He considered that the Church of England too readily tolerated the social inequalities at home, and began to hear 'voices' commanding him to accept Catholicism. These were reinforced by reading the life of St Brigit, which he came across accidentally on one of his journeys of inspection, and he wrote to Cardinal Newman saying that he wished to become a Roman Catholic.

During the ceremony Julia, a staunch Protestant and very angry about his conversion, collected a basket of stones from her yard, walked across to the nearby Chapel where he was being formally received into the ranks of Catholicism, and smashed the windows with this protesting ammunition. Even this failed to change his heart, though his conversion changed his prospects. Protestant Tasmania could not accept a Catholic Inspector of its schools, and he lost his job.

So the family returned to England in 1857. For seven years he taught at the Oratory School in Birmingham under Cardinal Newman; however, a difference of opinion about a prize (an unorthodox German book on theology) which Arnold wanted to give to one of the boys, caused a serious rupture between these two men of deep religious conviction.

As a result, Arnold decided to return to the Protestant Church. Taking his family, by now augmented to seven children (my mother being then three years old), he went back to Oxford, where he made quite a good living by lecturing on history and by private tutoring. This was perhaps the happiest time for them all, the parents sharing the same religion and the intellectual life of the university. My mother, called Julia after her mother (I was called Julian for the same reason) was one of Lewis Carroll's favourite 'little girls'. She was often photographed by him in fancy dress, and was presented with a signed copy of *Alice in Wonderland*, which I still possess. By the time she became a student of Somerville, my Aunt Mary, the first-born child, was too old to enter, and pursued her education under the guidance of her father.

But Tom Arnold's allegiance to the Anglican Church was fragile. He liked to keep in touch with his Catholic friends, preferably when his wife was not present. On one occasion she had gone to London, but returned earlier than expected, to find her husband entertaining two priests at dinner. Legend has it that she flew into a great tantrum, and the party broke up under a shower of plates.

On the eve of being appointed Professor of Anglo-Saxon, my tormented grandfather once again, and for the last time, gave in to the irresistible call of Rome, thereby throwing the family into great financial straits, for in those days no Catholic could hold a teaching post at Oxford. My mother used to tell us how she and her sister Mary had to go to parties in turn, as there was only one pair of best shoes and one evening dress for the two of them. He finally went to teach at the Catholic University in Dublin, and married again after the death of his beloved Julia.

Mary, the eldest girl, married Humphry Ward, then Fellow of Brasenose and later art critic of *The Times*. She was a person of great intellectual endowment and, in her late thirties, wrote her best known novel, *Robert Elsmere*. Not surprisingly, with her unstable father in mind, it was about a rector in her beloved Surrey, beset with religious doubts, a remarkable study of the religious turmoil, aftermath of the Tractarian movement and its bitter disputes over creeds and rituals, still raging in Oxford and indeed perturbing all England. Through her hero she expressed her own doubts of the validity of the miracles recorded in the New Testament, as well as those ascribed to later Catholic saints – how many really occurred, and what was the value of the testimony of those said to have been present? So many people, then as now, *wanted* to believe in miracles, even impossible ones, as seen in our own times when a huge gathering of pilgrims claimed that, at Fatima in Portugal, the sun had approached the earth, and then receded to its proper station!

In the end, Robert Elsmere resigns from his living but remains a believer in Jesus as an outstanding moralist, an apostle of love and forgiveness, but not of damnation for all sinners and non-Christians (that was added by Paul and the early Fathers of the Church). He ends by starting a vaguely Christian mission in the London slums.

My Aunt Mary behaved in much the same way. She attended church, but rejected belief in miracles, and helped to found the Passmore Edward Settlement – now called the Mary Ward Settlement – which was especially concerned with poor children in London.

The book had brought her fame and lasting rewards, and by the time my mother married, Mrs Humphry Ward was a famous writer and hostess in Belgravia.

And it was on that Jubilee night of fireworks and festivities that I was born in her large house, my mother's second child. Her first had died a few weeks after birth, causing great sorrow, and I was held very preciously, guarded from all dangers and given more than my share of love, attention and spoiling, until my brother Trev was born.

I adored my mother. How can I describe her? She wore pince-nez, had great charm and a tremendous sense of humour – I remember the way she used to throw back her head and explode with laughter when amused – but could pass from gay to grave as the mood took her.

Black-haired and dark-eyed, she had inherited Thomas Arnold's blunt nose, while Aunt Mary had come by her aquiline features and fair complexion from her grandfather's beautiful Cornish wife, Mary Penrose. It was this Cornish connection that made the Trevelyans our distant cousins, and prompted my parents to give my younger brother the Cornish name, Trevenen.

Her steady gaze was truth-compelling, but full of love, even when she had to reprimand us. But how can my poor words depict her? The best I can do is to quote the last stanza of Wordsworth's 'Perfect Woman', which I never read without thinking of my mother:

> And now I see with eye serene
> The very pulse of the machine;
> A being breathing thoughtful breath,
> A traveller betwixt life and death;
> The reason firm, the tempered will,
> Endurance, foresight, strength and skill;
> A perfect woman, nobly plann'd
> To warn, to comfort, and command;
> And yet a spirit still, and bright
> With something of angelic light.

Yet this omits her sense of fun, her gay participation in simple games, her enjoyment of acting, her infectious vitality and love of life.

As befitted an Arnold she was a great lover of literature and, long before I was twelve, instilled in me her passion for poetry, especially Wordsworth's and her uncle Matt's. She had a real vocation for and deep love of teaching, strengthened by her admiration for her grandfather, Thomas Arnold of Rugby.

In 1901, with her own and my father's slender capital and some bank loans, she founded a girls' school near Godalming, Prior's Field, which is still in full swing and now has over 160 students. After her too early death, at forty-six, many women who had been her pupils told me what inspiration they had gained from her teaching and character, and how uncannily understanding she had been with all their personal troubles.

She was the pivot of our family life, and used to organize picnic lunches in the Surrey countryside, and charades and all sorts of round games at night. She read to me – and Trev in due course – in the early evenings (as she did regularly to the Prior's Field girls later), first nursery rhymes and fairy stories, then a little history and poetry. Whenever possible, she would accompany my father and me on our walks, and the two of them did a great deal to instil a love of nature into me, partly Wordsworthian, partly scientific.

She kept a little notebook where she recorded various incidents of my early life, along with my weight and growth. She gave it to me when she was dying of cancer, in the dreary November of 1908. I still can't read its farewell message without tears: 'My dear, dear son, You have brought me only joy since you were laid in my arms, a little downy bundle, that June day in 1887. It is very hard to leave you all – but after these weeks of quiet thought, I know that all life is one – and that I am only going into another room "of the sounding labour-house vast of Being".[1] Use your great gifts of mind and heart unselfishly. You will do much for the world. My darling, how I love you. Your Mother.'

This little worn leather book gives a moving picture of her loving care for her children, and her deep sense of religion – not orthodox Christianity, but rather a pantheistic trust in the essential goodness of the universe, coupled with a sense of wonder.

This sense of wonder I have inherited, and though I cannot believe in the essential goodness of things as a whole, I have stressed the fact that evolution, including that of our own species, is essentially *progressive*. In spite of biological extinctions, human wars and cultural setbacks, and though today we are on the verge of a precipice, faced with the tragic threats of atomic destruction, over-population and total vulgarization, I still believe that we shall survive and, after a time of trouble, continue to advance towards a saner and more rewarding way of life.

My mother's notebook reveals her preoccupation for my welfare, and also what a strange, precocious child I was,

[1] From Matthew Arnold's poem 'Rugby Chapel'.

temperamental and full of resentment of my baby brother Trev, two-and-a-half years younger than I, who naturally absorbed much of my mother's attention. Like most elder brothers, I was jealous of my rival or supplanter, and pushed him about and slapped him. I must have had a sense of guilt about it, for she records that I said to him, after being punished for one of these outbursts: 'Did I hurt you, Baby? I am *de*sulated!' in a theatrical tone. However, I repeated the treatment a few days later, and said I wouldn't mind if he were to die 'because he is so very tiresome'!

When I was four, my eleven-year-old cousin Janet Ward wrote this letter to her elder sister, Dorothy:

Nov. 1st 1891

Dearest Dots,

. . . . . .

Julian is an awful fiend and is always scratching & poking & punching Baby so much that he often don't get any jam for tea. A day or two ago it came to a climax: after being read to in bed in the morning (I always go into Aunt Judy's room, mornings) he asked for some milk and drank it in bed. Soon a lot of milk trickled onto the sheet, & being told he was a pig, he promptly emptied all the rest of the milk onto the bed on purpose, whereupon he was told he wasn't to have any jam for breakfast, whereupon he seized the loose knob of the bed-post and sent it within a hair's breadth of Aunt Judy's face, whereupon he was told that 'Mummy would have to tell Daddy about him when he came down before breakfast school' (you know what that means!); whereupon he went into the nursery and scratched Baby's face so hard that it bled, whereupon Aunt Judy came in and told him that U.L. [Uncle Leonard] would have to whip him much harder now. Sure enough, as soon as 'Daddy' came in he went straight up to the night nursery & spanked him. Nurse asked him afterwards if he cried & he said saucily 'No, I beared it!'

No more news.

Love to people
Your affectionate Jan.

My Huxley grandfather, however, took an amused view of my

behaviour. One day, when I was about four, I deliberately walked on the wet grass after being told not to (he had been watering the garden that was one of his great consolations on his retirement at Eastbourne). He said to my parents: 'I like that chap! I like the way he looks you straight in the face and disobeys you! He looked straight at me as much as to say, "What do you mean by ordering me about?" and deliberately walked on the grass.'

This arrogance was, I suppose, a compensation for my sense of loss when I ceased to be the sole recipient of my mother's love and attention. It drove me to assert my 'freedom' by getting up at five in the morning and peeing in the corner of my night-nursery instead of in the proper receptacle. One morning my parents caught me in the act. I don't remember what punishment they allotted me – my humiliation lay in having been found out.

I was fond of exciting ploys, like staging an accident with a toy train and my little Dutch dolls, and was already in love with fine phrases, as I said: 'Look, the poor dollies are all lying on the ground crying for death!'

By the time I was four, in mid-1891, I was deeply interested in animals and plants. 'Why do all live things have natures?' I asked. Another time I said to Mother, 'Do come and see this *precious* spider.' I was very sensitive to nature's moods, and once, when rebuked for some absurd fabrication, replied, 'Well, of course, the sun's shining and I always *exaggerate* a little when it's a fine day.'

In a letter written to my father this same year, T.H.H. says: 'Julian evidently inclines to biology – How I should like to train him!'

My mother was teaching me to read, and records that I loved the lessons, and mastered even quite big words within four months. I discovered for myself that 2 plus 1 makes 3 and so on up to 16, and could read numbers up to 30 when only four and a half. Later, when I was nearly five, I read Kingsley's *The Water Babies* and was much intrigued by the picture in the book representing my grandfather and Professor Owen examining a bottled water-baby with magnifying glasses. I had by then learnt to write, and sent this letter to T.H.H.

Dear Grandpater have you
seen a Water-baby?
Did you put it in a bottle?
Did it Wonder if it could
get out? Can I See it Some
day?

　　　　　　　Your Loving
　　　　　　　　JULIAN.

Almost by return, and in printed lettering very different from his usual hasty and almost illegible scrawl, he answered with the letter reproduced on the next two pages:

Trev alternated between charming docility and sudden violence. I remember vividly one of our visits to Eastbourne; when Gran' pater came in at the dining-room door, Trev, then about four years old, rushed out from beneath the table, shouting fiercely, 'I'm a lion, I'm a lion!' and bit him in the leg. Gran'pater took it remarkably calmly, and merely said, 'Don't do that again.' Later, my grandmother told us that Trev had actually bitten through his trousers, and that some cloth fibres were embedded in the gash on his calf.

In June 1895 came the news of Gran'pater's death. I remember being seized with a terrible impulse to giggle (which I believe is common with children in such cases), and being much ashamed of it.

After his death, his many grandchildren frequently visited the

March 24
1892.

My dear Julian

I never could make
Sure about that Water
Baby. I have seen
Babies in water and
Babies in bottles; but
the Baby in the water
was not in a bottle and
the Baby in the bottle was
not in water.

My friend who wrote the
story of the Water Baby,
was a very kind man
and very clever. Perhaps
he thought I could
see as much in the
water as he did —
There are some people

who see a great deal
and some who see very
little in the same things.

When you grow up
I dare say you will be
one of the great-deal sort
and see things more

wonderful than Water
Babies where other folks
can see nothing.

Give my best love to
Daddy & Mamm, and
Trevenen - Grandmoo
is a little better but not
up yet -

Ever

Your loving

Grandpapa -

house at Eastbourne to which he and Gran'moo – Moo was my grandfather's nickname for his wife – had retired in 1890. Trev and I enjoyed it enormously: my dear grandmother with lace bonnet and shawl, the Alma Tadema engraving of Daniel in the lions' den, the amusing children's books, and a game we invented of racing marbles, each with its own name, round a solitaire board to see which stayed on longest.

Trev and I began to explore the beach and cliffs and the downs on Beachy Head, so wisely bought by the Eastbourne Corporation as an open space for ever. Later, we extended our walks to the Belle Toute Lighthouse, past the sheer and even overhanging 300-foot parts of the white chalk cliffs, interlayered with black flints, and down to Birling Gap, where one could walk down to the shingly beach. We would go far out on the reefs at low tide and see the great fleshy 'dahlia' sea-anemones, while below the cliffs we caught prawns for our tea.

One curious memory remains of this period. When I was about twelve, the eminent politician and literary man John Morley, who had become a great friend of T. H. Huxley, came to call on my grandmother, and took Trev and me on a long walk over the downs. We had tea at a little village, and here he recited the whole of one of Browning's long poems – I think it was 'The Ballad of Hervé Riel'. Here was another example of the all-round capacities of eminent Victorians.

By the time I was eight I began to be interested in birds. We had a bird-table, and there I learnt to differentiate the tits. Blue and great were easy enough, but it gave me great pleasure to 'learn' marsh and coal tits, one with all-black crown, the other with a white stripe down the nape. They especially loved sunflower heads, and sometimes even came into the dining-room for the seeds. And one day, down Charterhouse Hill, I saw a queer little bird, blue-grey above and russet below: it was just a common nuthatch, but to me it was a revelation.

Meanwhile the sight of the gold and silver pheasants bred by Mr Davies, the elderly Charterhouse master who was Trev's god-father, gave me my first vision of the improbable plumage and glorious brightness of some exotic birds. I had yet to see our British kingfisher – whose azure flight was to leave me dazzled and almost unbelieving.

One winter, after reading about Eskimoes and their habits, I built a miniature snow igloo on the edge of Charterhouse Green and illuminated it with a candle. I have never forgotten the little snow-house gleaming so romantically at the top of the lonely hill, and years later built a much larger illuminated igloo for my boys when wintering at Les Diablerets.

My first conscious memory dates from when I was four. I was being taken for a walk by the nursemaid. I was dressed in knicker-bockers with a fawn-coloured coat, and on my head was a red tam-o'-shanter – you know, the round cap with a little tail pro-truding from its centre, like the remains of a cut umbilical cord. And then out of the hawthorn hedge there hopped a fat toad. What a creature, with its warty skin, its big eyes bulging up, and its awkward movements! That comic toad helped to determine my career as a scientific naturalist.

But I must have been interested in nature even before that. In the little book where my mother chronicled my infant life, I found an entry to this effect, when I was barely four:

'There was a hailstorm today. Julian was watching through the window and suddenly said 'the little balls go hop, hop, hop, like little kanga-woos . . .'

Then there were the walks. The one I liked best was along the bank of the River Wey, entered and left by turnstiles. These were exciting in themselves; so were the big marsh horse-tails near the far end. Father told us something about their being related to huge trees that lived millions of years ago, and helped to make coal where they fell and died. But we didn't understand – not really; we were more interested to discover that we could pull their jointed stems apart, leaving a little spiky crown that served to enclose the base of the joint above. We began to learn the names of common flowers like the marsh marigold, which some people call kingcups, in the wet places, and the earliest flower of spring, the coltsfoot, bright yellow on the bank, with new species added every month.

Certainly a large number of my early experiences had to do with natural history. I am talking now of the time we lived at old Laleham, a house on the Peperharrow Road in the Wey valley. My mother chose the name Laleham because the village of Laleham-on-Thames had been the original home of her family. It was not until 1893 that we moved up the hill to new Laleham, built for us by Fred Waller (who married Jessie, eldest daughter of T.H.H.) architect-in-charge of Gloucester Cathedral. He also built North House in St John's Wood for the Hon. John Collier and my Aunt Ethel, youngest and favourite of T.H.H.'s girls, familiarly known as the Dragon by all the Huxley clan; and my grandparents' East-bourne house, named Hodeslea, after the traditional home of the Huxleys in mediaeval Cheshire, *Hod's lea* or meadow, later corrupted into *Huxley*. There is still a Huxley Hall near Chester, a fine Tudor farmhouse.

But to revert to old Laleham. A very early memory is of a wasp that lit on my hand. I kept absolutely still, filled with a mixture of excitement and fear, until it flew off again. Another is of standing in the front porch with the rain pouring outside, and saying over and over again, 'I hope it goes on, I hope it goes on . . .' This of course was on the theory that whoever or whatever controls events is essentially malignant, and will do the opposite of what one asks.

Not long afterwards, I was given a copy of Furneaux's *The Outdoor World*, which had on its cover the picture of a little boy looking outwards at the world of nature: I felt I had looked just like that when I tried to cheat destiny about the rain. Furneaux's book further aroused my interest in natural history – plants and animals, fossils and geography.

Another time, a young Frenchman who was living with us – I imagine as a paying guest – made me a train out of match-boxes and cotton-reels, the match-boxes actually loaded with real coal. Why that was so enthralling I didn't know at the time. I realize now that the pretence of grown-upness, the mimicking of adult behaviour, fascinates every child.

CHAPTER II

Early Boyhood

WHEN I was five I went to have some elementary schooling down the road with a Miss Daw. I remember nothing of it except the absolute misery of not being able to understand the process of subtraction as expounded by Miss Daw – carrying from one column to the next.

Next door to us lived the Petillauds. He taught French at Charterhouse (and once created a sensation by appearing in a dinner jacket and scarlet bow tie). Popping in and out of their house, I learnt that the French for potatoes was *pommes de terre*, and proceeded to impart this valuable piece of knowledge to our treasured Mrs Mills, who cooked and kept house for us. I was quite hurt that she wasn't in the least interested, and merely told me to get along out of the kitchen.

One thing I remember very clearly. Behind the house was a little glade in Charterhouse copse, very beautiful and very secret. I had the idea that it was part of Fairyland, and used to frequent it whenever I could, solitary within its magic circle – my first mystical experience.

The copse was indeed a wonderful place – a real copsewood, cut every seven years for poles, steep and full of primroses in spring. We used to go out and pick great bunches of them; they were sent up to London for some charity. I was early initiated into the mystery of there being two kinds of flower, pin and thrum, pin with the knobbed pistil in the flower's mouth and the anthers half-way down the corolla tube; and thrum the other way round, to cut down the risk of inbreeding by self-pollination. So I was told, but didn't really understand the mechanism until at Oxford I read Darwin's book on the subject of cross- and self-fertilization of plants.

Another thing I recall about the primroses, besides their delicate scent, was that they often had tiny black insects crawling over them. These rejoiced in the unforgettable name of thrips.

My mother used to read to us, sometimes a chapter from the Bible, but usually from story-books. But I learned to read by myself when I was four. Among my favourite books were *The Water Babies*, by Charles Kingsley, *The Story Without an End*, and various fairy tales. These included Grimm and Hans Andersen, Andrew Lang's series, *Celtic Fairy Tales*, Kingsley's *The Heroes*, and *Old English Fairy Tales*. This last volume had an appendix warning that any child who read it three times would go to sleep for a hundred years. I *did* read it three times, and went to my mother, very worried. Of course she comforted me and I went on reading. Indeed, I kept on enjoying fairy tales till I was twelve or more.

My first acquaintance with punning riddles came from a house-maid one spring morning, when she said things were dangerous on the road, 'Because the hawthorn is shooting and the bulrushes out'. I had to ask what shooting was, and discovered it meant sprouting.

In 1893 we moved into the new Laleham, close to Charterhouse. My Uncle Fred had built it in bogus neo-Gothic style, with an acre of garden containing a tennis-lawn, a nice rose-garden and a rockery, where my father could indulge his passion for exercise and gardening.

Our nursery was on the top floor, with a view of a hill towards Shalford which we called Horses Hill from the shape of the trees on it. The nursery boasted a rocking-horse with real rockers, the size of a pony. We managed to get four boys on it at once, two on top and two under its belly, taking great care not to get our fingers pinched. The nursery windows were fine outlets for paper darts, and we competed to see who could throw them furthest across the tennis court.

Aldous was born at new Laleham in 1899, and Margaret in 1899. All I remember of their births was a sense of something very strange going on in the house.

Being now too far away from Miss Daw's, Trev and I were sent to a governess at the house of Mr Parry, another Charterhouse master, where Aldous in due course followed suit. The lady was rather deaf, and this led to an immortal remark by Aldous: 'Deaf and dumb they may be, but contradict they must', referring to governesses in general.

Later we had our own German governess, Fräulein Frieda Salkowski from Königsberg. She had elaborate schemes for teaching ancient history, and made us draw up complicated tables of dates with coloured lettering, different colours for capitals. I have never forgotten her mnemonic for the date of the foundation of Rome: 'Sieben Fünf Drei, Schlüpfte Rome aus dem Ei' – which we anglicized as 'Seven-hundred and fifty-three, Rome hatched out of the E.G.G.'.

She also took us for walks, collecting and identifying flowers. Natural history continued to fascinate me. In the water-butt were young mosquitoes, the larvae flipping about and breathing through a spreading crown of tail filaments in the surface film. There were also the pupae, bulgy with a short tail, breathing through two horns on top of their helmet-like heads, and some sort of little red worm (I now know it as *Lumbriculus*) that propelled itself by throwing its whole body into contortions. And once, in a pit outside the cellar, we found a Devil's Coach-horse, rearing its tail forward over its head in a most alarming fashion.

I went on learning my field botany – I remember especially my first sight of the great white Convolvulus. It seemed to me wonderful that an ordinary English hedge could produce such splendid trumpet-bells; even today they give me a special thrill.

For a time, Roger and Tom Eckersley, elder sons of my Aunt Rachel (third daughter of T.H.H.), came to stay while their mother and engineer father were in Mexico. Roger was full of charm, and later rose to a high post in the B.B.C. Programme Department, smoothing down disgruntled performers. Tom was matter-of-fact and scientific, with a special gift for mathematics, later to become an F.R.S. Roger would tell tall stories of adventures in Mexico. One was of their encountering a wolf. 'Did we, Roger?' asked Tom. Another was of their climbing some enormous volcano, to which Tom's comment was the same: '*Did* we, Roger?' Clearly

Roger's tales were fantasies, but they certainly added to the gaiety of the household.

Once the whole family was mobilized to play scenes from 'The Pied Piper of Hamelin', organized by my mother. I have memories of painted cardboard rats in large numbers, affixed to bricks for their appearance on the stage of Charterhouse Hall, before a packed audience of boys and masters. I was about eight and cast for the part of the lame boy who is left behind when all the other children follow the piper into the magic cave. Was I priggish or vain? In any case, I remember relishing the applause when I was left pathetically alone on the stage, leaning on my crutch.

I fear I was certainly vain. When my grandfather was photographed with me on his knee in 1894, I was bitterly disappointed at the selected picture (which later appeared in his *Life and Letters*), for I thought I looked much nicer in one of the other proofs.

I was sent as a day-boy to Hillside when I was ten. It was a prep. school run by Mr Gidley Robinson, and situated conveniently close to Laleham, on the edge of a steep slope leading down to Farncombe. We wore strange little circular caps striped black and red. There was another prep. school in the neighbourhood, Sylvester's, with similar caps, but black and blue. Whenever we passed the Sylvesterites out for a walk, we would hold our noses and put out our tongues.

When my sister Margaret was born in 1899, I was sent to sleep for a few nights at Hillside, my first and only experience of a schoolboy dorm. It upset me, and I learnt that such experiences could have physiological effects; there was a nasty taste in my mouth in the morning.

For some reason I was not allowed to cycle until I was twelve. (Trev was allowed to at ten, and Aldous even younger). What a joy it was! After one afternoon on Hillside playing-field, I felt perfectly at ease with the machine, and next day went on a twelve-mile ride along country lanes, through Shackleford and Peperharrow. The joy of being master of a new dimension and the glory of coasting down a long hill were unforgettable. In those days, motor-cars were virtually non-existent; up to 1895, they were limited to 5 m.p.h., and had to be preceded by a man with a red flag! The roads of south-west Surrey were all mine for my delight. So far as I know, H. C. Beeching is the only man to have preserved this pleasure in verse, in his Boy's Song: 'Going Downhill on a Bicycle'.

In the 1960s I remember Aldous recalling the same joys and lamenting the fact that boys of the present generation are virtually cut off from this carefree recreation, with the roads dangerously crowded with cars and trucks.

I soon explored all the heathlands and commons of south-west Surrey, from the top of Hindhead on the south to the Hogsback on the north, and from Frensham in the west to Vackery Pond in the east. I discovered cyclable paths across common land, including one which led ten miles from near Milford to Little Frensham Pond (with its great crested grebes), crossing only one road in its course. I discovered a spot near Tilford where the River Wey had undercut the high bank to make a sheer cliff nearly a hundred feet high – a place of wonder which I still delight to visit.

Cuttmill deserves a passage to itself. It is notable to me as the place where I first consciously discovered beauty. I was about seven years old, and we were on some sort of a picnic, walking along the path that led to General's Pond. There was a hedge of honeysuckle in full bloom, with Scots pine on a knoll at one end of it and the open heath alongside. It came into my little head that this was beautiful, something to be enjoyed for its own sake.

The Cuttmill area contains a series of ponds in the middle of heathland. At one end there is the Millpond, with a mill beside it which is now converted into a country house. The next pond is the Tarn, with its pine-crowned bluff at the far corner. Then a real lake, Royal Pond, runs along below a large eighteenth-century mansion, Hampton Lodge, approachable only by a private road from the top of the Hogsback. And finally, the product of a swampy spring, lies General's Pond (who the General was I have never known).

The tussocky growth at the end of the swamp was a great excitement to us boys. When we jumped on the tussocks they swayed up and down – just a mattress of soil floating on a reservoir of liquid yellow mud. One day we cut a ten-foot stick and poked it down without reaching solid bottom. Suppose one fell through? . . .

I loved Cuttmill, and would bicycle there by the shortest route, through Puttenham and over the hill, four miles in under twenty minutes.

Cuttmill taught me a good deal of natural history. There were carp in the Tarn and a pair of swans in the Millpond. One year, Trev and I drove the sitting bird from the nest – not without some trepidation, having heard that a blow from a swan's wing could break a man's arm – and extracted an egg. The blowing of it was a monstrous task; I shudder to think of blowing ostrich eggs as the Bushmen do! There were, of course, coot and mallard on the ponds; one hard winter there was skating on the Tarn, and all the waterfowl were concentrated in a little stretch of open water. It was exciting to skate near them in their agitation. I found my first mallard's nest near the Mill, marvelling at the duck's camouflage; but this time I took no egg.

I learnt a good deal of botany too. It was here I first learnt to distinguish the three kinds of heather. In the marsh above General's Pond I saw my first sundew, with little insects trapped in its clutching tentacles. Then there was the lovely Water Avens, a Geum with drooping, purplish flower cups; and the not very common Petty whin, an excellent name for this curious miniature gorse.

Much later, when I was reading biology at Oxford, I found General's Pond full of minute green specks which turned out to be the strange *Volvox globator*, a globular colony of green ciliate algal cells rotating through the water. Later, I used a drawing of it as the frontispiece to my first book, *The Individual in the Animal Kingdom*, as it was the best example of an assemblage of single cells becoming an organized individual whole.

The Mill itself was another great fascination. To start with, it had an undershot wheel which, my father explained, was much less common than the overshot type. The miller had no objection to us invading the place. We would watch the flour dropping from the grinding-stones, and inhale its queer, rather hot and musty smell. Then we would go right up to the grain-store, and leap into the semi-fluid mass – a strange sensation. Years later I read one of Frank Norris's books, where the villain is drowned in the grain in the hold of one of his own ships; and I thought of Cuttmill magnified and made horrific.

When I was an undergraduate at Oxford I took a small reading party to what had been the miller's house, on the bank of the Mill-pond. One evening there was an incredibly brilliant red and yellow sunset with pink clouds in a pale blue sky, and flaming sun-rays reflected in the water. I was enchanted; but the others derided it as just a picture postcard. My romantic spirit was painfully pricked.

To come back to natural history, I had heard snipe in a bog beyond the Millpond, and one day took up a position there with a volume of Charles Lamb's *Essays*. Just as I was reading about Mrs Battle and her whist, I looked up to see a snipe advancing towards me, only a few yards away, plunging its long beak into the mud and leaving it there quite a time before moving on to repeat the performance. It was only later that I learnt that the soft tip of the snipe's bill is curiously sensitive and supplied with nerves, so that it can detect any movement of a worm in the neighbouring mud. I felt that I was being let into the secrets of an alien creature, which is one of the great attractions of bird-watching. My first experience of this took place in new Laleham. There was a box-room off the nursery, and a pair of starlings had made a nest in a corner of it. I used to creep in and spend hours watching the parents take turns in feeding their brood, to the accompaniment of greedy chattering, completely unconscious of my presence. It was a privilege to share the private life even of these common and noisy creatures.

One day, armed with my first pair of binoculars – an old-fashioned Goertz $\times$ 12 prismatic, so old-fashioned that the prisms were wedged with thin strips of wood and were extremely tiresome to adjust – I walked along the path to General's Pond, to be astonished by an enormous bird flapping off a few yards away from me, leaving a half-eaten pheasant on the ground. It completely foxed me; but by good luck I met another bird-watcher, also with a pair of field-glasses round his neck, who told me that it was a juvenile white-tailed eagle, off course in its migratory wanderings. Alas, this noble bird is now extinct in Britain, and no one will again have the same thrill of excitement that I had over seventy years ago.

On the main road to Cuttmill was a handsome house called Mitchin Hall, lived in by a man who had been captured by Barbary pirates, and sold into slavery. I was told about this by Sir Philip Gibbs, who lived on the Puttenham approach to Cuttmill, and warned me that the man much disliked being reminded of his bondage, so I never heard the full story of his adventures.

Butterflies and moths soon began to play a part in my life. What a fascination they exercised! Apart from the common creatures like tortoise-shells and cabbage whites, there were the blues. I particularly remember the little blue, so absurdly tiny; the brilliant chalkhill blue, and the strange holly blue, with a very restricted habitat. We once caught a rare green hairstreak on Puttenham Common. A great thrill was provided by the fritillaries, with the glistening silver wash on their underwings, and I never forgot my first sight of a peacock butterfly sunning itself, slowly vibrating its wings and showing their startling false eye-spots. These seem to be a warning of nauseous taste, or perhaps a lure to attract birds, so preventing them from attacking the creature's body.

But the moths were perhaps the best. There were the poplar hawks, wonderfully camouflaged to match the tree-trunks on which they rested; the lime hawks with their lovely pink bodies; and one stupendous day a convolvulus hawk arrived on our terrace, its body so big that it completely upset my ideas about lepidopteran anatomy.

Puss-moths existed in the grounds at Hillside. The caterpillar, when frightened, swelled up its head in an alarming manner, with false eyes prominent, and waving red filaments extruded from its posterior end, all as warning that it possessed unpleasant properties of taste.

So the list goes on. Even their English names were fascinating:

the lackey, the burnet, the angle-shades, the burnished brass (living up to its designation), the ghost swift, the goat moth, uncannily like a rotten willow twig. Yellow underwings were common, and there was a tiny and almost uncatchable little yellow underwing on one of the heaths. The rarer red underwing, with its flashes of crimson hind-wings, was a real winner. The bright hind-wings attracted birds when the moths were in flight, while when the creatures dropped to the ground, they became indistinguishable from the surrounding dry herbage.

One tragedy befell us. Among the potatoes, we found a full-grown death's-head hawk caterpillar which pupated under our eyes. We carefully buried it for protection till its emergence, but later discovered that the gardener in his digging had cut it in two. I had been looking forward so much to seeing the moth with its big body mysteriously marked with skull and crossbones.

As a surprise for my little sister Margaret, I skinned a poplar hawk caterpillar and varnished the skin as a hearth-rug for her dolls' house. It was rather a tricky bit of work, but the result, I felt, was magnificent, and would have done very well in Titania's fairy palace.

Now I must pass to another of our haunts – Stocks, near Tring, under the scarp of the Chilterns. My Aunt Mary, Mrs Humphry Ward, had bought it from Sir Edward Grey, who wanted rivers to fish in. We usually spent several weeks there in the summer and around Christmas. How often memories of it have cheered me out of fits of depression! It was a big eighteenth-century house, very dignified, with a lovely garden. Beyond was a fine group of tall beeches called Aldbury Nowers, and in front of the house an open space where a cricket pitch was laid down for my cousin Arnold, a fast bowler who had just failed to get his Blue at Oxford. Arnold was not one of my favourite cousins; he had a brusque and arrogant manner. He got into a fast set at Oxford and took to gambling. Eventually his debts became so great that my poor Aunt Mary had to sell the Nowers, and see the woodmen cut down those lovely trunks whose canopies soared so purely upwards. I remember walking up and down in the kitchen-garden with her when I was an undergraduate, grieved for her, but proud that she was confiding her worries to me.

At the edge of the road was a splendid avenue of limes, a pleasure both to my nose (then more sensitive than now) and eyes. At the far end of the garden a gate led to a secluded mossy walk. In the little wood around were ash saplings, which I once cut to make bows – only moderately efficient! It debouched into a patch of grass, dotted in winter with snowdrops and shiny yellow aconites, a welcome sight in the Christmas holidays.

Facing the south front of the house was a ha-ha with a low wall in front. It was a test of prowess to leap over this wall into the field beyond. Aldous, then a growing toddler, once went out into the dense shrubbery bordering the wood walk and came back with the fascinating report: 'I was walking along when I saw a mouse – and I *fled. . . .*'

Aunt Mary had two daughters; the eldest was dear Dorothy, who never married and devoted all her life to looking after her mother, then her family, and finally her brother Arnold. Her sister Janet was eight years older than I, vigorous and active; she later married George Trevelyan, the historian. As a girl, she went in for archery, and I can see in my mind's eye the multi-coloured circular target with the golden bull's eye in the centre, so neatly pierced by her arrows, so seldom by mine.

It was at Stocks that I learnt to play the letter game – alias Word-making and Word-taking (which is still one of our favourites); you turn up letters from a blind heap until a five-letter word can be made from them; whoever shouts first takes the word and places it, facing the enemy, on the board before him. The turning up of letters continues, making it possible to take fresh words from the pool and also to take words from your opponent by adding one or more letters to his words, changing them into new anagrams. Or you can do the same with your own words, so making it harder for your enemy to take them from you. This fascinating evolution can continue until you have words of as much as twelve letters. Janet was a great dab at this, and both she and I used to lie awake thinking of new combinations: to give an example, I once changed *western* into *wet-nurse*, just by adding a *u*. It is a good game to train both memory and quick reaction, and, incidentally, to reveal the curious quality of words in themselves.

On one of our visits, when I was about eight years old, I slept in Janet's bedroom. Waking up early to read in bed was one of the good moments of my day. One of Janet's books was Carlyle's great satire, *Sartor Resartus*. I ploughed through it, but all I remember was something about a duck-pond, a German count whose epitaph recorded only that he had eaten a hundred thousand partridges, and the wonderful phrase about 'the Everlasting Yea and the Everlasting No'. I also found and read Janet's diary. Unfortunately I mentioned the fact, was told that to read other people's diaries was very wrong, and was henceforth forbidden to begin my day at five. So ended my matutinal excursions into literature.

Stocks was the great house of the neighbourhood, and on Christmas Eve all the village children assembled with their mothers in the big hall to be given presents. On Christmas Day we had our own Christmas tree in the library. What rustlings of tissue paper, what lighting of candles! And then the thrilling moment of ripping the coverings off our presents and seeing what was inside – a knife, a toy, a book – and comparing it with what the others had got.

In those late Victorian times it was, of course, a class-ridden society. My mother sometimes took me visiting among the villagers. At one cottage was a rather nice little girl, and my mother asked if I didn't think her pretty. I remember saying: 'I am no judge of female beauty.' I was about eleven at the time. Was it embarrassment or priggishness – or both? Maybe I even considered a little girl living in a humble cottage as belonging to another sphere – like the menservants at Stocks, who, though we enjoyed chatting with them, were kept behind green baize doors, only emerging into the main rooms for their particular duties.

The gardener, Mr Kean, was in a different category. Trev and I stood in awe of him, for he had the power to keep us away from his stoke-hole, his grape-house and other forbidden places. However, we did sometimes manage to get the better of him, as when we hid our childish selves – I was seven and Trev just over five-

under the gooseberry nets and had a marvellous time stuffing ourselves with the best of the fruit, while all the household was
running about in search of us.

On one unforgettable day I spotted a little blue butterfly on a
grass stalk. I plucked the stem without disturbing the delicate
creature, and carried it tremulously all the way home, feeling in
this small success a sense of achievement – I had become part of
the butterfly's world. On the other hand I still remember my sense
of guilt and shame when Trev and I threw stones at a half-grown
pheasant and killed it: we concealed it in the thickest part of the
bramble hedge and slunk home.

I have described elsewhere (in my *Bird Watching and Bird Behaviour*) how, at the age of thirteen, the sight of a green woodpecker
at Stocks, with his green and yellow plumage, red head and black
moustache, gave me my first full awareness of the wonderful
creatures in our countryside and set me to serious bird-watching.
From then on, I used to go off into the woods and commons nearly
every day in the holidays, and try to learn not only the appearance
but the language and habits of birds.

CHAPTER III

Eton

AT Hillside School I went on preparing for my scholarship exam
at Eton. I knew how anxious my parents were for me to
succeed, and as a result of hard work and anxiety about my
possible failure, a couple of nervous mannerisms began to affect me.
Whilst walking I used to match my cadence to a pentameter and,
contrary to usual practice, instead of avoiding cracks in the pavements, I deliberately trod on them. I shudder to think what a
really ingenious neo-Freudian would make of this.

I had two tries at the exam, when I was twelve and thirteen. My
mother and I stayed at Eton with a Jewish watchmaker called
Alexander. I shall always remember my first awareness of Jewish-
ness in Miss Alexander – the long brown face, the deep black eyes,
the big hooked nose.

The examination was held in Upper School. At my second try
in 1900 it was supervised by the famous Dr Spooner – albino and
extremely short-sighted. Spooner, when marking the papers, would
take up one of them, bring it close to his nose, and then put it down
with a great slash of red pencil across it. Of course I would be certain
that it was mine. However, I got in all right – and there was much
jubilant preparation of Eton jackets, top hats, stiff collars and gowns.

My first two halves at Eton were spent in Chamber, once the
infamous Long Chamber that originally housed all the seventy
scholars, and had at one time such a bad reputation that not even
the free board and lodging allowed to King's scholars by the
founder, Henry VI, kept the numbers up. In my time it was
divided into fifteen cubicles, with curtains for privacy, basins, flat
tin baths and rubber syphons to be affixed to taps. Old George the
man-servant brought hot water.

Chamber was presided over by a captain – Knatchbull-Huges-sen, with whom later, in 1906, I went sketching on the Neckar, and who when ambassador in Istanbul was tricked by the famous German agent in his employ, with the code-name Cicero.

The social anthropology of Chamber was complex. Only the captain could beat other Chamber boys, and did it not with a cane but a syphon – which could be quite painful. He alone had the privilege of making sulphurous 'Chamber Stink' by throwing water on the fire. On the fine oak table was a big jug of drinking water: if the captain shouted 'Cloister P.' the junior boy would have to rush across School Yard, fill the jug with water from the pump in the Cloisters and be back within three minutes. If he shouted 'Chamber curtains', the second junior boy had to go scrambling round, drawing all the window curtains against the approaching night.

Small boys, like primitive tribesmen, are highly legalistic. If you wanted privacy, you called out: 'Nobody annoy me or my curtains; nobody cause anything to annoy me or to annoy my curtains.' This of course was to deter neighbours throwing objects over the partitions, or pulling one's curtains open. Transgressions of such commands were reportable to the Captain of Chamber, who could then 'syphon' the offender.

I wish someone could write a history of Chamber sociology. I gather that within a few generations of boys the old customs had completely changed or died out. Here is a field for a Ph.D. thesis in one of our modern universities!

After two halves (Etonian for terms, though there were three 'halves' in the year) in Chambers, I was moved to Passages, where the other fifty-five scholars were housed. Note that this was the twentieth century. Yet there was no gas in the rooms and the boys were rationed to one candle a week each. My parents were horri-fied and presented me with a superb candlestick, fitted with an extra thick candle and a reflector throwing light on the page. Gas was put in some time in the next year, and work at night became easier. But I have always sympathized with the mediaeval scholars who had to work by candle-light.

Lights out at ten (half past ten for the older boys). Old George called us at seven and we had to be in early school by eight (I saw in the papers of August 1967 that early school was to be abolished, and a good thing too). Most of us were able to snatch a bit of bread and butter and perhaps gulp down a cup of tea, but some went hungry, until real breakfast at nine.

The fagging system was in full blast. At any moment one could be summoned to go on an errand or undertake any task. Once I was made to copy out a long passage of Homer by a boy called, appropriately, Pallas. And of course, we had to make toast for our fag-masters' breakfasts. (The only time I was caned was for making toast so burnt as to be uneatable!)

It was now that I and Neville Bland, later our ambassador in Holland, became fags of Timmy Jekyll, who inhabited Top Tower, which eventually became my own room. Dear Timmy – he was a nephew of Miss Jekyll, the famous gardener, who once told my father of driving to the Punchbowl on Hindhead and coming back with masses of king-fern, *Osmunda regalis*, trailing behind: it is practically extinct today in southern England.

Timmy, who had one leg shorter than the other and clip-clopped up into Hall, did what I am sure no other fag-master ever even thought of: he read to his fags on Sunday evenings. I have forgotten what he read – was it *Treasure Island*? – but I have always remembered his kindness.

I wasn't very happy my first year, and remember my embarrassment when my father, in the presence of a visitor, asked me how I liked Eton. I answered guardedly, 'Rather.' My father made it worse by saying, 'He means ra-*ther*.'

Next year I was free of fagging, but missed my spring half almost completely. First we were in quarantine for Trev's mumps, and I was sent with Aldous to Stocks Cottage, at the bottom of a steep scarp crowned by the monument of the Duke of Bridgewater, 'Father of Inland Navigation'. There I had my first close-up of a cock bullfinch, and had the same sort of thrill as with the green woodpecker. I also tried to teach Aldous long division of money, without any success whatsoever. I invented different coloured counters for pounds, shillings and pence, but they were all useless, and his mathematics remained *in statu quo*, as earlier reported at his dame-school.

When the three weeks were over, I hurried back to Middle Fifth, presided over by A. C. Benson. He had a very aggravating inscription over his class-room door: 'Someone must be last, but no one need be.' He was a remarkable man, who dreamt a poem about the Phoenix which has found a place in *The Oxford Book of English Verse*, and later had a distinguished career as master of a Cambridge college, and I was looking forward to working under him.

But after only a few days I was seized with violent flu, and spent the rest of the half in College Sanatorium. I can still hear the ostler below perennially whistling, 'You are my honey, honeysuckle, I am the bee' – a poor substitute for Benson's words of wisdom.

I had made another discovery while in mumps quarantine – masturbation. It is really unfair of nature to build into young boys this capacity for excruciating pleasure. I can never forget my first overwhelming shock. I hope modern boys are not so much tormented – sometimes devastated – by this problem. It certainly haunted me through my time at Eton. I didn't believe the old wives' tales about its bad effect on health – I just knew it was wrong. For years I had a little notebook marked with crosses and ticks each day, recording whether I had succumbed or not. I imagine all the boys were affected, with the exception of Charles Lister, Lord Ribbledale's son, who for some reason was exempt – or so he told me.

Charles Lister was, in my opinion, the most remarkable boy of my time in College: not sparkling like Ronnie Knox or toughly brilliant like Shaw-Stewart, but just remarkable. He had a striking long face, with a fine bony framework. His behaviour was quite unpredictable: early in our first half we were walking in the playing fields when he suddenly threw himself down on the grass and screamed. And who else but he could, while still at school, organize a trade union among the shop assistants in the little town?

Ronnie Knox became head of the school, in spite of being bad at mathematics, and as such became a member of Pop, the exclusive Eton society, originally devoted to debating, but now merely a self-elected club of senior boys, chosen chiefly for their popularity or athletic ability, though automatically including the academic head boy, and enjoying sartorial privileges like wearing coloured waistcoats and sporting flowers in their button-holes. Ronnie was very High Church and later became a Roman Catholic, ending up as a monsignor. His knowledge was impressive and versatile until he canalized all his activities into the service of the Church. Soon after his conversion, at the age of twenty-five, he wrote his autobiography: presumably he thought that the rest of his life concerned only God. H. K. Marsden was good at mathematics, and came second while I, with reasonably good all-round abilities, came third.

Are boys inevitably coarse? Certainly our language was full of dirty gossip. 'There's Mrs X in pod again', and various quite unprintable remarks about the anatomy of one of the house matrons. And there was homosexuality – not much in College, I think, but there was one house where it was rampant and horrible. This was reported to me years later by a distinguished old Etonian I knew well. 'Luckily,' he said, 'I was large and ugly, but the pretty little boys . . .' and he broke off.

Romantic love, as opposed to physical homosexuality, was common enough. In College, so far as I know, it was purely platonic. I shall have more to say about it later (p. 54 f.).

Meanwhile my mother had started Prior's Field School for Girls, with very little financial backing. She once said to me, 'Don't be afraid of borrowing money', which rather shocked me, and I have never borrowed except on mortgage. However, the school was a great success from the start; the numbers swiftly went up to eighty and the borrowed money was soon repaid. My mother picked an excellent staff, among whom was Miss Neroutsos, a rather formidable woman with a horsey face, of Greek origin; the mild and sentimental Miss English; and a very handsome and athletic gym mistress, whose name I have forgotten.

Among the girls were Valerie Barker, who later achieved notoriety by undergoing a change of sex and becoming 'Colonel' Barker; Isabel Vernon-Harcourt, the witty daughter of the professor of chemistry at Oxford; Enid Bagnold, future authoress and playwright, with whom I exchanged poems. She was a dare-devil who rode a bicycle from her home in Chatham all along the Old Kent Road to get into London. She also jumped from the loft of Prior's Field stable on to the concrete pavement and dared the Wetzlar-Coit girl to do the same, with the unfortunate result of a broken leg. Then there was lovely Bridget Hole, who later married Stephen Tallents and remained a much loved friend of ours until her death fifty years later; and a long-limbed, athletic girl with whom I had my first love affair, running round to the copse to meet her before breakfast. More about her later.

While on vacation from Eton and Oxford I was rather like Achilles among the virgins, for the girls at Prior's Field stayed on for some time after my vacations had begun. I played hockey with them sometimes, and that exciting game lacrosse, while in summer I joined them at cricket, resplendent in white flannel trousers and my Etonian blazer.

After three or four years, my mother took Mrs Burton-Brown into partnership. She was a fine classical historian, and established herself firmly in her position. When my mother died in 1908, Mrs B.B. became sole headmistress, and was in due time succeeded by her daughter Beatrice.

The rest of my time at Eton must be told in snatches as it comes into my head. It seems extraordinary, but one afternoon, in the autumn of 1900, I saw Queen Victoria herself, driving along the Slough Road, a dumpy old woman, dressed in black, an epitome of a fading epoch. When she died, early next year, the College boys lined the last stretch of the route along which her coffin was carried into St George's Chapel in Windsor Castle (Eton was after all a Royal college). It was followed by an astonishing array of crowned heads, but the only one I remember was the Kaiser, with his plumed helmet, his white and gold uniform and withered arm, and arrogantly cocked-up moustaches. He passed so close that I could have touched him – even then a striking but unpleasant figure.

During the spring holidays of 1901, a memorial statue of T. H. Huxley was unveiled by the Duke of Devonshire in the Natural History Museum. (The Prince of Wales, the future Edward VII, had regretfully declined to perform the ceremony because of my grandfather's unorthodox views on religion, though he remained as Honorary President of the Memorial Committee.) The statue still stands on the right of the entrance, looking up at the memorial figure of T.H.H.'s great opponent, Professor Richard Owen.

My own family was there, together with Gran'moo and hordes of Huxley aunts, uncles and cousins. Aldous was not quite five years old, and found the lengthy ceremony very trying. Suddenly my mother whispered, 'Give me your top hat.' 'What for?' I muttered. 'For Aldous to be sick in – he's turning green.' 'I won't,' said I, unwilling that my sacred headgear should be so profaned. 'But you must,' she said, 'we can't have him making a mess on the floor before all these grand people.' 'No, No,' I hissed, clutching the precious object, carefully ironed for the occasion, behind my back. And then Aldous miraculously restrained himself, and my hat was saved. . . .

The memory of those awful moments has stayed with me all my life. I told the Duke of Edinburgh of the incident when he, standing by the same statue, was inaugurating a special Huxley wing of the Museum in the late 50s. By then I was able to see its comic side and we both enjoyed the joke.

I was inducted into the mysteries of Eton football, where forward passing is not allowed. I remember one match of Chamber against the lower boys of another house where the written record states that Marsden, who had been relegated to the post of goal-keeper, 'failed to hit the ball with his leg': Marsden was tall and lanky, with little control over his awkward limbs. He was very peculiar. He knew Bradshaw's railway guide by heart, and used to go on long solitary walks sending postcards to himself, to add to his collection of postmarks. He was passionately devoted to Eton:

in Chapel, on the last day of our last half, tears were rolling down his cheeks. He returned later as a housemaster – one of a queer but, I think, quite successful sort.

The ushers, as we called the masters, certainly included many oddities. The master in College, and my tutor, was Mr Goodhart. He wasn't a very good tutor, but I owe him two things: one is my first glimmer of understanding music, the second the gift of an *Oxford Book of English Verse* presented in 1904, 'Honoris causa' – though what the honour was I have quite forgotten. This has been all over the world with me, and is still at my bedside.

Hugh McNaughton was really inspiring. Under him, in Upper Fifth, we read Aeschylus' *Prometheus Bound*. He got me so excited that I read it all through again in the original Greek during the holidays. Ah, what one has forgotten! . . .

Edmund Warre was headmaster – deep-voiced, big and burly, once a great rowing man, and always keen to get good athletes as assistant masters. He had a queer little wife, who was always saying odd things. She was even reported to have asked, while walking to see a cricket match in the playing fields: 'What is that bird that always says Cuckoo, Cuckoo? . . .' And once, when my cousin Gordon Selwyn, then head of the school, was breakfasting with the Warres, she burst out with the question, 'Edmund, what are cigarettes made of?' To which embarrassedly he replied: 'Tobacco, my dear, tobacco', and quickly changed the subject.

Warre-Cornish, the vice-provost, was a learned little man with white hair, a slightly red nose, and a large and formidable wife, about whom many legends sprang up, for she was always making extraordinary remarks. Her eyes fixed on her husband, she once announced to a group of boys who had been lunching there: 'How sad the fate of the carrion crow: it mates for life!'

Other characters among the masters were Luxmoore and 'Toddy' Vaughan. Luxmoore was extremely impressive, very handsome with beautiful white hair. He was very kind to a few selected boys, of whom I was lucky to be one. He was something of a funda-mentalist, and when I began talking about protective resemblance and natural selection, said to me: 'How do you account for the fact

Henrietta Anne Huxley, painted by
[h]er son-in-law John Collier

[I] Thomas Arnold, second son of Dr
[A]rnold of Rugby: a memorial plaque
[i]n Dublin

[V] T. H. Huxley at the age of 32,
[w]hen Professor of Zoology, South
[K]ensington

V Julia Arnold, photographed in Chinese dress by Lewis Carroll

VI Leonard Huxley, in 1928

that a potato may look exactly like a stone? Is that due to natural selection?'

He had a beautiful garden opposite Baldwin's Shore, with bridges over the little stream that issued from under the main road, arbours and pergolas, and a lovely view across the Thames. I much appreciated the privilege of being able to wander in it, a refreshing escape from hustle and other boys. I am glad to say that it has now been preserved as a permanent monument to him. You don't get masters like that nowadays.

Vaughan (why nicknamed 'Toddy' I never knew) was a very different kettle of fish. I forget what his speciality was, but he was a little man and somewhat comic. He was adjutant of the Eton College Volunteers, and on field-days boys would fire blank cartridges at his horse and try to make it run away with him. There was a tale that he once had to take command of a company and instead of giving the order: 'Rear rank, about turn, shoulder arms', said, 'Back row, turn round and pick up your guns'.

He was wonderfully enthusiastic. One winter the Thames froze over. On hearing of this, he rushed back from his holiday abroad and insisted on skating on it, though by this time the ice was beginning to thaw. Luckily he was small and succeeded in his ambition without falling through. He was devoted to Shakespeare, and organized a Shakespeare society for sixth form boys, which met at his private house. One evening we were reading *Othello*, with the captain of Oppidans taking the title part. When he was accusing Desdemona of her unfaithfulness, a surprising modesty overtook him, and instead of bursting out with, 'You have played the strumpet in my bed', he rather hesitatingly mumbled: 'You have played the . . . trumpet in my bed', upon which the Shakespeare society dissolved in explosive laughter. I owe Vaughan a great debt for introducing me so thoroughly to Shakespeare's works.

There were three science masters. The rubicund Dr Porter taught chemistry, and was a great showman. He had a high-vaulted classroom, and his special 'turn' was to blow bubbles of pure hydrogen and explode them with the aid of a long bamboo pole, smouldering at the tip, just before they reached the ceiling. Then there was the physics master, Mr Eggar, whose experiments always seemed to go wrong. And finally there was the biology master, Mr M. D. Hill, generally known as Piggy from his protruding nose. I owe him immense gratitude. When the time came for me to take so-called 'extra subjects', I wrote to my parents saying that German and Biology were the obvious alternatives, and suggested that I should take German, as it would be useful for the Civil Service examination, as the Civil Service then appeared to be my future career. My parents wrote back very sensibly, saying that I could at any time learn German by going abroad. So I took Biology.

They were right – and I was lucky, for Piggy Hill was a genius as a teacher. He soon made me understand the excitement of Zoology (he had got a First in it at Oxford), and I decided to specialize in the subject. Dear Piggy! He settled my career for me, and I have always been grateful to him. Paul Methuen, one of the Meinertzhagen boys and I were his three specialists; but I often used to spend the two hours after twelve alone in the lab, dissecting and drawing.

My parents had a report from him, which somewhat embarrassed me: 'Huxley ma. K.S.[1] Barring a tendency to think himself infallible, I have no possible fault to find in him. (This remark about infallibility later delighted my wife.) For one of his years he has a remarkable insight into zoological principles, and his power of writing good English is exceptional.'

It is curious to think that at one remove I owe my zoological training to my grandfather, who surprisingly was put on the governing body of Eton and insisted on having the school build science laboratories. They were known by the more conservative masters as Huxley's Folly, but have turned out a number of eminent scientists.

Piggy Hill was a fussy little man, but inspiring. My brother Aldous also began biology with him, and thus laid the basis for his constant fascination with science. In one of his early novels Aldous

[1] Short for King's Scholar, since the original school of seventy boys had been founded, like King's College, Cambridge, by King Henry the Sixth.

launches into a marvellous metaphysical disquisition, which actually derived from his hearing Piggy asking the lab boy for 'the key of the Absolute' – the absolute alcohol being safely locked up in a cupboard, as the word Absolute is hidden in mystery.

I spoke twice at Speeches in Upper School, when sixth form boys in knee-breeches declaim to privileged visitors. The first year I chose Matthew Arnold's *The Forsaken Merman*; the second time I broke with tradition by going across the Atlantic to Walt Whitman's *Pioneers, O Pioneers*. Many boys chose classical pieces. One performance I shall never forget was that of Hubert Young (later Governor of Northern Rhodesia) reciting the ghastly passage from Marlowe's *Faustus*, where Faust knows he has but one hour to live before being taken by the Devil to eternal damnation, and ending: 'See where Christ's blood streams in the firmament – One drop would save my soul – half a drop – Ah my Christ! . . .' It was a triumph of horrific acting.

In house matches I got my College Field, and was so childishly proud of it that I wore the blue-and-white cap, blazer and scarf when bicycling to Cuttmill in the next Christmas holidays – but relieved that there was no one, at least no one that mattered, to see me. I also got my Mixed Wall as 'lines', ready to kick towards goal, in the traditional Wall Game between Collegers and Oppidans on St Andrew's Day. But I never achieved School Field colours. I shot twice at Bisley, but the Eton team failed to bring back the Ashburton Shield. I was especially keen on hurdling and high-jumping, and used to spend hours in the Lent half practising (I couldn't even resist going over the Charterhouse hurdles during the holidays, in my ordinary clothes). It was long before the technique of straight-leg hurdling, or of rolling over the bar in the high jump instead of straddling it. On my last School sports day I was chagrined to be beaten in the hurdles by a yard or so by Twiggy Anderson, a boy much younger than myself, and so missed the privilege of wearing a gold shield on my watch-chain.

I did, however, win the high jump (alas, no gold shield for that), in the presence of my mother. I had previously strained a muscle in my right thigh when practising, and had to have massage. But the strain was still there, and after my victory, I achieved a melodramatic touch by fainting flat out at my mother's side.

In my last summer at Eton, I amassed three school prizes – the Poetry Prize, the Shakespeare Prize and the Biology Prize. The subject for the poetry prize was *Camoens*, and my poem, written in the tricky Spenserian stanza form, wasn't very good. But the award fanned my poetic ambitions; and reading for the Shakespeare Prize rekindled my enthusiasm for the great historical plays, especially *Henry IV* and *Henry V*.

In November, 1905, I obtained a Zoology scholarship at Balliol in rather unusual circumstances. Playing in a College Field match, I got an agonizing kick on my shin (the dent is there to this day) and could only hobble, so that it was impossible to walk to the examination. Luckily my parents knew Percy Matheson, a kindly New College don, and I was allowed to take the examination under his supervision in his house in Mansfield Road.

It was on this occasion that I demonstrated my early interest in conservation. Besides dealing with questions on their special subjects, all candidates had to write an essay on a set problem. This time we were asked, 'What would you do if you had a million pounds?' and I suggested buying up as much as possible of the unspoilt coastline of Britain.

I was later told that this unusual answer helped in getting me the award. Denys Finch-Hatton spoiled his chances by writing that he would start by pensioning off the older Balliol dons: this showed a bit too much originality! Finch-Hatton, by the way, was without doubt the handsomest boy in the school. I remember seeing him on my return from a before-breakfast Sunday run, standing on top of College Wall in a red silk dressing-gown – an unforgettable Antinous. He had an exciting and very unacademic career. He went to Kenya as a big-game hunter and safari leader, fell in love with Baroness Blixen, the well-known Danish authoress who was also mad about East Africa, and was tragically killed in a plane crash while still in his prime.

After getting my scholarship I felt I should broaden my mind, and moved back into the Classical Sixth Form, away from biological specialization. It seems extraordinary now, but it *was* entirely classical – nothing but Latin and Greek. Once we had to write a Latin poem in any metre we preferred. I thought I would be clever and chose galliambics, that extraordinary metre with each line ending in five short syllables, of which only one example is known, by Catullus, about the priests of Attis, who voluntarily castrated themselves. I still remember the first line: 'Super alta vectus Attis celeri rate maria'. Unfortunately, Alan Parsons had the same idea: we each thought the other too original by half.

Another time we had to translate an English poem into Greek iambics. Today, it seems incredible that I should have been able to do anything of the sort.

Warre had now been succeeded as headmaster by Edward Lyttleton – a curious character, not always successful in keeping order. He had the habit of scrawling the word *Fluff* across any piece of work that seemed particularly stupid. One day a group of Collegers, headed by Ronnie Knox and Charles Lister, played a trick on the Oppidan Sixth Form. I must explain that we were subject on the Sabbath to a discipline called Sunday Questions. The questions, on biblical matters, written by the headmaster in his own hand, were put on the letter slab in College, and the Oppidans sent their fags to transcribe them. On this occasion, one question was: 'Which is the oldest part of the Bible? Discuss and give your reasons.' The plotters converted *oldest* into *oddest*. There are indeed many odd passages in the Bible, especially in the Old Testament. The Head was clearly a bit suspicious, but contented himself with explosions of *Fluff* over the Oppidans' answers.

There were changes too, among the ushers. Goodhart had become a housemaster and the master in College was now Cyril Alington, later Dean of Durham. He was a witty man, an immense change from most masters, and had a capable, warm-hearted and hospitable wife, Hester. Tea with the Alingtons was a real treat.

My love life coincided with the onset of my desire to write poetry, and that began on manoeuvres on Salisbury Plain, when I was just seventeen. On the great flat expanse, one summer evening,

I was seized with an oceanic feeling and wrote my first poem, in which the words 'away to the farthest horizon' recurred at the end of each stanza. It wasn't a very good poem, but it started me on a mild career – the excitement of actually creating a poem of my own was overwhelming.

Love affairs can be just as devastating between boys, just as romantic, as between young men and women. The boy I fell in love with was Eric Forbes-Adam. He was really beautiful, with an oval face, fair hair and blue eyes, and a lovely mouth. I was so obsessed by him that on the way to school I would follow at a safe distance, just to have him in view. And of course I wrote poems about him, including one about the 'Cupid's bow' of his mouth – it takes time to rid oneself of clichés! It is a terrible thing to recall that in the prime of his life he committed suicide, in one of our embassies in the Middle East. But why?

His younger brother, Colin, inspired equally passionate devotion, though totally different in looks – dark, a little impish, with quite unclassical features.

I was not the only one to fall under the Forbes-Adams' spell. I remember Alan Parsons clutching the back of a chair on which he was perched and demanding why we wretched boys should have such violent passions which were impossible to gratify. I mumbled something stupid about inborn biological urges, but it was not very satisfying.

Alan certainly was passionate. He became engaged to Viola Tree while still an undergraduate at Oxford, and used to write to her twice a day, often with a telegram thrown in for good measure. And I remember Aldous saying how embarrassed he was when, between the leaves of a book Alan had lent him, he came upon photographs of the young couple on their honeymoon, both in the nude.

As I write these pages, other memories of Eton, disconnected and often trivial, surge up. Between obvious growing pains and the stress of constant new adjustments I remember a clear night when, coming back from my tutor's, I found myself alone in School Yard. Lying between two buttresses of Chapel, I looked at the stars and felt I could in some way *possess* even their immensity. The joy of it filled my heart like a revelation, a reassurance that the world of natural beauty meant something important to me, and to the world. Another peaceful and penetrating glimpse of what I may call nature's poetry came on College Field when, waiting my turn to bat, I stalked off towards the arches spanning a brook. There I saw the pure blue of the wild meadow geranium in the lush grass – an unforgettable discovery of beauty in a common plant.

These moments, when I felt mystically united with nature, were very precious. The most extraordinary came to me at a dance at Shackleford. Wandering out into the fragrant night air, the sky crowded with stars, I had a strange cosmic vision – as if I could *see* right down into the centre of the earth, and embrace the whole of its contents and its animal and plant inhabitants. For a moment I became, in some transcendental way, the universe.

The great mystics and visionaries, like St Catherine of Siena, have recorded the piercing joy of such moments, and today, too, many people attempt to produce such ecstatic states artificially, by drugs such as lysergic acid, often with unfortunate after-effects. (My brother Aldous told me that he only once experienced unpleasant effects – all his other experiences with lysergic acid were of liberation and overwhelming beauty: this was doubtless due to his gentle and loving temperament. Other acquaintances of mine have been plunged into a hell of misery, and I, subject as I am to occasional fits of depression, have never dared to take this or any other hallucinogenic drug.)

When we were fags, we were sometimes ordered to betake ourselves to the Copper Horse by our superiors as punishment for some misdemeanour. It was always on a Sunday afternoon, and we had to be back by four, when the College roll-call, misleadingly called 'Absence', was held by a master. The Copper Horse was an effigy of one of the Georges, about two miles up the great avenue stretching south from Windsor Castle: it was quite an effort to get there and back within an hour and a half. Once, when recovering from an infection, and free from temporal restrictions, I determined to go right on beyond the Copper Horse to Great Meadow Pond.

And there I saw a miracle of a bird, no less than a goosander, with lovely dark green head, a hint of a crest on it and brilliant white flanks.

I had my own binoculars by then. My parents had taken me to see the Kearton exhibition of bird photographs, one of the very first to be held. They gave me a print of a sedge-warbler on its nest, which I framed, and early prismatic field glasses, which I have already described, a pair of very early Goertz ×12's. With this precious aid I often went birding. Once I ran to Haymills Pond near Taplow. One end of it was full of reeds, and I spent an hour there looking for the nest of a reed-warbler, whose strange up-and-down jerky song I had heard. It was an uncomfortable hour, for the sharp stumps of dead rushes protruding from the mud were very painful to my bare feet. But at last I found the nest: a deep cup, carefully woven on to the surrounding reed-stems, so deep that the eggs could never be shaken out by the wind. The bird-watcher's reward is to discover the intimate facts of bird life for himself, and I felt amply compensated for my discomfort by finding this miracle of adaptation.

All through my Eton and Oxford days, even when travelling, I kept an elaborate bird diary, noting which species of bird I saw each day, their approximate number, whether they were singing, the nests I found (with the number of eggs or young) and notes on peculiar behaviour.

Out of this elaborate note-taking by myself and other pioneers like Eliot Howard, with whom I became very friendly, and Edmund Selous, there grew the British Ornithological Union's scheme for detailed nest-recording, which has yielded interesting facts concerning the effect of weather on clutch-size and number of fledglings reared, and the nation-wide tallies of birds seen on particular dates, which have told us a great deal about migration and fluctuations in bird numbers. These early bird-diaries of mine, together with all Howard's notes, which he bequeathed to me, have now been deposited in the Edward Grey Institute of Ornithology at Oxford.

My last two halves at Eton were sadly marred. Sixth-form boys used generally to mess together in little groups for breakfast. I was in a mess of three, and was suddenly informed by the other two that I wasn't wanted any more. I never discovered why, but it was a bitter blow to my esteem. I remember going down to the little room where I used to get the extra milk my parents insisted on, and bouncing a squash-racket ball against the wall, up and down, up and down, until I recovered a reasonable equanimity. But it was a dreary business, eating alone, endeavouring to console myself with a book.

Looking back, I can see how fruitful were my years at Eton, in spite of such minor troubles. To start with, Eton was then the only school where every pupil had a room to himself. This permitted uninterrupted study, and time for quiet thought and private reading. In addition, College was an élite – it needed brains to get a scholarship, and it was valuable to have the companionship and stimulus of one's intellectual equals. Thirdly, there were no compulsory English lessons in Upper School (all Collegers started at that level). This sounds like a disadvantage, but was really a benefit. We were spared the tedious business of being taken through a set of so-called masterpieces of English prose and verse, and were free to indulge our own tastes. It was thus that I learnt to love poetry – Wordsworth, Coleridge, Milton, Walt Whitman, Chaucer, Marvell, Donne, and many others. The one compulsory bit of English was the writing of a weekly essay for my tutor. This undoubtedly helped me to develop a reasonably good prose style, and the habit of rapid thinking.

Eton could afford to pay high salaries, and so the masters were mostly men of high academic and social standard, whose teaching was stimulating and whose company was agreeable. And then the beauty of the mediaeval buildings round School Yard – Chapel, Cloisters, Hall and the gigantic kitchen with conical roof – and also those at Windsor Castle, especially St George's Chapel with its banners, and the Horseshoe Quadrangle, kindled in me a love and some understanding of fine architecture. Finally, the amount of free time available permitted me to explore the countryside and enlarge my knowledge of birds and plants.

I am all for helping boys of poor families to enter Eton, but I hope fervently that the general system of education will remain.

During my school and undergraduate days the summer vacations loomed as large as term, but were much more pleasant. They were an education in themselves, an education in the beauties of nature and its varied geology, in the diversity of animal and plant life, and in the splendours of architectural history.

Mortehoe and Clovelly, with its steep street available only to donkeys; Alnmouth with its shell-strewn beach and neighbouring mediaeval castles; a sad holiday at Stocks when my mother had typhoid, yet redeemed by the beauty of the garden and the beech-woods on the downs; Swanage, with its fossil ammonites on Dancing Ledges, its rare butterflies like the Lulworth skipper, and Corfe Castle nearby with its donkey-operated winch for its well; Saundersfoot and Tenby, with splendid bathing beaches and strange marine creatures in the rock-pools; later to Switzerland, where my father and I had our first experience of real mountaineering with rope and ice-axes, and I learnt to love the Alpine flowers and birds – dwarf rhododendrons, gentians and saxifrages, crossbills, wall-creepers with wings flashing crimson, Alpine swifts and choughs and the great black woodpecker, scarlet-crested, the Romans' sacred bird of war, with a blood-curdling, screaming call.

In October 1904, while still a seventeen-year-old schoolboy, I was invited to Loch Rannoch to coach the very backward Etonian stepson of a very brilliant stepmother, Mrs Violet Hammersley. I did my best for the boy, though he couldn't even spell properly (*cushion* became *coochon* in his retarded brain), tried my hand at fly-fishing and was given a day's deer-stalking. The crawling approach was very exciting, but the sight of the lovely antlered creature falling to my rifle made me disgusted with myself, and I vowed never again to kill a large mammal (and I never have, except once in Kenya, when I shot a Tommy gazelle for supper).

The chief result of my visit was the beginning of a friendship which lasted for sixty years. Violet was the sister of Agnes Williams-Freeman, Aldous' godmother, but totally different in every way – slim, olive-complexioned, and looking, as someone once said, 'like a Siamese princess'. She was painted by Steer in a billowy dress, and later by Duncan Grant, sitting at her piano, brooding and dark. Her husband was a rich bank-director, and silently adored her. They had a lovely country house on the Thames, near Marlow, where they kept a four-oared racing skiff and a sandalo from Venice, complete with its gondolier, Giulio. In London she gave wonderful parties in her house in Cadogan Square, where one met all kinds of interesting people. She had the knack of fascinating men and dominating women, and by sheer egocentric volition obtained from most people every imaginable service, which she took as her due. She was witty without being malicious, intelligent and flexible, and avidly interested in everything. '*Do* tell me', she would ask – and one told all one knew.

She was left a young widow with her three children and a large fortune, most of which unfortunately was later lost in the bank-ruptcy of her husband's bank. Plunged into ruin – relative ruin, for she was still quite comfortably off – she became a prey to every sort of anxiety, afraid of imagined destitution, afraid of being alone in a taxi, afraid for her health, wrapping herself in shawls and veils even on hot days – yet her adventurous spirit led her into formidable travels in India and Africa, where she became a legendary figure. She was indeed a strange and fascinating character, and an unforgettable friend. Someone should write her biography: maybe she was, in fact, a princess? . . .

CHAPTER IV

Oxford

In the summer vacation of 1906 I was sent to Germany to learn enough of the language to tackle the mass of German biological literature that I should have to go through when I read Zoology at Oxford. I was to stay with a Fräulein Groh (it was carefully explained to me that I must not call her Fräulein Grob, which means coarse and vulgar) in the suburbs of Heidelberg.

I had a very interesting time there. Heidelberg itself had not been spoilt by hordes of tourists, and its castle stood out splendidly on the bluff above the Neckar. The Neckar itself, in its delightful valley, was waiting to be explored. Once I went out with Knatchbull-Hugessen (who had been Captain of Chamber during my first half at Eton), up to Neckarsteinach, a charming little mediaeval hill town by the river, and drew it. My pencil sketch still hangs in my bedroom as a reminder of the happy and distinguished Germany of pre-Hitler days.

I was introduced to Professor Hans Driesch, a notable experimental embryologist with a taste for the mystical. For instance, he ascribed the capacity of portions of early embryos to regulate themselves and develop into normal wholes, to an indwelling vital force or *entelechy* – a term borrowed from Aristotle.

One day, when he and I were walking along the celebrated Philosophenweg where the professors took exercise and discussed their learned problems, the subject of the talking horses of Elberfeld came up. One in particular, Klüge Hans – Clever Harry – seemed able to spell out words and do sums, even cube-roots, indicating the answers by scrapings of his fore-hoof. (It was later shown that he took his cue from the involuntary signals of his trainer; the man was quite honest but the horse stopped scraping when the trainer's face showed a minute change of expression – a proof that animals can make up for their lack of speech by surprising sensitiveness to their trainer's looks.)

I had been much impressed by what I had read, and was inclined to believe the story. But Driesch, who by that time had gone over to what we now would call parapsychology, was so emphatic that the facts could only be explained by some supernormal faculty, like telepathy, that he drove me into the position of *advocatus diaboli*. I said: 'But, Professor Driesch, if horses are so clever as to be able to extract cube-roots in their heads, how is it that they are so stupid in ordinary affairs?' To which he replied: 'Perhaps, Mr Huxley, because they have such an intense inner life.' This was too much for me, and we passed to other subjects.

When I first saw the students in their tasselled caps, proudly displaying sabre scars on their faces, I thought that their duels were just boisterous but harmless ritual, part of the fun of being young and enthusiastic students of a great traditional university. It was only later that I realized that the duels were an initiation into arrogant violence, a precursor of Hitlerism.

Up the Neckar I also explored a little town on a lonely hill called Dilsberg, where the population was so heavily inbred that the place was full of defectives. I realized then that the idiots so common in English villages before the railway age were the unfortunate victims of similar isolation.

In Speyer, just across the Rhine, there was an opera house, and there I attended my first opera, perched high up in the gallery. It was Richard Strauss's *Salome*, and I was much impressed. Salome's Dance of the Seven Veils was a slightly shocking revelation. I seem to remember that the opera was banned when it first came to London.

As a reward for getting my Balliol scholarship my mother took me on a spring cruise in the Mediterranean, together with Mrs Burton-Brown, who had just joined her at Prior's Field.

I saw porpoises for the first time, disporting themselves round the ship's bows, obviously enjoying their leaping and racing, just as the herons at Avery Island which I saw some years later certainly enjoyed their aerial flight-games. I realized how stupid the behaviourists were in denying any subjective emotional experience to animals.

I was immensely impressed by the ruined temples of Sicily and by mediaeval Palermo, especially the exquisite cloisters at Monreale. We passed through the Straits of Messina between Scylla and Charybdis, no longer dangerous to modern ships, and had the frustrating experience of staying at Taormina when the clouds were so low that I saw nothing of Etna's 11,000-foot cone. This was a serious annoyance, as I was a great admirer of my great-uncle Matthew Arnold's *Empedocles on Etna,* where the mountain is so beautifully described.

For me, the high point came at Capri. My mother and Mrs Burton-Brown drove up to the little white town, but I walked. At once, I found myself surrounded by scented wild narcissi in flower, and I was shaken by a kind of ecstasy: it was one of the most moving and transporting experiences I ever enjoyed, more moving even than the Greek temples on their lonely hillsides.

That autumn I went up to Oxford. Arriving at Balliol with my luggage, I asked where my rooms were. The porter was the redoubtable Hancock, whose reputation for omniscience was famous. 'Ah, yes, Sir,' he said, 'your rooms are on staircase so-and-so, at the left, in the front quad. Yes, I remember your father had the same rooms when he came up in 1882.' I wondered whether he might perhaps have looked it up, but quite possibly he did remember. His greatest achievement was when he was asked an undergraduate's whereabouts, and replied: 'He's just gone out, and by the look on his face, I should say he was going to the tobacconist's' – which turned out to be true.

I duly settled in, and found that the man in the rooms below me was Tavistock, Lord Russell, the Duke of Bedford's son and heir, one day destined to take over Woburn Abbey. He had a long sad face and always wore the off-white narrow linen neckties affected by the Russell family. I did my best to be friendly but found him so unresponsive that I gave it up.

For my general tutor, I was assigned to Harold Hartley, the Balliol physical chemist, still going strong today at ninety in spite of a game leg. He did me a great service by insisting that I should read the life of Pasteur. It was an eye-opener about the methods of scientific discovery – a mixture of intuition, pertinacity and occasional good luck. I later found that the chief role of intuition was in the selection of the problem to be investigated, though sometimes the solution came as a flash of insight – but only after much donkey-work – observing, altering conditions, and mathematical calculation.

Strachan-Davidson was Master of Balliol, a lovable, rather vague man, with a beard which he would stroke while talking, putting an 'er' before every word. He had all the newcomers up in Hall, obviously trying to memorize us. When he left he absent-mindedly let fall his notes. We pounced on the paper and found a list of our names annotated with descriptive reminders. The most memorable was of Ward, a dark, short fellow, with a round, rather shiny face. Strachan-Davidson had written 'a little black tea-pot', and Ward remained 'Teapot' for the rest of his career.

We were lucky in the Balliol dons. In philosophy there was young Sandy Lindsay, later Vice-Chancellor of Keele, passionately interested in public affairs; and also the white-haired J. A. Smith, passionately uninterested in anything but metaphysics; Pickard-Cambridge in Classical History – a learned dry stick; Cyril Bailey, a really sweet man, who afterwards married Gemma Creighton, in Classical literature (he introduced me to the wonders of Lucretius' great scientific poem); and, most especially, F. F. Urquhart in Modern History. For some unexplained reason, he was always called Sligger. His rooms were open to all and sundry every night, and provided a wonderful mixing-ground and a stabilizing and civilizing influence.

He also had a chalet in the French Alps south of Geneva, to which selected undergraduates were invited during the summer. It was about three thousand feet up from the local post-town, and every morning a stocky French maid would climb those three thousand feet with the eggs and milk and the day's letters, and go down in the evening to sleep.

One year both Trev and I were invited. The Alpine pastures were delightful, with masses of Alpenroses and a miniature golf course. We also wanted to demonstrate our prowess in downhill running: here Trev, with his long legs, easily beat me: I remember he did the three thousand feet down in under half an hour.

At the chalet, the mixing process continued, with excellent results – many new friendships were made on those airy heights, with their superb view of Mont Blanc.

My first sense at Balliol was one of relief – relief at being free of the shackles of the smaller world of school, able to choose my own friends and venture into all kinds of adult interests. I largely lost contact with my Etonian companions like Ronnie Knox and Charles Lister, who belonged to the smart and rather rowdy set. But I made great friends with George Fletcher and especially Bob Brandt, ex-Harrovian and great cricketer; we used to go bicycling together. I remember once going with him to the upper Thames in May, swimming, and then lying face down on the turf: filled with a magnificent cosmic feeling, I said, 'I am fertilizing the earth . . .', to which he quietly replied, 'Nonsense'. He was killed in the war, as were so many of my contemporaries and predecessors, a crippling loss to Britain's cultural and political life.

I became a member of the Brakenbury Society, which held weekly debates on all sorts of subjects, and joined the Oxford Bach Choir as a bass. Sir Hugh Allen was the conductor, a strict taskmaster. I shall always remember singing in Bach's B Minor mass, spurred to achievement by his caustic comments. This seems to me the greatest of all vocal compositions, even more rewarding to sing than to hear. I also attended the Musical Club's performances, there to enjoy Schubert and Brahms and Beethoven, as well as modern composers like Butterworth. It was like entering a new

VII Julia Huxley, about 1903, with
her daughter Margaret then aged
about 4.

VIII Aldous Huxley with Mrs
Humphry Ward, his aunt and godmother, about 1898

IX Julian 9, Aldous 2, and Trev 7, taken in 1896 at the country home near Tring of their Aunt Mary, Mrs Humphry Ward

world. Aldous later introduced me to Beethoven's posthumous quartets, which to me represent the deepest profundity and most glorious tenderness of all instrumental music.

I haunted the bookshops, especially Blackwell's, and penetrated further into the world of poetry – Donne and Marlowe, Cowper and Burns (whom I never really liked), Housman and Bridges, and a host of others. Nor must I forget Dante's *Divina Commedia*, which gave me intense pleasure in its interleaved translation; and Goethe's *Faust*, that extraordinary torrent of Germanic imagination.

Thanks to my parents, I had numerous senior acquaintances in Oxford, and used to go to tea or supper with remarkable people like Gilbert Murray, Professor Sedgwick and the Haldanes. This was my first introduction to the intellectually adult world, the international intelligentsia.

I learnt to punt, of course – and never fell in. Later a group of us took to Canadian canoes and even ventured to punt these, upright in the unsteady craft, using a long bamboo as pole, through the maze of waterways towards Cumnor.

Once, with Ronnie Knox and George Fletcher, we heard the bell of Cumnor's little church tolling for evensong, and at Ronnie's suggestion attended the service. The parson and handful of villagers, unaware of Ronnie's devoutness, were visibly surprised at this irruption of undergraduates in blazers and white flannels. Indeed we surprised ourselves.

Today a stream of cars whizzes along the bypass that has re-placed the rustic lanes of the Cumnor slopes, and the view of Oxford from the tree above, where Matthew Arnold's *Scholar Gipsy* rested, is no longer one of spires and domes and ancient houses, but of factories and suburban villas. Indeed a watcher could no longer detect 'the line of festal light in Christ-Church hall', for the view is blocked by ugly warehouses and blocks of flats.

At one of the after-supper Sunday concerts in Balliol Hall I heard Jelly d'Aranyi playing the violin. She was then only sixteen, a lovely creature with hair hanging down her back. After the concert, I was introduced to her; but as we emerged from the

Senior Common Room, Jelly was overcome by excitement, thrust her fiddle into my hands and started running round the Quad, her hair streaming. I had to rush after her and rescue her from the guffawing crowd of undergraduates. I didn't understand then, but later I learned that it had been a display of sheer exuberant joy that it was her birthday, and she had played in wonderful Oxford on that auspicious day. Jelly was entrancing. I found myself on the verge of falling in love with her, but although her exuberance and enthusiasm were her greatest charms, I was a little frightened of them, too. She was devoted to all the family, and both my brothers as well as myself fell under her spell.

She never married, but achieved firm religious faith, and a deep happiness in her friendships, and of course in her music. I corresponded with her until her death a few years ago. In 1966 I asked her if she had any of Aldous' letters to add to a collection of them.[1] She sent copies of twenty-three which, as she rightly said, revealed him as a 'very young and sensitive and most lovable Aldous'. She also sent drafts of some of his earlier poems.

I worked very hard at Oxford, under excellent teachers. J. W. Jenkinson taught us Experimental Embryology. E. S. Goodrich handled Comparative Anatomy: he drew so beautifully with coloured chalks on the blackboard that once we prevented the lab attendant from erasing the drawings until someone had taken a photograph of them. There was a hesitant young don called Schuster who did his best to explain to us the study of statistics as applied to Biology, but I am afraid without much success. And of course I had to do weekly essays for my brilliant Zoological tutor Geoffrey Smith of New College, soon, like Jenkinson, to be killed in the First World War. What hours I spent in the Radcliffe Science Library, digging out material! My German often came to my aid, enabling me to read even such enormous works as Haeckel's Monograph on jellyfish and corals.

I took protozoa (single-celled animals) as my special subject. This was a new idea; one could choose a particular group or topic in the zoological field, do some small piece of research, write it up,

[1] *The Letters of Aldous Huxley*, edited by Grover Smith. Chatto & Windus (1969).

and the resultant thesis would be taken into account in one's Final Examinations.

During all this time I continued to write verse, and in 1908 entered for the Newdigate Prize poem. The subject was Holyrood; I had never been there, but read all I could lay hands on about its romantic history. Again, as at Eton, I chose the Spenserian stanza. After an anxious period of waiting, I was told I had won the Prize. Then came the ordeal of having to stand up in a little balcony in the Sheldonian Theatre, and read it aloud to the assemblage of dons and visitors, at the Encaenia. My mother came to hear me. She was especially proud of my attempts to follow in Matthew Arnold's footsteps, notably by my quiet last stanza on a flowering horse-chestnut tree and its beauty. Arnold had achieved this same peaceful close in his sad *Scholar Gipsy*, with the simile of the Phoenician trader escaping from his Greek competitors and sailing to the Pillars of Hercules to bargain with the barbarians; and also in *Sohrab and Rustum*, when he takes the tragic edge off the poem with some lovely final lines on the majestic Oxus flowing into the Aral Sea.

Curiously enough, Aldous, who was a much better poet than I, never won the Newdigate. This was because, caught in the cynical post-war mood, he referred in his entry to the Kaiser as 'Sweet William with his homely cottage smell', a phrase borrowed almost verbatim from Matthew Arnold, but ludicrously misapplied in this context. It was too much for the examiners.

So far as I know, I am the only winner of the Newdigate to have spent the prize money on a microscope. It was a binocular microscope of a very old-fashioned kind, but very helpful in revealing stereoscopic views of the miniature world of algae, polyps and protozoa.

Each May a group of Balliol friends cycled over Cumnor Hill and down the Long Leys to Bablockhythe on the upper river. There we had dinner at the excellent pub and then recrossed by the ferry to settle down and listen in silent enchantment to the nightingales. There were many more of them than today – pesticides and hedge-clearance, combined with suburban spread, have killed or driven them away from most of their old haunts. It was our festival of spring – alas, no longer available to Oxonians.

Our 'nightingale' group also organized a 'Nebuchadnezzar Club'. A Nebuchadnezzar is a form of charade, in which one side wordlessly acts a set of historical scenes, and the other side has to discover the final name-word, compounded of the initials of the protagonists of the separate scenes. My rooms in the Tower between the two quads were ideal for this purpose, with two doors, and a window-seat which could be screened by a curtain. We met on Sunday evenings after hall and the concert. I remember once doing a scene of Elijah and the Prophets of Baal. An erection of chairs in a flat bath served as sacrificial pyre. The prophets danced madly round and nothing happened – no fire descended from heaven. Then water was poured into the bath, Elijah made an appeal to his God, and the curtains were drawn back, revealing the fat figure of Finlay as Jehovah. From under his surplice he produced a new box of Club matches and hurled it at the chairs, upon which it duly exploded into 'divine' flames.

My wife and I continued the charade tradition long after we were married, giving a 'Nebbers' party every New Year's Eve.

That summer was a high point in my life. I had just come of age; I had won the Newdigate; was doing well in my Zoology; and in the early weeks of my summer vacation I was the only male among the eighty or so girls at my mother's school and thoroughly enjoyed striding about on the playing fields in straw hat, my Etonian blazer, and white flannels.

I fear I took advantage of my position, and used to wander into the copse with one of the girls in the evening. A little kiss was the usual result. But one evening I went into the wood with K., a gay, athletic, fair-haired girl, and not only kissed her but rolled on the ground with her. Such was my contrariety of spirit that, though I was deeply attracted, at the same time I was repelled by the sexuality of the action; I can still remember her black stockings and the femininity of her smell. Why is the human mind so complicated as to be repelled and attracted at one and the same time? Why is sex both an inspiring blessing and primal curse, inflicting guilt as well as joy?

This did not deter me from going on with this intriguing ambivalence. We used to get up before breakfast, she strolling casually to the wood while I ran out on to the road, out of sight, and so into the copse from its far side. That was the beginning of a sad story which I shall take up later.

Both the summer vacations of 1907 and 1908, the family spent in Switzerland. In 1907 my father and I walked with our heavy rucksacks over the col to near Champex. I was so tired that I staggered to bed and slept a good ten hours. Next day, we marched with a guide up the mountain path to the *cabane de tours*. From there we made the ascent of the Aiguilles Dorées – spectacular pinnacles, climbable only with the aid of a rope over a chock-block, with a sheer drop to the northwards. The next night we spent in a *cabane* close to the Italian frontier, and were joined by a solitary Italian, equipped only with an alpenstock. We got talking and discovered that he was smuggling a load of dynamite! He assured us that it was quite safe, but we did not envy him as he started off next morning, down the rocky descent with his potentially explosive rucksack.

In 1908 Trev accompanied us to the Graian Alps in Italy. There we climbed the Grivola, a fine peak of about 11,000 feet. On the way up we saw chamois running up the steep slope, but I was not a creature of the heights – I found it heavy going in the snow and began to feel palpitations of my heart, while Trev began to be affected with mountain sickness. But a rest on the summit, with a view of the Gran Paradiso and the great line of the Swiss Alps like buttresses above the Lombard plain, quite set us up. We came back by way of the Val d'Aosta, and so to Courmayeur, with the formidable wall of Mont Blanc looming high before us. We toiled up the 9,000 feet to the Col du Géant, the only negotiable gap in the great rock rampart, then down steeply to the Mer de Glace, the enormous glacier. At last we came to a meadow, and there in the sun we all slept for an hour before proceeding to the valley and the hotel at Argentière, where my mother was waiting for us.

It was a gloomy time for me, for not only was I worried about my relations with K., but felt that I had physically strained my heart, so had to lounge about while my father and Trev went off on another big climb. To cap everything, my mother was not feeling well. On the way home I accompanied her through the pleasant, sunny little towns on the French shore of Lac Léman, but she was always out of sorts, and often in pain. And so home; and there, all too soon, my Uncle Harry and a specialist diagnosed cancer. . . .

I went back to Oxford, but latish in the term was summoned to her bedside at Prior's Field. Never shall I forget how wasted she looked, nor the terrible cry she gave: 'Why do I have to die, and die so young!' She was only forty-six; the same age at which her grandfather Thomas Arnold of Rugby had died of heart-failure. I was overcome, and ran out into the drive – anywhere in the open air, away from that doomed bed. Mr Judson, a Charterhouse master, came to ask how she was: I just couldn't answer coherently and rushed out into the fields with my misery.

And then, only a fortnight later, came the news of her death and another summons home. I reproached myself bitterly for having forgotten about her, even for a day, and for having enjoyed myself in a normal way at Oxford while she was dying. The tragedy of her death seemed unbearable, and I was overcome by a sense of overwhelming loss. She had always been the loving and loved central figure in our home life.

At the funeral all the Prior's Field girls followed after the family, two by two, many of them in tears, to the Watts Memorial Chapel in the lovely village of Compton. There my mother was buried, with my poor father standing solitary by the grave, in which he too was later to be laid to rest. Trev and I were on the verge of tears, and Aldous, then at the critical age of fourteen, stood in stony misery. We know now, from several of his early novels, what sense of irreparable bereavement occupied his mind and soul; I am sure that this meaningless catastrophe was the main cause of the protective cynical skin in which he clothed himself and his novels in the twenties.

Margaret, then only eight, looked bewildered and frightened, and well she might, destined at her early age to a bereft existence, until my father married again four years later.

The move to a gloomy London house in Westbourne Square, away from our beloved Surrey, was a blow to us all: but it came early in 1909. For the first half of that year I was very busy at Oxford, preparing for my Finals, but I managed to get out into the country on most week-ends, generally with Bob Brandt. Once on the way to Beckley we flushed a water-rail from under a culvert; and in Beckley were delighted with the sight of an old man, comfortably perched on the seat of his out-door privy in Roman fashion, surveying the landscape and greeting the passers-by. And in the little pub where we had lunch was a visitors book, where we read:

> I went to Noke and never spoke.
> I came to Beckley and spoke direck'ly.

This is a good characterization, for Beckley is a cheerful village on a hill, while Noke lies isolated on the flat marshy edge of Otmoor.

This dreary plain must once have been the bed of a lake. Right in its centre, where four rough tracks meet, there was a wood with a heronry in it. And here one spring, I witnessed the strange social gathering of the herons, jumping around with flapping wings. No one knows exactly what this signifies, save that the urge takes them just before the breeding season: I expect that here they recognize their old mates, or, if need be, choose new ones. Later, we saw the same kind of social dance in the crested cranes of Uganda, though they nest singly, not in colonies like herons. This confirms my idea that the prime function of these dances is the choosing of mates – just as in the ballrooms of our own societies.

I was by now thoroughly bitten by the excitement of mountaineering, the pitting of one's human self against inhuman nature. As I wrote in Arnold Lunn's anthology, *Oxford Mountaineering Essays*, published in 1912: 'The mountains can give the climber more than climbing. . . . From them there will come to him flashes of beauty and of grandeur, light in dark places, sudden glimpses of the age, the glory and the greatness of the earth.'

I recalled lantern-lit tramps over the pre-dawn snows, imagining the incredible crumplings and foldings that had attended the birth of the Alps, forty or fifty million years ago, and seeing the fantastic shapes into which wind, water and ice had eroded the Alpine ranges and our own Lake District into their present peaks and valleys.

As a substitute for real mountaineering, I had done a good bit of roof-climbing in Oxford, usually with a friend but sometimes alone. This was in some ways more challenging than ordinary mountain-climbing, for it was undertaken without ropes, in darkness and silence, for fear of the college authorities or the police. There was a particularly nasty bit at the back of Balliol Hall, where one had to put one's leg round a corner, trusting that the foot would encounter a projecting water-spout. The man who first surveyed this route must have been a cool and daring fellow.

There was a splendid climb to the north face of Trinity clock. This started alongside the Balliol science lab, where I had to grip the coping-stones to pull myself over the gables. On one occasion the stone I was pulling on started to give way: luckily I was able to throw myself forward into position, otherwise I could easily have fallen back on to a *cheval de frise* with the stone on top of me – an unpleasant idea! Then up the west wall of Trinity, with the possibility of being confronted with a don looking out of his rooms; and so on to the clock, setting its hands wrong before returning.

But we were not confined to Balliol and its neighbouring colleges. There was a reasonably simple exit over the back gate into St Giles', and one night two of us climbed out and started scrambling over the Ashmolean Museum. Making our way along a ledge, we were suddenly faced with a lighted room and an Ashmolean curator, looking at us through the window. We beat an unorthodox retreat, slipping over the balcony, wedging ourselves between the wall and the grooves of the classical pillars, and glissading down to the safety of the street.

My last exploit was solo. I was determined that, whatever happened to me in my Final Examinations, I would put myself, at least physically, above the Examination School. I just managed to get up the sham Tudor building and had a splendid and triumphal view of all Oxford, with its spires and domes and quadrangles gleaming in the clear light of a June dawn.

Finals at Oxford are a formidable trial, for the candidate has to be prepared to answer questions on anything that he has learnt in the Honours course of two or even three years. I felt the strain of last-minute cramming, and on the Sunday before my Schools, went for a long walk to clear my head along the upper river. It was a beautiful June day, with a profusion of wild roses in bloom, but I got back over-tired and far from clear-headed.

Next week, however, I successfully faced the ordeal of my Finals, and to my own and my father's pleasure was awarded an Honours degree – B.A., First Class.

At Cambridge, in July of that same year 1909, there was a great international gathering to celebrate the centenary of Charles Darwin's birth, and at the same time the fiftieth anniversary of the publication of the *Origin of Species*. As a Huxley and a budding biologist, I was invited, and was deeply impressed by the stream of addresses stressing the importance of Darwin's many-sided work.

I thought of my grandfather defending Darwin against Bishop Wilberforce, of the slow acceptance of Darwin's views in face of religious prejudice, and realized more fully than ever that Darwin's theory of evolution by natural selection had emerged as one of the great liberating concepts of science, freeing man from cramping myths and dogma, achieving for life the same sort of illuminating synthesis that Newton had provided for inanimate nature. I resolved that all my scientific studies would be undertaken in a Darwinian spirit and that my major work would be concerned with evolution, in nature and in man. This was not so much a turning point in my career as a crystallization of my ideas, a clear vision and inspiration which I can truly say remained with me all through my life.

Two veterans of Darwin's epoch were sitting side by side on a dais – my dear Huxley grandmother, then rising eighty-five, and the bewhiskered and heavily eye-browed Sir Joseph Hooker, Darwin's botanical mentor, older than she. Gran'moo was in her bonnet and bombasine, very dignified and worthy of the great honour. T.H.H. had been dead for fourteen years, but she survived him with amazing vitality. Even after this, I remember her reading the weekly science journal *Nature* assiduously, and discussing with me various biological problems as they came up, and physico-chemical issues with Tom Eckersley, her mathematical grandson. She also wrote some of her best poetry in her old age, and published an anthology of T.H.H.'s most striking phrases. And yet when she first came to England as a bride the doctors warned her husband that she should not have children and would in any case die within a year! She actually bore him eight children and only towards the very end of her life (she died at eighty-nine) did she take to her bed.

In August the family went, with the Harry Huxleys, to Cotherstone in Teesdale. K. joined us for a week. We were not officially engaged but it was recognized that we were devoted to each other. I had not breathed a word to her about my difficulties – this battle between sexual attraction and a puritanical sense of guilt, which prevented me from achieving a complete emotional relation with this attractive and uncomplicated girl. The whole climate of the Edwardian age, with its hypocritical suppression of everything 'nasty', fostered this conflict between instinct and reason. My schooldays, with their smutty stories and my concern over masturbation, had induced an underlying sense of moral guilt about sex which took me years to outgrow.

Today my grandchildren and their friends live in a 'permissive society'. Sometimes it seems a little too permissive, but at any rate most of its younger members are spared the anguished conflicts of my own time. Their inner lives are rarely complicated by repression or guilt feelings about sex – though they are often troubled by the violence and stupidity of the adult world.

My passion for unspoilt nature helped me, as so often, to get over my inner troubles. I fell in love with the wild Yorkshire moors and their beautiful streams and rivers. I especially remember a long walk with K. and my cousin Gervas, Uncle Harry's elder son, past High Force, a splendid waterfall with the rare pink *farinosa* primroses growing near its lip, past the even more romantic cascade of Caudron Snout, and up across peat hags to High Cup Nick, assuredly one of the strangest places in Britain, a U-shaped valley in the north face of the Pennine scarp, bordered by vertical basalt cliffs, with the Lake District mountains on the far horizon. On our return in the hot afternoon, we spotted a solitary farmhouse in a fold of the moors and knocked at the door to ask for a glass of water. After a long wait, an ugly old woman grudgingly fetched a pitcher for us. We later found that the place was called *Hagworm Hall* – a fitting name for such a Brontë-esque habitation!

The river near our lodgings was beautiful, with banks eroded into miniature grottoes, locally styled the Fairy Cupboards; and there were still salmon in its unpolluted waters. One three-footer I found wedged between the stones and tried to capture it with my bare hands. But its muscular strength was enormous: it wrenched itself free and was off in a flash, robbing me of my triumph.

In the evenings I worked on my first scientific paper, an account of an aberrant protozoan parasite which Geoffrey Smith had found in the primitive little freshwater shrimp *Anaspides*, a survivor from the carboniferous epoch dating about three hundred million years back, which he had found in Tasmania, preserved by its isolation.

This was our first holiday without my mother, and we were hard put to it to cover our hearts' grief.

CHAPTER V

Naples

AFTER this sad holiday, I set out for Naples in September, having been awarded a 'Naples Scholarship', provided by a fund set up by learned societies in various countries to enable biologists, even young ones, to do research at the Naples Marine Biological Station. Its founder was the German biologist Anton Dohrn, backed by my grandfather T.H.H.; he was succeeded as Director by his son Reinhardt, a delightful and truly international personage – born in Naples, married to a Russian, and master of most European languages. We soon became friends and our friendship lasted till his death.

The saying 'See Naples and die' can be taken in two senses – either that you will never again see such beautiful scenery, or that you may catch some fatal disease like typhus in the city slums or malignant malaria in the adjacent marshlands. I got off with a bout of hepatitis, nasty but not fatal, though it made me very ill-tempered.

I don't want to usurp the functions of Dr Baedeker, but must mention one or two points about this wonderful area. The volcanic soil was so rich that it supported three crops at once – olive and orange trees, with grape-vines slung between them, and vegetables below. The scenery was a never-ending joy: Vesuvius towering up to the old crater of Monte Somma, whose head was blown off in the great eruption that destroyed Pompeii and Herculaneum; the limestone cliffs of Sorrento and Capri; and the volcanic tufa islands of Procida and Ischia, the latter with the 2,000-foot Monte Epomeo towering from its centre, and *fumaroli* emitting sulphurous steam – even through chimney pots in the peasants' gardens. These *fumaroli* are also found abundantly in the

Campi Flegrei on the mainland. They fascinated me: when you lit a piece of paper over one hole, sulphurous smoke was emitted by a number of others. The physicists 'explained' to me that it was due to ionization, but I never really understood how this curious pulsation of gas could be instantaneously induced in separate vents.

I was also fascinated by the crater lake of Avernus, reputed by the Romans to be the entry to the subterranean world of the dead. Myth and geology made their unequal claims, but I was romantic enough to enjoy both.

The scrub beyond was a Royal preserve, full of wild boars, and when 'my' Professor Goodrich came out in the spring to work at the *Stazione* I went to Cumae with him, left him painting (he was as good a water-colourist as he was a blackboard draughtsman) and went off to explore the ruins. As I returned I was intrigued by seeing a wild sow and her brood advancing on the mild little Professor, and wondered what would happen, for an old sow can be pretty vicious. What *did* happen when the brood reached his easel was quite unexpected; he dipped his brush in water and flipped it in their faces, upon which they beat a disorderly retreat.

In the wooded crater of Astroni, also a Royal preserve, I witnessed a congregation of black snakes, up to five feet long, convoluted in their mating ceremonies, writhing and coiling, with a flicker-tongued head poking out here and there. I was fascinated and also repelled by this extraordinary spectacle. It clearly had something to do with mating, but I only learnt later that it occurs in numerous species, including our British viper, wherever they are abundant. A number of males gather round a female, and try to push each other away, often with intertwined bodies (hence the Roman medical symbol, the Hippocratic caduceus, with a pair of snakes twined round Aaron's magic rod), while at the same time they 'court' the female by licking her with their darting tongues. I consider myself very lucky to have witnessed this rare ritual, stranger even than the social dances of herons and cranes. The copulation of giant boa-constrictors must be equally amazing, but they are solitary creatures one would never find in a crowd.

Another unforgettable sight I enjoyed was Halley's comet,

which I saw one evening from the ruins of Tiberius' cliff-top palace on Capri, apparently diving into the glowing centre of Vesuvius. It was easy to understand why comets were regarded as miraculous portents of disaster.

Nor shall I ever forget what I saw one December evening in one of the Naples *bassi* – single ground-floor rooms that served as shop, eating-place, sitting-room and bedroom – a whole family asleep in the one bed with a goat in a corner and a turkey on the bedrail! It was a moving spectacle, a revelation to a comfortable Englishman of how the poor were forced to live in what was then the largest city in all Italy.

At least they had the consolations of religion – there was a lighted picture of the Virgin in every dwelling, and I saw plenty of *zampognari*, the cross-gartered bagpipe-men who come down from the Abruzzi every Christmas to play their pipes before these images, even in the slummiest houses. They were much more picturesque than our own carol-singers: but why, I asked myself, are bagpipes so generally associated with mountains?

I was lucky to see the liquefaction of St Januarius' blood, which takes place twice yearly. His church was packed, with a special enclosure reserved for the Saint's *parenti* or relatives (who included a number of extremely unprepossessing women of the lowest class).

The Saint's coagulated blood was brought up from the crypt, contained in a sealed glass tube within a splendid monstrance, and held up by the officiating priest, facing an acolyte holding a large candle. After a minute or so, he reversed the reliquary – but the reddish mass stayed solid, and the priest solemnly intoned '*Non Liquesce*' – the blood is not liquefying. The process was repeated several times, without liquefaction. The Saint's relatives began to get impatient. Instead of gentle implorations – 'Dear San Gennaro, *please* liquefy your wonderful blood', and the like – they became more and more peremptory, and eventually were threatening their patron, even shaking their fists. 'Liquefy your blank-blank blood, or else . . .', they were shouting; for it is very unlucky for the city and all its inhabitants if the 'miracle' fails to occur.

At last, however, the priest proclaimed the auspicious word,

Liquesce. You should have seen the orgy of satisfied superstition that ensued. The *parenti* screamed for joy, the general congregation crossed themselves and shouted, while some respectable gentlemen went down on their knees or waved their top hats.

The obvious explanation of the 'miracle' is that, when the substance (whatever it may really be) is brought from the cool crypt and exposed to the heat of a large candle in a crowded place, it melts. But how the priest regulates the time before the liquefaction takes place we do not know – perhaps by varying the distance between the blood and the candle.

Regulation is certainly possible. When Nelson brought his fleet into the harbour, the British were extremely unpopular and the holy blood refused to liquefy, as token of the Saint's displeasure – until Nelson sent a message intimating that if the miracle didn't take place, he would bombard the city. The priest was soon able to say *Liquesce.* . . .

In Ischia, the peasant guardian of the old castle above the circular harbour told me of another 'miracle'. The port area has a special patron saint, who protects his worshippers from earthquakes. But his power does not extend to the neighbouring parish of Casa Micciola, which has another celestial patron. And so, when the great earthquake of the 1880s struck the island, its effects stopped precisely at the parish boundary: Porto d'Ischia was unscathed, while Casa Micciola lay in ruins!

He also told me of another portent – the return to the harbour, each year at the same time, of a particular porpoise called The Monk, from his curious cowl-like head-markings.

This, if not miraculous, is certainly mysterious. We know that porpoises and dolphins can detect submarine obstacles by echo-sounding, and also that they are highly intelligent. But, even so, how can they remember the echoes from a particular stretch of coast, and find their way in to one favoured refuge?

But to my work! Dr Mayer drew my attention to two exciting projects. One concerned the fact, first recorded by an American, H. V. Wilson, that the tissues of sponges, if pressed through fine cheese-cloth, came out as isolated cells, singly or in small groups, which then slowly coalesced into two-layered solid spheres, with the dermal ('skin') cells outside, and the flagellated collar-cells packed in the centre, unable to use their microscopic whip-lashes.

I took this further, and showed that the masses eventually expanded, the dermal cells produced protective spicules, entry pores, and a space within, together with an osculum for the exit of the water driven by flagella of the collar-cells lining the interior, whose sticky 'collars' entrapped minute food-particles from the passing flow. Each random mass of cells became a perfect minia-ture sponge.

I also found that when I carefully teased out sheets of pure collar-cells, these would form hollow spherical masses with their whip-lash flagella directed *outwards* – the reverse of normal. Apparently collar-cells put out their flagella and sticky proto-plasmic collars whenever there is access to sea-water, so that their fate is not predestined, but a function of their position. This was a new and interesting fact, and the paper I wrote on my experiments was eventually accepted for the Phil. Trans. – the Philosophical Transactions of the Royal Society – a real honour for a biologist only twenty-three years old.

Meanwhile my old loves, the protozoa, were not forgotten. I came across some specimens of a rare mud-living Foraminiferan, a peculiar flattened tubular creature encased in a thin skin, over a centimetre long (pretty big for a single cell) with only two fora-mina or openings, one at either end, from each of which pro-truded a network of fine-drawn sticky pseudopods, designed to capture minute protozoa and algal spores. By a combination of luck and patience I was able to describe the multiple reproduction of this species for the first time. After a slight injury, one specimen divided up during the night into over five hundred miniature organisms, each like its parent in having an opening at either end, but their body ovoid instead of elongated.

Then there was the story of *Clavellina*. Again, it was Paul Mayer who drew my attention to Hans Driesch's startling work on this social Ascidian 'sea-squirt'. He found that, when the thorax with its gill-slits and miniature brain was cut off and left in a small container, it was gradually poisoned by its own waste-products, lost its visible differentiation and shrank into an opaque mass, in which the heart-beat alone remained as evidence of normality. If replaced in clean water, it re-differentiated, not into a new thorax, but a normal whole individual.

By leaving whole zooids in unchanged water for a longer period (I used very small animals, grown from pieces of the stolon-tube joining the entire colony), I got the dedifferentiation process to proceed to its limit, until only tiny solid whitish balls were left, a skin of epidermis over a solid blob of undifferentiated mesenchyme, with no trace of heart or other adult organs. Even these could redifferentiate into a normal adult, but with a gill-slit pattern quite different from that of the original zooid: the old individual was reborn, but in a new form. Thus mesenchyme acted as reserve germ-plasm – a substitute but multiple ovum, if you prefer this term.

This was the beginning of a whole series of experiments, carried out later at Plymouth and Wood's Hole. Some of the results were quite startling. Thus in Perophora, another social Ascidian, I isolated zooids still attached to a length of tubular stolon, the living pipe connecting all the zooids of the colony. When its little bath of sea-water was changed every day, the zooid maintained itself at the expense of the stolon, which gradually shrank. But when placed in unfavourable conditions (by adding very dilute poisons or not changing the water) the zooid would dedifferentiate and might eventually be entirely resorbed into the stolon, which could actually grow as a result of absorbing the zooid's tissues.

Still later, I was able to take advantage of this differential sensitivity to obtain precocious metamorphosis in sea-urchins. As is well-known (to zoologists!) the sea-urchin larva is called a *pluteus* – a flimsy, floating creature with elongated arms covered with a delicate membrane, edged with bands of cilia for swimming. At a certain stage the solid rudiment of the future urchin is formed in its interior. In slightly toxic conditions the delicate pluteus dedifferentiates and its arms shrink; while the solid urchin-rudiment is not affected and may even develop prematurely into a miniature urchin. Thus the differential sensitivity of pluteus and urchin-rudiment is responsible for normal metamorphosis. When the increased weight of the urchin-rudiment brings the whole complex down into conditions unfavourable to the pluteus, away from surface oxygen, it can continue to develop on the sea-bottom, while the pluteus disintegrates, and its tissues are resorbed into the growing urchin.

I must mention the *Stazione*'s porter, who had to be a member of the notorious Camorra, in order to ensure success in any dealings with the municipal authorities – I myself saw him handing out half-lire, worth then about fivepence, even to senior officials in the Mayor's office when I was being registered as an approved visitor.

An interesting visiting worker at the *Stazione* was the young Otto Warburg, a few years older than myself, but already a remarkable scientist, who later won the Nobel Prize for his work on respiration. I got on well with him and we went one day to visit the subterranean grottoes on the Sorrento peninsula, full of the skulls of monks from the local cemetery – a macabre sight. Later, in 1913, I worked in his laboratory at Heidelberg. He had a strange career; though of Jewish origin, he managed to keep his stable of Arab horses during the worst of the Hitler regime, and to employ several Jewish assistants on the staff of the Max Planck Institute, of which he was Director, without incurring any trouble from the Nazis. I suppose that his international reputation was too high for them to risk interfering with his work.

Between days of hard work at my bench I explored the exciting neighbourhood. There was Amalfi with its university founded by the Moors, and patronized by that strange Emperor, Frederick II; and I explored the remains of the Greek colony of Paestum, standing then on a deserted plain, so malarial that even the solitary station-master's house had mosquito netting all over it. What a revelation were the Greek temples, virtually intact after more than two thousand years. The Temple of Neptune was the grandest, with its massive Doric pillars. I had no idea that some Greek temples were like the later Christian basilicas, but here was a nave with side aisles, and on the pillars separating them were other smaller pillars, like those on the clerestory of our Gothic cathedrals.

In the spring I took a week's holiday with my Aunt Mary Ward, who had rented a lovely villa at Fiesole, above Florence. It was a great refreshment of the spirit, as shown by the letter of thanks I wrote her:

'. . . I feel much set up, physically and mentally. What is more, I learnt twice as much of Florence as I should have done alone, and now really understand something about the growth of Italian art, which I had never grasped at all before. And last, but not least, all you told me about your work and yourself made me understand you much more than I ever did before and gave me another ideal to help me along through the mush of "ordinariness".'

And so my year at Naples came to an end. It had taught me several lessons, mainly the importance of choosing an interesting problem: if it had not been for Paul Mayer, I should not have known what to investigate, or got involved in the basic subject of progressive differentiation and its occasional reversal. Selecting a problem for oneself is largely a matter of intuition. In pursuing one's investigations, however, one must persevere with every available method, and also be ready to take advantage of a chance happening, as I did when I found that some of my sponge cell-masses were entirely composed of collar-cells. Finally, one must be prepared to read all previous work on the subject, in order to evaluate one's own results correctly.

It also taught me the value of discussing problems with other people, and the mysterious catalysis of ideas that results. This is now well recognized, and most major scientific projects are carried out by teams, basing their work on just such interplay of ideas and methods. The era of solitary exploration, in the laboratory or the field, is now largely a thing of the past, but it was not so in my early days.

CHAPTER VI

From English Bird-watching to Texas Festivities

I RETURNED to Oxford to take up a lectureship at Balliol (£200 a year), and an equally poorly-paid demonstratorship in the Department of Zoology. My memories of that time are rather fragmentary. I demonstrated away, mostly in the Elementary Lab. During one spring vacation, I organized a reading party at Mochras, near Harlech. I remember stupidly wading my way through Bütschli's enormous German work on protozoa, but in my spare time doing something that I knew intuitively would be of much greater importance for my future career – scientific bird-watching. I watched and noted the courtship of redshanks on the mudflats through a telescope and my treasured binoculars. I was able to follow all stages of the process, from the long drawn-out pursuit of the hen by the cock, terminated by the hen stopping in her tracks. Then began the male's remarkable display, in which the wings were opened to show the white undersides, and the bird advanced slowly towards the female, his conspicuous red legs repeatedly raised, while he emitted a continuous rattling note. Finally he vibrated his wings even more rapidly, until he raised himself into the air, settled on her back and, still fluttering, succeeded in copulation. I also repeatedly saw the conspicuous display-flight, warning rival males off the chosen nesting area, in which the male indulges in a series of switchbacks, giving vent meanwhile to a loud and melodious song.

As a result of these observations, I published the first of my many papers on bird courtship in relation to Darwin's theory of sexual selection. I am not a little proud that I used the word 'formalized' for some of the male's actions, for we now know that much courtship behaviour is indeed stereotyped in a special formalism; and much prouder of having made field natural history scientifically respectable.

At Balliol, I now had nice rooms in the main quad. I made various new friends, but my main tie was still with Bob Brandt, who had become a Fellow of Brasenose. For two years we lunched together every week in term-time, alternately in Balliol and BNC, and discussed poetry and politics.

Meanwhile my affairs with K. were getting very complicated. I had by now become formally engaged to her, had bought a ring, and was a frequent visitor at her home. Her father was a charmer, but her mother was difficult. The terrible fact was that I still had the same ambivalent feelings about her, still torn between attraction and a sense of guilt. There were times when, after she had gone to bed, I would wander out into the garden of their comfortable Regency house and be seized by the deepest despair and horror of myself – and the intolerable situation I had created for her. Self-torture is a terrible thing.

Suddenly, my prospects changed. In the summer of 1912, when I was just twenty-five, President Lovett of the newly-created Rice Institute in Houston, Texas, offered me the Chair of Biology there, with a salary far beyond what I could look forward to in Oxford – the equivalent of £750 a year. I accepted, but said I would need another year studying on the Continent to fit myself for this challenging job.

Meanwhile I was bidden to the formal opening of the Institute in November. But before this I had spent a strenuous spring fortnight at Tring with my brother Trev to pursue the study of the 'courtship' of the great crested grebe, *Podiceps cristatus*. Their spring antics, much stranger than the redshanks' displays, had long aroused my curiosity. We slept at Stocks Cottage, which had been lent to us by Aunt Mary, and bicycled off every morning to the reservoirs

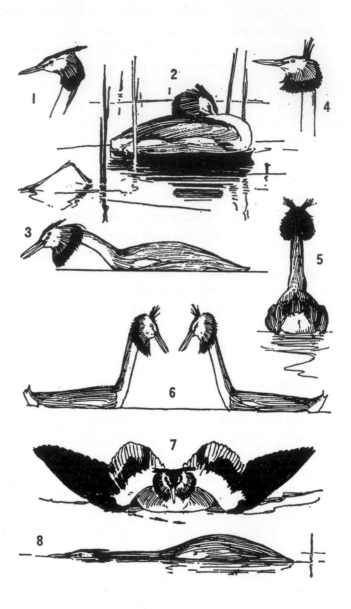

Opposite

Drawings by Miss Woodward, based on my own sketches from 'The courtship habits of Great Crested Grebe', *Proc. Zool. Soc.* 1914.

1. Head and neck, showing ruff and ear-tufts relaxed.
2. Resting attitude. Note the position of the head, and the curve of breast and rump. In most figures these are erroneously represented.
3. Search (Dundreary) attitude. Ear-tufts relaxed, crest spread longitudinally; sometimes it may touch the water.
4. Head and neck in shaking attitude: ear-tufts erected vertically, ruff pear-shaped.
5. Shaking attitude, from behind. Note the curious shape of the lower part of the neck.
6. A pair in the forward (excited) shaking attitude. Note the head bent down, the neck strained forward; the slope of the body and cock of the tail are also very characteristic.
7. The cat attitude (display). The general attitude is very well represented. More white should show on the breast; and the dark portion of the wings should be grey. To represent them black lessens the effect of the real black on the crest, which in actual life is the central and most conspicuous part of the picture.
8. The passive ('female') pairing attitude. Note the strange stiff appearance, the humped back, and the total closure of the crest.

Overleaf

9. The 'ghostly penguin' attitude of the emerging bird in the display ceremony.
10. The same as Fig. 9 in side view.
11. A pair in normal shaking attitude, necks out, tails slightly raised.
12. Display ceremony: the diving bird just fully emerged.
13. The penguin dance. The birds have dived for nest material (water-weed), met, and leaped up breast to breast.

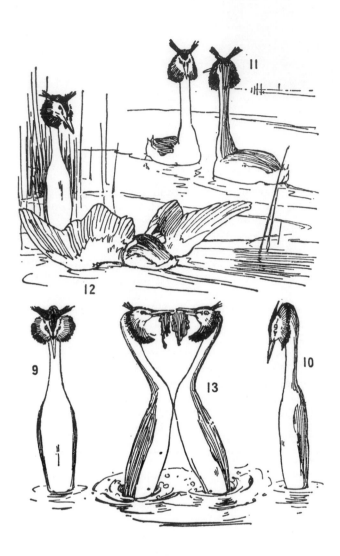

at Tring to watch and make notes on the grebes' behaviour. This was facilitated by a contraption I invented – an × 30 telescope mounted between two strips of wood on a tripod with a ball-and-socket joint, which permitted observation and note-taking at the same time. Even so, it was an exhausting job, and Trev took my place when I got tired by this dual concentration: the continuity of the record owed much to his help.

The resultant paper, published in 1914, proved to be a turning point in the scientific study of bird courtship, and indeed of vertebrate ethology in general. In the crested grebe the adornments of the sexes, ochre ruff and black ear-tufts, only grown in spring, are essentially identical in male and female. I discovered that the use of them in display was equally so; the courtship was *mutual*, not one-sided as in most birds. Even in coition, the behaviour of the two sexes was interchangeable: after the male had mounted the female, prostrate on a special pairing platform of water-weeds, he would slide off into the water, reascend the platform and the proceedings would be reversed, with the hen bird in the masculine position.

The displays were many and various. There was the common one of head-shaking, with necks erect and ruffs fanned out. There was the threat attitude with ruff spread and neck forwardly directed. There was an astonishing display when one bird dived, to emerge vertically before the other, which had its ruff opened and wings spread out to show the flashing white patches. And, even more extraordinary, a ceremony that I christened the 'penguin dance'. This occurred rarely, always after a very prolonged bout of head-shaking. First one bird dived, then the other; they emerged, with some of the water-weed used for nest-building in their beaks, and swam straight at each other. Just when a collision seemed inevitable, they leapt up and met breast to breast, slowly sinking down, dropping the weed, and ending with a further short bout of head-shaking.

In all this, ritual played a prominent part. Indeed, I was the first to apply the term *ritualisation* to these formalized ceremonies. I also was the first to record what is now called a *displacement activity*. Sometimes, towards the end of a long spell of head-shaking, the birds would make as if to preen their wings – not actually preening, but just raising the tip of the wing with their beaks. This meaningless activity was also ritualized, releasing inner tensions into new and irrelevant channels, when the urges to continue displaying and to break away were in conflict. Scratching our own heads when puzzled is a similar human 'displacement activity'.

I have recently been much gratified by an English firm's republishing my original paper, illustrations and all, as a pamphlet. This was indeed an honour after fifty-four years. (See sketches, pp. 86, 88.)

Another thing I discovered on the main reservoir was that the ducks were badly molested by the mallard drakes. Some were trodden so repeatedly that they were drowned. This happens when there is too great a concentration of mallard, due to over-protection by the owners of the shooting rights. I published a note on this in the *Biologische Zentralblatt*, and was able to point out an analogous incident in man, as recorded in the Bible in Chapter 19 of Judges.

In late September I took ship for America. I landed in New York and stayed at Miss Spence's; she was a friend of my youngest Arnold aunt, Ethel, and kept a girls' school, so I was in a familiar atmosphere. Here I earned my first money from lecturing – fifty dollars for a talk to the girls on biology.

Looking at my diary, I am astonished at the number of American biologists I was able to see on my journey to Houston and back. My first visit was to the famous 'fly-room' at Columbia University, where T. H. Morgan and his famous team, Sturtevant, Bridges, Muller and Altenburg, had just completed their first great piece of work on *Drosophila*, the now famous little fruit-fly. They had proved that the genes existed in groups on the four pairs of chromosomes and, what is more, that they could be located relatively to each other by the frequency with which they crossed over from one member of a pair to the other. This meant that one could now make a 'gene-map' of Drosophila's genetic constitution. It was an immense step forward from Bateson's work, admirable though that was.

It also led to my inviting H. J. Muller to come to Rice as my assistant – one of the most sensible things I ever did. Muller was a tower of strength, and managed to carry on with his genetical researches as well as helping me with teaching and demonstrating. He was later awarded the Nobel Prize for his splendid work on mutation and its artificial induction by X-rays and other agents.

I also met E. B. Wilson, the great authority on cell biology, and his charming young wife, who had previously been his ward; and Flexner, who was, I think, Head of the Rockefeller Institute for Advanced Biology in New York City. Also Peyton Rous, a noted research worker there. He had just discovered the first microbial cancer-producing agent – a virus that causes sarcoma in fowls. During his work on this, he had found that he could cultivate the virus, or even grow fragments of chick embryos, on the so-called allantoic membrane, richly supplied with blood-vessels, that grows out from the developing chick to act as a lung on the inner surface of the egg-shell. I wasn't interested in cancer then, but was excited by the new method of grafting tissues on to the egg's surface-membrane.

New York thrilled me with its skyscrapers (though they were nothing compared to the later giants); and the grandeur of its two main railway stations, Pennsylvania and Grand Central. (Pennsylvania resembled a Roman basilica, while Grand Central reminded me of Piranesi's drawings of gigantic imaginary buildings, now realizable through the invention of reinforced concrete); with my first taste of American food – soft-shell crabs, corn-on-the-cob and pumpkin pie; with the beauty of Brooklyn Bridge; and with New York's admirable Museum of Natural History which, under the direction of Henry Fairfield Osborn, had achieved a much higher standard of display than we had in London. It also sent out research teams to excavate and study the rich fossil deposits which revealed the evolutionary secrets of past animal life on the North American continent. Osborn was a proud man, occasionally arrogant, but very kind to me, as he had studied under my grandfather at South Kensington.

From New York I went north to New Haven (by boat, a wonderful trip up Long Island Sound, with a splendid view of Brooklyn Bridge from below). At Yale University I called on my second cousin Arnold Whitridge (a grandson of Matthew Arnold), and on the head of the Biology department, the distinguished embryologist Ross Harrison, a gaunt but generous-hearted man.

From there to Boston, where I noted in my diary my admiration for the gilded dome of the State House, a marvellous gleam in the centre of this rather drab puritan city; and so to Harvard. Here I met Professor Parker and other zoologists, and also the many-talented mathematician, Griffith Evans, who was to be one of my colleagues at Rice. I also saw my first game of American football, so much rougher than Rugby, and watched the winning Harvard team dance the traditional 'snake-dance' of victory round the goal-posts.

Back through New York and so to Princeton, where I renewed my acquaintance with the genial Conklin, an embryologist whom I had met at Naples; and admired the beauty of the University campus, while reflecting that the place seemed over-full of rich young undergraduates.

Further south to Baltimore, with its famous Medical school, which was linked to the equally famous Johns Hopkins University, the first solely post-graduate university in the world, with Ramsden, the brilliant medical administrator as President, Welsh as Dean, and Osler as head of the Medical school. They were all most cordial to me. Here again, my ambivalence about myself came to the fore. I knew I was able, yet could not believe that I was really worthy of all this praiseful recognition: I thought that it was merely because I was T.H.H.'s grandson, and because he had delivered a famous speech at the inauguration of the university.

Though his speech dealt primarily with educational problems, T.H.H. had given several lectures on evolution while in the USA, and was widely known as the champion of Darwinism, a blasphemous believer of the descent of man from apes. Ramsden told me of a letter he had received from a Presbyterian minister in New York, regretting that the proceedings had not been prefaced by a prayer, and still more, that Huxley had been invited to give the inaugural lecture. I remember the precise words: ' 'Twas an ill thing to have invited Professor Huxley. 'Twere better to have invited God. 'Twould have been impossible to have invited both . . .'

Then I started the long journey west and south to Houston. I was busy writing up my notes on grebe behaviour and was intrigued by an astrologist-banker (something one could only find in the US) in the same coach, who was astonished that I was actually writing by hand, instead of dictating to a stenographer. So on to St Louis, with just time enough to walk through unpleasant slums to see the junction of the two great rivers, Missouri and Mississippi – even more impressive than my later sight of the Nile dividing to fertilize the Egyptian delta.

From St Louis I went on by the Katy Flier, the star train of the M. K. and T. – the Missouri, Kentucky and Texas railroad. This was a lesson in social geography. The Flier, I found, 'flew' at an average of 34 m.p.h. This slow rate of locomotion was partly due to the poorness of the rails – it is hard to lay a perfect track across a thousand miles of sparsely populated prairie; but also to the delightful habit of meal-stops. Instead of eating on the train, joggled from side to side, we would draw up at a station – I should say 'deepo' – scramble out, and be served excellent home-cooked food on big tables by motherly ladies in white aprons. Meal-stops are now a thing of the past – the frantic desire for speed has abolished this leisurely custom.

In 1912, Houston was still only an overgrown town, not a real city. It was called after Sam Houston, the famous but eccentric general who had won the first round of the Mexican war after Texas had proclaimed itself a North American state, by his victory of San Jacinto, close to the future site of Houston, in 1835. (Texas was not incorporated into the Union until much later; it commemorated its independent origin by retaining a single star on its flag – the Lone Star State.)

The muddy San Jacinto bayou ran through Houston, but the land was so dreadfully flat that one area was called Houston Heights because it was eleven feet higher than the rest of the town!

The buildings of the Institute were very fine. They had been entrusted to the architect Ralph Adams Cram, who had drawn the plans for the Cathedral of St John the Divine in New York. He was a fanatical gothicist, but even he could not contemplate erecting a Gothic building on a semi-tropical coastal plain in Texas. Accordingly he had gone to Illyria for his inspiration, and the buildings were in rich, almost Byzantine style, with coloured tiles and marble capitals grotesquely carved among the bricks – and very effective they were.

At that time the Institute was a mile beyond the eastern border of the town, with nothing but prairie and a few pine-groves near by. Now, it has been swallowed up by the enormous growth of the city, which started with the digging of the ship channel to Galveston Bay and the sea, thus converting Houston from a railroad centre to a port, and incidentally spelling Galveston's downfall. Today, as I found on a lecture tour in the mid-sixties, a rash of smart suburbs, a huge medical school and a Hilton (which once, it is said, advertised itself as the most expensive hotel in the world), stretch well beyond the Institute, now re-christened Rice University.

If there was one thing President Lovett was good at, it was organizing a show with as many notables as possible. There were nearly a hundred distinguished professors from American universities, and a galaxy of outstanding savants from Europe, including Borel, the French mathematician; Benedetto Croce, the Italian philosopher, who looked more like a prosperous butcher than a savant; de Vries, the co-discoverer of Mendelism, from Holland, and Sir William Ramsay, the eminent British chemist and physicist, accompanied by his wife.

Some of the celebrations were held down-town, in the first and, at that time, the only skyscraper in Houston, the ten-storey Rice Hotel. At a lunch there the Governor of Texas, Colquhitt by name (who, by the way, was later impeached for corruption!) was the guest of honour. His speech boiled down to something like this: 'Ladies and Gentlemen, the State of Texas is the largest State of the Union. It is a thousand miles long from El Paso to the Red River, and eight hundred miles broad from the Panhandle to Brownsville and the sea.' (He exaggerated slightly, but it is true that the area of Texas is as great as that of France, with Alsace-Lorraine thrown in.) 'Ladies and Gentlemen, I am the Governor of this great State; and yet, amid my multifarious dooties as Governor of this vast territory, I have found time today to come to the Inauguration of the Rice Institoot'. . . . One could almost feel the shudder of horror that went through the ranks of the northern professors. What would the great men of Europe think of their country? I was not a great man, but I thought quite a bit about this amazing piece of braggadocio, which could only have happened in the self-glorying atmosphere of Texas.

The lunches, dinners and receptions continued inexorably. At the final one, which was held at the Institute, I was sitting next to Lady Ramsay. After a few formal speeches, the architect was called on. Cram rose to his feet, produced an enormous roll of typescript from his pocket and proceeded to read implacably on. After twenty minutes, the lady could stand no more: 'Oh, I am so tired! . . .' she said, and let her head fall forward on to her hands on the table. President Lovett had had his triumph. . . .

On my way back, via New Orleans, I was intrigued by the palmettos dotted about the coastal plain of Louisiana, looking as if they had been dropped from a wagon on the way to a concert or reception. In New Orleans itself, I caught a glimpse of the old Creole part of the city, picturesque but dirty, with circling vultures spying for carrion – very uncivilized, I thought.

And so back to New York, where I bade farewell to Miss Spence and my Columbia friends and took passage on a Holland–America boat for home in early November. After the dusty plains of the USA and their already withered grasses, the perennial greenery of Plymouth Hoe and the Devonshire countryside was a welcome reminder of Charles II's dictum – that England has worse weather but a better climate than any other country.

CHAPTER VII

German Studies and
Home Troubles

O N getting back to England, I had to fulfil my pledge to the
Rice Institute, and polish up my comparative biology in
Germany. I started by working with Otto Warburg in
Heidelberg, once more lodging with Fräulein Groh. There are two
things I recall from that visit – not the biochemical work, for it
largely went through my head, without affecting my research programme: I was always much more interested in the behaviour of
living animals and their past evolution than in the physico-chemical
basis of their activities.

Once as I was walking back to my lodgings in winter, I saw a
company of rooks in a field, all cawing away in chorus. At short
intervals, a few would fly high up in the air, and then plummet
down, dropping with closed wings almost to the ground, when
they opened their pinions and zigzagged in all directions before
landing. I later found, by a careful search of the 'literature', that
this so-called 'shooting' of rooks had been recorded earlier; but the
favourite time for this sport (and I do believe that it is a sport, and
really enjoyed by the birds) takes place in early autumn. On one
occasion, the whole flock went up so high before shooting down
that they reached the limit of human vision.

The other incident was when an aeroplane passed over the lab
(remember that this was in 1913). One of the students said sneer-
ingly: 'It won't be long before aeroplanes like that will be bombing
English cities.' I was already a fervent internationalist, and this
came as a great shock to me, especially from a research student at
the most famous German university. It was my first introduction

to the unpleasant fact of Germany's increasing military power and chauvinism – though my earlier visit to Heidelberg had shown me the students' violence expressed in sabre duels and beer-drinking competitions instead of games or sport.

I was still very unhappy in myself about K. and also about my own powers, and used to go on long walks in the winter mornings soon after dawn, up and down the little lanes and pathways of the vineyards, to dispel my doubts and miseries. But all they did was to tire me, and I got little comfort from them, save the dubious one of demonstrating my own physical toughness at the expense of my mental and spiritual energy.

From Heidelberg I went to Munich to work in Hertwig's laboratory. Here too I failed to profit very much from the work I was put to do – indeed I have forgotten what it was. But I remember a beautiful walk over dazzling snow towards some lake – was it the Starnberger See? – with snow mountains rising beyond. But again I was overtired, and now began to feel quite ill. There was a nice English girl in the pension who looked after me very kindly, and when I recovered I took her out to dinner to eat boar's head – an exotic symbol of the mediaevalism still surviving in Germany.

When I got back to my father's new house in Hampstead, my troubles with K. became intensified. I wasn't well, and was more and more torn between attraction, loyalty and guilt. It must have been clear that I was not in love with her, in the true sense of the word; the ambivalent situation was becoming increasingly difficult for both of us.

One afternoon she came into my room as I was resting, and broke off the engagement. It was a painful scene; she took off her ring and thrust it at me, got up, kissed a photograph of me hanging on the wall, burst into tears and rushed out of the house.

This was all my fault; but it was also the last straw, and I relapsed into a real 'nervous breakdown' – in modern terminology, a depression neurosis. Whatever it is called, it was a horrible experience, a hell of self-reproach, repressed guilt, a sense of my own uselessness and the futility of life in general. My Uncle Harry, the doctor, was called in; I expressed a desire to be treated by hypnosis and went to a psychiatrist in Primrose Hill Road. However, his treatment proved totally ineffectual and I was eventually sent on a 'rest cure' at a sanatorium near Godstone, under the North Downs in Surrey. There was no special regimen, apart from lying in bed, being well-fed and given tonics; the value of electro-shock treatment had not then been discovered. After what seemed an interminable time, I was allowed to take little walks, gradually increasing in length. The one incident I remember from that depressing interlude is of a robin perching on my window-sill and, after some effort, disgorging a tiny black pellet. This proved to consist of the wing-cases and other hard parts of small insects, so I was able to add a mite to my ornithological knowledge.

The net result was that I regained my physical health and was drained of the acute depression and guilt-feeling, but also of much of my intellectual and general self-confidence. However, I had to take up my duties at Rice, and in the early autumn of 1913 sailed for New York, and then by coasting steamer to Galveston – a dreary voyage, with the crew inclined to make fun of the callow young Britisher, so obviously unsure of himself.

On reaching Houston, however, I was stimulated by the multifarious activities of starting a biological department from scratch. Hermann Muller's presence was reassuring, and I had had the foresight to secure an excellent and energetic laboratory assistant called Davies, who had been Piggy Hill's lab boy at Eton. He and I got the microscopes out and all the paraphernalia of slides and stains. There was a little stream at the far side of the campus, and Davies and I used to go down to it and look for specimens. My chief recollection is of the local grasshoppers, which had the unheard-of habit of jumping into the stream when scared and actually swimming under water to escape. And the damp ground near by was beset with little towers of mud pellets, which turned out to be the breathing holes of the local land crayfishes. Terrestrial crayfish were as new to me as aquatic grasshoppers.

Like my grandfather, T. H. Huxley, I used earthworms as one of my zoological types, but had the greatest difficulty in getting hold of any for dissection, as the black moist soil of the prairie and campus held none. Eventually we heard of a market-gardener who had some in his greenhouses, and managed to secure a supply. I duly lectured on the anatomy of the familiar European earthworm, and then moved to the practical lab for dissection. After a few minutes one of the students said: 'Professor, these worms aren't like what you told us in your lecture.' I looked, and found him right: the organs and apertures were all in the wrong places! I eventually found that these worms belonged to a South American genus called Perichaeta, as different from the European earthworm as a gull is from a heron, or an eagle from a sparrow-hawk. I suppose they came with some tropical bulbs. Slightly put out, I was, however, able to use them as a text to demonstrate the variability of living things, even within the limits of a single zoological family.

My chief difficulty was one prevalent in most American universities at that time – to make my students realize that the two-year advanced course was a unity, as it had been at Oxford. They clung to the idea that all they had to do was to pass their exams at the end of each semester, and if I asked any questions concerning earlier work, would protest: 'But, Prof, we've *done* all that.' However, I persisted, and did something to establish biology as a unitary study, not to be chopped into unrelated chunks of knowledge. I later found that Harvard and Amherst were working along similar lines; but the 'dollop' system still prevails in many junior colleges and some universities in the USA.

With my love of varied scenery I found it difficult to get used to a country so uniformly flat that it rose only a foot a mile for fifty miles from the coast. But I must admit that in spring, when the prairie was full of flowers, the air blowing across its boundless space had a soft and scented character which was exceedingly pleasant.

After a year, three of us young bachelor professors decided to live together, and rented a house about three-quarters of a mile away, with sugar-pines all round it. Griffith Evans, the distinguished mathematician I had met at Harvard, proved to be well-read and musical, and became an intimate friend; and we both got on well with A. L. Hughes, a Welsh physicist. Evans invited young

Norbert Wiener to stay, the future pioneer of cybernetics. He was brilliant at mathematics and had got his degree at Harvard at the age of fifteen. But in all other subjects he was childishly ignorant; he spent his time mooning about and prattling to the Tsanoffs' infant daughter. He was also untidy and rather dirty.

Professor Tsanoff, the philosopher, had the house just opposite ours. He was a Bulgarian with a striking hooked nose and an un-ending flow of talk. I once heard him discourse for half an hour on the fact that the Bulgarians were the most taciturn race in Europe, without my being able to get a word in!

Soon after renting our house, I bought my first car – an original Model-T Ford, costing about £100, with petrol at 5d a gallon! It was a gallant little machine, which I could drive across the prairies; though I had to get out now and again to check that the hard dead stalks of last year's plants had not hit the sump-cock and let out the oil.

In the winter vacation, I drove with a colleague in my new car to see Stark Young, Professor of Comparative Literature at the State University at Austin, who had called on me in Oxford on hearing that I was coming to Texas. Americans today, accustomed to well-surfaced four-lane highways, will hardly believe how bad the Texas roads were fifty years ago. This important route from Houston to Austin soon turned into a 'dirt' road, so bad that at one swampy place I had to turn off into a field, and later, when we reached the heavy black cotton soil, the car stuck in a muddy mess on the slightest of slopes, and one of us had to get out and push. . . .

Stark Young was a remarkable man and became a real friend to me, and later to my wife. His appearance, with his long pointed nose and small chin, was rather like an aristocratic goose, but he had immense charm and a great sense of humour. He later moved to New York and became one of the most notable dramatic critics as well as an accomplished painter.

On another occasion, I was invited to stay with an eccentric millionaire near San Antonio, scene of the famous last stand of the little 'gringo' garrison of Los Alamos. My host kept a kennel of wild coyotes to howl him to sleep, in memory of his early days, when coyotes and hostile Indians roamed the plains and he never rode far without a rifle as protection against Indians, and to shoot prong-horned antelopes, then abundant, for his meals. In the mornings he was woken by his butler playing sacred music on a pianola-type organ. He also owned a fantastic barge, christened Noah's Ark, to which he would invite friends. I once went with him and an Austin professor on a cruise through the coastal bayous, a lovely trip on which I had my first sight of wild yuccas (Spanish bayonets), with their formidable spikes and beautiful white bell-flowers.

In 1914 I had a mild fit of depression and spent a gloomy spring vacation at a seaside boarding-house in Pass Christian. I was still far from well in the summer, so decided to return to England in the long vacation, and take a few weeks further 'rest cure' at the nursing home where I was treated the year before.

My brother Trev had had a breakdown too, and was at the same nursing home. After I had finished my spell there, I went first to stay with the George Trevelyans in the Lake District. Here came the news of Archduke Ferdinand's assassination, and the threat of war. George was an ardent pacifist, and rushed down to London to see Sir Edward Grey, the Foreign Secretary, and other friends in Government circles. He came back, haggard and drawn, on the 3rd of August, after an all-night train journey, buried his head in his hands on the breakfast table, and looked up weeping. 'It will be war, and millions of human beings are going to be killed in this senseless business.'

Next day came the German invasion of Belgium, and Britain joined in the struggle. I went on to Connel Ferry, near Oban, where my father and my new stepmother, Rosalind Bruce, were spending the summer. They had married in 1912, just after I had gone to Houston.

The time was full of rumours; we actually went out to the mouth of Loch Etive to look for the famous but imaginary Russian soldiers 'with snow on their boots', who were supposed to be coming to our assistance.

Then came the disquieting news that Trev was missing from

the nursing home. We thought that perhaps he had enlisted in the Army on a sudden impulse. But the news soon came that he had hanged himself in one of the dense woods near by.

Trev's suicide was one of the most ghastly things that could have happened. He was brilliant, good-looking, athletic, especially as a mountaineer, wrote good poetry, and was very popular. What horrible burden of suppressed guilt had driven him to take his own life? I was full of remorse, for as I knew nothing of his troubles at the time I thought that perhaps my successes at Oxford, and in getting this exciting job in the USA, compared with his own failure to win the Newdigate and to achieve a First in Greats, might have contributed to his depression: perhaps I should have been more encouraging to him in the nursing home; anyhow, the calamity still haunts me.

It was not until many years later that I heard why Trev had been so distraught, since, no doubt for his own good reasons, my father did not discuss the tragedy with me, and anyhow I was soon back in Texas, carrying my own remorse about K.

Trev had become deeply attached to an attractive and intelligent young housemaid working at the new family home in Bracknell Gardens, and was secretly trying to educate her by taking her out to plays, concerts and lectures. After a time he realized the hopelessness and unsuitability of the situation; and so did the girl, who gave in her notice. The break between them was to be final, but she wrote him a letter full of despondency, just as he was recovering from his breakdown. It was too much for him, and he chose to die. Sarah, our faithful parlourmaid, knew about the affair, and was able to explain the girl's letter found in Trev's pocket. Aldous must also have known, for he wrote to his cousin Gervas soon afterwards:

'It is just the highest and the best in Trev – his ideals – which have driven him to his death . . . Trev was not strong, but had the courage to face life with ideals – and his ideals were too much for him.'

CHAPTER VIII

Teaching and Research at Houston

I N September I returned to Rice, to take up my duties. The work absorbed me a good deal, and helped me to carry on, but again it was natural history which brought me my moments of joy. It was at Houston that I saw my first humming-bird, hovering in front of a spider-lily, itself a miraculously beautiful flower with white streamers protruding behind the main corolla. And I realized that humming-birds can do something beyond the reach of any man-made aeroplane (even the clumsy helicopter, which had not yet been invented): they can reverse without turning and can actually keep sucking from a flower swaying in the wind.

I made the acquaintance of many other new birds. Among them was the western gnat-catcher, a blue-grey little bird which reminded me of home, for (apart from the tiny kinglets and gold-crests) it is the only American representative of our European warblers. But my favourite was the crested fly-catcher, ash-grey and pink, with a long forked tail. I enjoyed seeing them in spring, sitting on the telephone wires and flying up in courtship display, their tails fluttering behind as they descended.

However, my most exciting (and scientifically profitable) ornithological experience was a study of the egrets and herons on McIlhenny's Reserve on Avery Island in Louisiana. One of my students, Finlay Simmons, was a first-class field ornithologist, and after getting permission, we set out in the spring of 1915 in my Ford with camping equipment, binoculars and a clumsy but efficient quarter-plate camera.

Mr McIlhenny owned the whole of the island, and cultivated most of it; it was here that the famous Tabasco sauce originated. Many of the labourers were French-speaking negroes, descended from slaves expelled (with their French masters) by the British from Acadia, as the French part of Nova Scotia was called in the eighteenth century. This was well before Wolfe's final victory over the French at Quebec. It was strange to hear garbled French issuing from their black faces in this alien setting.

McIlhenny exercised a feudal authority over them, much more arbitrary than anything I had seen in agricultural England. His great virtue – to me – was his love of birds. Some years earlier he had constructed a large pond in the low-lying part of his estate and planted it with willows and other semi-aquatic shrubs. Here he introduced about a dozen snowy egrets. They went off in the fall on migration, and he wondered if they would come back. Most of them did; the colony quickly grew and attracted new species – lesser egrets, Louisiana herons, little blue herons (which are white when young), reddish egrets, night herons and small bitterns. The pond also held some snakes and alligators, which fed mainly on the baby herons and egrets when they fell out of their nests.

When we arrived there were at least 100,000 birds of the heron family breeding there. It was a wonderful sight to see them come home to roost. They flew straight in from their feeding grounds, a couple of hundred feet up; when over the pond, they simply let themselves drop, spreading their wings when near the trees to side-slip and twist (like rooks in their aerial tumbles) in a moment of enjoyable emotion before searching out their own nests.

We had a punt moored in the middle of the colony, with a hide built on it; every morning we would go out there in a little canoe and watch the birds, taking elaborate notes on their behaviour and snapping away with my camera.

The only trouble was the mosquitoes. They were so abundant that we had to tie scarves over as much of our faces as possible, and wear gloves. On really bad days, when it was still and muggy, so many of these pestilential insects rose out of the grass round the pond that our khaki trousers were almost black, and McIlhenny couldn't take his horse out because their bites maddened it.

But the trip was well worth it. I corroborated what I had already established in the grebes, namely that in herons and egrets, and indeed in all birds in which secondary sexual characters are equally developed in both sexes, there exists a mutual courtship, with the two birds displaying to each other. And we ran across a nice bit of adaptation – the organs used in display in each species are particularly well-developed. Thus in the Louisiana heron, the reddish-blue neck is displayed, and its feathers are long and very conspicuous when bristled up; while in the white egrets the plumes of the back are erected in display and have been converted by natural selection into the beautiful fan of filmy aigrettes that used to decorate ladies' hats. (It was this commercial slaughter that induced McIlhenny to re-introduce these lovely creatures, and later, I am glad to say, forced Britain and other countries to prohibit the sale or import of aigrettes.)

We were also able to get some insight into the emotional life of the birds. When a pair was reunited after one partner had come back from fishing, there was great vocal excitement with bobbing of heads and fluttering of wings. The returning bird went off to gather twigs, which he or she ceremoniously presented to its mate, who then built them into the nest. Real affection was apparent between the couple: when they had a quiet time together on the nest, one would often rest with its head pressed against the other's neck, in mutual comfort.

I later incorporated our observations and some of my photographs in a comprehensive paper on bird courtship and display, published by the Linnaean Society.

In the summer of 1915, the Tsanoffs and I set off for Estes Park in the Colorado mountains, fully equipped for camping. We pitched our tents at 10,000 feet, with humming-birds all around sucking the mountain flowers (it is extraordinary that these tiny creatures, with such a large surface-volume ratio, can survive in the cold mountain air), and ground-squirrels and camp-robber jays stealing from our tents. We explored the neighbouring peaks with delight and great benefit to our physical well-being.

On Long's Peak, I had an extraordinary sensation – a series of pricks in my head, as if some being from outer space was trying to communicate with me in some curious code. Eventually I found that the 'messages' ceased when I took off my hat – I had some damp flowers in the hat-band, and so was acting as a lightning conductor when standing on the actual summit.

A party of Americans refused to believe me, so I got one of the men to put on my hat and scramble to the top. He was flabbergasted by the prickings and threw my hat back, muttering something about witchcraft.

Thence I went alone to a dude-ranch in the Bighorn Mountains of Wyoming. The scenery was even more fascinating than in Estes Park; canyons with narrow gorges, between open downlands and streams fringed bright with huge forget-me-nots, with immense cotton-wood trees, and sandstone buttes rising like castles over the sage-brush dry-lands to the east. An immense solitude, peopled only with the ghosts of Indians and the early American settlers trekking and fighting their way through to the Far West. There were tracks of long-dead bison on the lower slopes, and not far away was the scene of General Custer's last stand.

I was not unmindful of my biological department at Rice. I shot a prairie dog and stuffed it, after preparing its skeleton for mounting; and, even at the cost of some painful pricks, skinned a porcupine which had been shot by a forester, macerated its bones and took them back. So far as I know the two skeletons still stand in the biological collections at Rice.

This was the most restful holiday I ever had. I was out all day in the bracing air, often on horse-back, and slept up to ten hours every night.

Up in the mountains the pine-woods were bright with scarlet Indian paintbrush and our party fed luxuriously on trout that we caught ourselves in the clear streams, using grasshoppers as bait.

My usual breakfast was a couple of half-pounders followed by waffles and maple syrup and huge mugs of coffee.

Meanwhile I did a lot of thinking, and decided that I ought to get home next year and do something about the war. So long as I was resident in the USA, I was not liable to be called up, but I felt that to go on like this was shirking my duty.

Aldous advised against it, writing from my father's house in the spring of 1916:

'I cannot help thinking it would be unwise to come home. There is very little to be done unless one means to fight: and in these days, when one cannot get commissions, it is impossible to fight with that elegance and efficiency which, in the old days, as an officer, were within one's reach. Work in munitions factories is intolerable. They are destroying the potential value of thousands of workers by systematic over-working. Government departments are sometimes interesting, but of a fearful strenuity. I thought of going into the Foreign Press Department of the W.O. last winter, which would have been v. nice, but found that 12–14 hrs per diem was normal – so that it would have been quite beyond my ocular abilities to stand the strain. The longer this war goes on, the more one loathes and detests it. At the beginning I should have liked very much to fight: but now, if I could (having seen all the results), I think I would be a conscientious objector, or nearly so. But I shudder to think what England will be like afterwards – barely habitable.

Yours, A.L.H.'

Nevertheless I felt it more and more unbearable to be out of Britain now, and not to bear my share of its miseries and discomforts. I determined to go back to England in September, but first I went to Wood's Hole to finish the research work I had begun in 1913.

Wood's Hole, on Cape Cod, boasted the largest laboratory of marine biology in the New World, as well as an official Oceanographical Institute. Many biological professors, like Morgan, Wilson and Conklin, had built houses there, so that they could enjoy a good holiday while getting on with their research, and I was privileged to be admitted to their homes. I particularly enjoyed the Wilsons', whom I have already mentioned. He was the world's greatest authority on cytology (I had been biologically brought up on his splendid book *The Cell*).

Davies and I had various exciting sails in the swift-flowing sound, once kicking off our shoes in anticipation of capsizing. In the intervals of work, I was invited to the neighbouring island of Naushon, summer home of the New England aristocrats, the Forbes. The island was still as unspoilt as when the Indians lived there, or indeed when the Norsemen discovered what is now Massachussetts about a thousand years back, and christened it Vineland, country of vines, for Naushon was full of wild grapes.

Commodore Forbes took me out in his beautiful yacht, which was called the *Kalinga* – I suppose because he had visited north-western India, where the Kalinga dynasty once held sway. Little did I know that I should later be the recipient of the Kalinga Prize, a UNESCO award for popularizing science; and, at the invitation of the founder of the award, Mr Patnaik, actually visit the Kalinga area.

I also managed to get across to the outlying island of Martha's Vineyard, where, in company with Floyd Dell and other writers and artists concerned with the socialist weekly, *The Masses*, I bathed in the tremendous Atlantic swells on its sandy east coast, and enjoyed really civilized talk on books and politics and the American social set-up.

One natural history incident I vividly remember. It was the time when the tawny monarch butterfly sets forth on its extra-ordinary migration to Central and South America. Martha's Vineyard is mostly bare, and the solitary tree near the port was so crowded with monarchs that it looked like a gigantic orange chrysanthemum.

As my ship drew into Plymouth Sound I was again overcome by the greenery of England, greenery that continues throughout the year, unlike the prairie grasses that wither to brown every autumn; and this rediscovered luxuriance was a joy all the way to London.

The question was what sort of job I should take on. It was first suggested that I should go into a chemical factory turning out some substance important for the war effort; but this, luckily, fell through (the nature of the substance was kept secret, so I had my suspicions that it was something toxic). I was then given a post in the Censor's office in Carey Street. Here I learnt how to open letters and seal them up invisibly after reading them, and was able to report a few, as it seemed to me very minor, indiscretions – not an inspiring job.

It seems absurd now, after World War II, to remember what horror was caused by the first German bombs to fall on London. One came down on the Embankment close to the flat I shared with my old friend David Pye and my cousin Will Arnold-Foster. I ran down to see what had happened. A tram had been overturned; human brains lay scattered on the roadway, and Cleopatra's Needle was pockmarked with flying fragments. We were all deeply shocked, and the bomb-scarred Egyptian obelisk remains as a lasting monument to German barbarity – though the stupid and militarily useless destruction of rococo Dresden at the close of the Second World War reminds us that the Allies could be just as barbarous.

However, we soon got used to the bombs. I remember taking Agnes Murray, Gilbert Murray's beautiful daughter, to hear *Figaro* at Covent Garden. During one of the lovely duets a bomb fell close by. A few spectators half rose from their seats, but the conductor's baton never wavered, and after a momentary pause the singers continued and the audience relaxed again to enjoy the delights of Mozart's music, punctuated by the Beethovenish bangs from outside.

The censorship was a boring and frustrating job from which I soon resigned, and in the spring of 1917 I enlisted in the Army Service Corps, for my health record prevented my being drafted for front-line service.

I went to Aldershot for basic training, including riding and the care of horses. I thought I rode pretty well, but my pride was taken down several pegs by the riding-master. If anyone's riding was at fault, the riding-master would correct him and then ask his name. One day he shouted at me to keep my knees on the saddle, then asked my name. 'Huxley, Sir,' I answered. I had got used in the States to being asked if I was a relative of the famous zoologist whose name I bore, but the riding-master said: 'Are you related to the celebrated jockey of that name?' When I replied in the negative, he finished me off by saying, 'I thought not . . .'

Meanwhile I informed President Lovett that I would not be coming back to Rice. As I wrote from Aldershot to my bird-watching student Finlay Simmons, it was a difficult decision to make, 'but inevitable. Much as I enjoyed Houston in many ways, I'm not made for Texas – I want, or rather need, to be at the centre of things if I am to do good work: besides, they are going to be very short of biologists at Oxford after the war, and I have been practically offered a very good post there.' (This refers to a conversation that I had had with my old Professor, G. C. Bourne, Goodrich's predecessor.) 'At any rate, I think I did something towards starting a tradition at Rice – a frame of mind on one side, and people on the other – Davies, and you and Dr Muller.'

This was quite true – the Honours-type tradition of comprehensive biological teaching, backed by research, continued; and, when Muller left, his place was taken by another pupil and co-worker of Morgan's, Altenberg, an excellent geneticist, though perhaps not so good a field naturalist as Muller or myself.

Hearing that Simmons was proposing to continue his scientific work, I gave him some advice which shows how my mind was working. 'When writing or preparing a paper, treat detail *as* detail, put it in its proper place. The fault of a great deal of American scholarship today is the worship of fact *qua* fact, and not as something which has no intrinsic value until it is put in its right place – an ultra-German overloading with detail, which results in quantity without quality. When you have got a leading idea, as T. H. Morgan has, and string all your facts on to that, you get quantity *and* quality.'

I think that this was good advice, and also that I was all too right about American theses, especially on arts subjects. Many American

examiners seemed (and still seem) to think that facts, however
trivial, are more important than critical evaluation of the subject.

I went on to describe life at Aldershot, 'quite stiff – eight hours
work at drill and lectures, besides all the clearing up and working
over your notes – you never get much time to yourself . . .'
However, I added, 'I really am beginning to feel physically fit.'

In the spring we were sent to a camp at Upstreet, near Canter-
bury. I remember well riding about the peaceful Kentish lanes
lined with white may bushes and pink-flowering horse-chestnuts,
in strange contrast with the distant boom of heavy artillery from
across the Channel.

About the only other thing I remember of that dull spell,
redeemed only by the beauty of spring and occasional glimpses of
the cathedral, is of a private having his face smashed by a kick
from a draught-horse – a foretaste of the multiple horrors of
actual war.

I was getting thoroughly bored with the stupid drill of the Army
Service Corps, and pulled various wires which got me transferred
to Intelligence. This was certainly more interesting, though one of
my friends reminded me that, in the Army, *Intelligence* only means
Information. We had courses in map-reading, forecasting enemy
troop-movements, and gleaning various types of information
from prisoners and their letters. Eventually I was posted to Colchester at the H.Q. of a brigade which, so rumour had it, was to be
landed behind the enemy's lines in Belgium, to draw off some of
their manpower while our main force attacked from the south.

This too was a dullish time, and I remember little of it: I didn't
regret rejecting Aldous' advice about coming home, but I was
restless, and frankly worried – it looked as if the brigade was to be
sacrificed for short-term tactical advantage.

I made few friends among the military, but became acquainted
with the Mayor of Colchester, a self-made furniture-dealer and
antiquarian who rejoiced in the name of Jarnim and ascribed his
success to his wife's clairvoyant powers – a real 'character', he
could have stepped out of a Dickens novel. From the hill on which
Colchester stands, he showed me where the Roman road ran

nearly two thousand years ago – the corn grew less well over the site of the paved *strada*: a reminder of another empire's overseas military commitments.

I took a spell of leave with David Pye at Lake Ogwen in North Wales. It was a joy to see fine mountain scenery again, after the flatness of Texas and the dusty boredom of Aldershot and Up-street. One day we caught a long-nosed shrew just outside our tent and I was so much impressed by its strange twitterings that I wrote a poem about it – 'The Captive Shrew', which I used as the title of a book of verse, published by Blackwell in Oxford a few years later. To my surprise, the little collection went on selling for over thirty years.

THE CAPTIVE SHREW

Timid atom, furry shrew,
Is it a sin to prison you?
Through the runways in the grass
You and yours in hundreds pass,
An unimagined world of shrews,
A world whose hurrying twilight news
Never stirs but now and then
The striding world of booted men.
Fear and greed are masters there,
And flesh and blood go clothed in hair;
Life hurries without Power, and Mind,
Cocooned in brain, is almost blind.
And yet 'tis wild, and strange, and free –
And all that shrews can ever be.
What is it, Shrew? I fain would know . . .
– Dumbness and fright, I let you go!
'Tis not by holding in the hand
That one can hope to understand;
Truth was never prisoned yet
In cage of Force, in Matter's net.
The body of a shrew is small,
Of man is big; but after all
Not so am I more great than you –
It is the soul that makes the shrew.

X Julian Huxley with his grandfather, T.H.H., in 1893

XI Aldous Huxley in his early twenties

XII Julian Huxley as a lieutenant
in the Intelligence Corps, 1918

Go back to twitter out your life
Of obscure love and timid strife!
To learn the secret of your kind,
I will pursue you with my mind.

I also read the sad story of Abélard and Héloïse in French – sad both because of the monstrous penalty inflicted on the brilliant friar, and for the way in which his love receded so much faster than hers, but glorified by Héloïse's enduring constancy.

David was an experienced climber and led me up the face of Tryfan. I was looking forward to real climbing after years of inactivity, but something had cracked in me as a result of my breakdown. My nerve gave out when we got to the famous overhanging pitch and we had to return ingloriously.

During this period, a theological essay by William Temple, the liberal-minded Archbishop of York, set me on a study of philosophy and religion. I wanted to understand how the religious mind works, and what induces changes in doctrine. I am astonished to see from my diary what a mass of reading I undertook – not merely the story of Abélard, but St Thomas Aquinas' *Summa Theologica*, the *Confessions* of St Augustine, the lives of various saints and mystics, notably St Francis, and translations of some very iconoclastic German theologians; also works of liberal English bishops like Gore and Talbot. It was a refuge from the thought of war and helped to clarify my own mind. It also laid the foundations for the work I wrote later on the role of religion in present-day society, *Religion without Revelation*.

I also find that, foreshadowing the work on war aims that I and other members of the planning organization PEP were to undertake on a larger scale in the Second World War, I had made contact with numerous people interested in post-war reconstruction, both in America and Britain – in the USA, people like Norman Kellogg, the biologist Loeb, the New Republic crowd, and Lord Bryce, our ambassador at Washington; and Toynbee, Nevinson, Norman Angell, G. D. H. Cole and Gilbert Murray in England. Murray, I noted with interest, was pushing a scheme for an international peace-keeping organization. With President Wilson's urgent encouragement, this was the start of the original League of Nations, with Murray as head of the League-sponsored Institute for Intellectual Co-operation – the precursor of UNESCO, with which I was later to be concerned.

While plans for our departure matured at GHQ, I got leave to go to Garsington Manor, near Oxford, to see my brother Aldous. He had wanted to enlist, but was debarred from active service because his sight was so bad after an eye-infection at Eton (an inflammation of the cornea, *keratatis punctata*) which left him with one eye completely out of action, and the other only three-quarters unimpaired), and was unhappily wondering what would happen to Britain in general and to himself in particular. Meanwhile, in order to feel of some use he was working on the Morrells' farm at Garsington.

Lady Ottoline Morrell was the focus of the place. Very tall, fantastically dressed and enjoying the wearing of exotic clothes acquired in her travels (I saw her once in Turkish trousers and a turban), with something equine in her long intelligent face, she dominated the Manor and its inhabitants. She and her husband had given asylum to a number of intellectuals and artists, mostly Bloomsburyites, who were either conscientious objectors or, like Aldous, rejected for health reasons. There was Lytton Strachey, Mark Gertler, Middleton Murry, D. H. Lawrence, Gerald Shove and his poet wife Fredegond, and Bertrand Russell, while Maria Nys, a beautiful Belgian girl, was living there as a refugee: she later became Aldous' wife.

Garsington was a beautiful place, an old Tudor manor with mullioned windows, lemon-yellow curtains across their grey stone frames, approached through an avenue of great yews with pea-cocks screeching about. I was shown into the drawing-room, the Tudor panelling glowing scarlet, with gilding round the edges of the panels. And there, warming herself before the log-fire, was Brettie, as she was generally called by her circle – the Honourable Dorothy Brett, a daughter of Lord Esher, who had rebelliously taken to painting – wearing a pink sweater and riding breeches, with light-brown hair cut in a bob round her head – an apparition very different from anything I had seen in the last few years.

I was introduced to Lady Ottoline and Philip Morrell, her husband, a tall handsome man with an eighteenth-century look; their young daughter Julian (named after the saintly nun, Julian of Norwich) and her governess-companion Juliette Baillot, a French-Swiss girl from Neuchâtel. This young woman was exceedingly pretty with her fair hair coiled in delightful flaps over her ears; she also had a sense of humour and was very intelligent, with a good knowledge of English as well as French literature. Lytton Strachey had helped her with her reading, and she was going to Walter Raleigh's lectures on English Literature in Oxford. Later, when I became engaged to her, she told me how surprised she had been at my spending so much time in the schoolroom – what could I have seen in a little girl like Julian? She was, and still is, much too modest about herself and her many human, intellectual and artistic qualities, and never guessed that *she* was the attraction.

When I got back to Colchester, it turned out that the plan for landing behind the enemy's lines had been abandoned (luckily for me and the whole brigade) and we were to be sent to the Italian front instead.

So in October, I set off in the train for Padua, where our HQ was situated on the eastward slopes of the lovely Euganean hills. My work consisted largely in piecing together information obtained from prisoners and captured letters, and then plotting on the map the probable disposition of the enemy forces, in this case Austrians, for their German allies had retreated to make their last stand in their own country.

The war here had reached a sort of polite stalemate, leaving us with a good deal of time on our hands, which I filled in by learning Italian and exploring Padua and the neighbourhood. Padua was the first north Italian town I had seen: it still retained its mediaeval flavour, with its arcaded streets and busy markets, but with smart modern cafés thrown in, taking the place of our London clubs.

As a biologist, I was fascinated by the old School of Anatomy. It was founded when dissection of human corpses was prohibited by the Church, so that it had to be built windowless in the thickness of the wall. Light was provided by the students on the steeply ascending benches, all holding candles, and the corpse had to be brought up by pulley from a mortuary chamber below. It was fascinating to recall that the great Harvey had once been a candle-holder here. Perhaps in this very place he had begun to ruminate about the circulation of the blood, which he later was the first to demonstrate scientifically.

Equally thrilling were the Giotto frescoes in the little Arena Chapel near the station, covering the whole interior. It was like being inside a painted ark under God's captaincy, with Jesus and the Virgin Mary as fellow-passengers, participating with the weeping cherubs above the Crucifixion in their cosmic mourning: and spiritually I felt that I was *inside* the New Testament. And it was all executed with a new force, a new pattern of painting close to the realities of human life, transcending the stylization of Cimabue and earlier artists with their stiff ritualized figures. I sat on and on, fascinated by the power of artistic truth in the work of this forerunner of Renaissance humanism.

On my walks I made the acquaintance of numerous peasants, and was much struck by their Lombard vigour. One old materfamilias had even gone on a walking tour in the mountains (Neapolitans rarely walked, except to church or the nearest café).

Their mythopoeic faculty was very evident; one old peasant 'explained' the bronze cannon-ball supporting the fore-leg of the horse in Donatello's splendid equestrian statue of the Paduan condottiere, Gattamelata. He spun a long rigmarole about the horse having belonged to St Anthony, Padua's patron saint, and miraculously stopping this very cannon-ball with its fore-foot when the Saint was leading the Paduan troops against an enemy attack. And then, because the horse had shown such military sagacity, it was given to the great warrior Gattamelata. Yes, the cannon-ball was there to this day, to prove the truth of the tale. . . . The dates were all wrong, and St Anthony certainly never rode into battle, but it made a good story.

In the summer I got the flu badly and after some days in hospital was sent to recuperate in a sanatorium at Sirmione, near the south end of Lake Garda. It was a strange situation, for the northern tip of the lake was in Austrian hands. We speculated on the possibility of the enemy launching a submarine on the lake and cutting the railway from Verona to Venice. Actually, everything stayed completely peaceful. The only aggression was against the small birds netted for food in the circular tree enclosures called *roccoli*, which rose all over the countryside.

Once my colonel took me up the 6,000-foot Monte Grappa, to the front line. We were made to take off our caps with the green band of the Intelligence staff, for fear that the Austrians would think us particularly important and open fire. But we were able to look quietly at the enemy trenches, watching the Austrians unconcernedly moving about, without a single shot being fired by either side: there could not have been a more complete contrast with the Western front.

Forty years later, in the spring of 1968, I drove up Monte Grappa again, this time with Juliette. It was strange to see the same old trenches and barbed wire scarring the grassy slopes, now covered with gentians and narcissi.

George Trevelyan (who was married to my cousin Janet Ward) was running an ambulance unit south-east of Padua. I went to see him because I felt so useless in my job at HQ, and wanted his advice about finding something more valuable to do, but he gruffly told me it was my duty to carry on.

He took me to Abano, '*il Grande Bosco*', the sheltering forest as the Italians called it, because the Italian GHQ there harboured so many '*imboschati*' – men with staff jobs who managed to keep out of the front line. It was close to sulphurous mud-baths, for which it was famous in peace-time. There I saw Geoffrey Young, the famous Alpine climber who had lost a leg in the retreat from Caporetto and was now helping George, diving one-legged from the high board of the swimming pool. I was running around naked after a swim when I came upon an old woman, also with nothing on, immersed up to the shoulders in one of the natural mud-holes with which the place was dotted – just like a human frog.

I also visited Petrarch's house in which the great poet had spent his last years, now preserved as a national monument. It was just a big cottage, but attractively built, and over the door was a glass case with a badly stuffed animal in it. I asked the guide what on earth it was. He replied, '*la gatta mommificata*' – the mummified cat. When I asked why it was there, he said, because it was the last living creature to see the poet before he died. '*Italianissimo*,' I murmured to myself; only in Italy could the authorities kill and stuff a pet animal for such a reason.

Later came the final push, with the crossing of the Tagliamento and the eventual recovery of Trieste. My colonel again took me to see the crossing. We were all in considerable anxiety, for the enemy had heavy artillery on the heights above, with which they could have bombarded the whole position. But they had lost all heart for the war; the masses of Allied troops were left in peace and crossed the stony river in good order. It was in fact the end of the Italian campaign: soon afterwards came the armistice with Austria, and our little unit, together with others, was withdrawn to Lonigo, north of the Vicenza-Verona road.

There the problem was how to pass the time. I filled it by exploring the Palladian architecture and Tiepolo frescoes abounding in and near Vicenza, collaborating in writing a farce for the troops, trying to justify my new appointment as education officer by reading poetry to them and giving talks on natural history; also by learning the Venetian dialect, reading Goldoni's plays with an attractive peasant girl who had risen to become a very efficient schoolmistress.

The more I saw of the district, the more I was surprised at the tourists' habit of going straight on to Venice from Verona, without stopping to see cities so richly and diversely endowed as Vicenza and Padua. Quite apart from their architecture and store of paintings, there is the fascination of the scenery. The Euganean hills are lovely and unspoilt, and in early spring their groves are covered with a carpet of wild snowdrops.

I got leave to go to Venice for the Thanksgiving Mass in San Marco. The great church was still sandbagged against air-raids, and was indeed lucky to have escaped damage. Venice was beautiful as ever, but ramping with prostitutes, prowling in wait for the troops.

The Mass with all its pomp made a deep impression on me; I thought gratefully how lucky I had been to escape without a scratch, and mourned for so many of my friends and contemporaries who had been killed, leaving an irreparable gap in Britain's intellectual and cultural life. But there was some hope, now that the senseless carnage of war had come to an end, that constructive work could begin again, and I resolved to set myself the task of doing what I could to clear up some of the confusions of thought and feeling that brooded over life.

I still had a long time to wait in Italy, but we were finally demobilized and sent back – by the longest route – to London. At the turn of the year I dumped my gear at Bracknell Gardens, and in early January of 1919 made straight for Scotland.

CHAPTER IX

Marriage and Return to Teaching at Oxford

ALL this time, I had been keeping in touch with Juliette Baillot, who had struck me so much during my visit to Garsington two years earlier. We had exchanged letters during my time in Italy, hers full of an impromptu charm and a sensitiveness to natural beauty which fascinated me further. She was now living at Callander in Perthshire, as governess-in-charge of Lord Esher's grand-daughters, while their mother, the Ranee of Sarawak, elder sister of Brettie, whom I had met at Garsington, was vainly trying to rejoin her husband, the last white Rajah, in northern Borneo.

I found rooms in the little town, and daily visited Juliette and her charges. She had a good deal of free time, as the children had a nurse and nursemaid, and we managed to go for long walks in the wintry landscape. After a few days, I proposed to her and was accepted. This provoked a whirlwind of happiness in my heart, and I spent much of my time writing to all my friends and relatives telling them of my good fortune. The only one to show annoyance was my father, who thought that I should have told him of my intentions before going north. But when I brought Juliette home, all his objections disappeared, for, like all my friends and other relatives, he was completely captivated by her.

Callander is a lovely place, even in winter. One day we went up Ben Ledi in the snow and mist, a world of whiteness, where we put up an Arctic hare in its white winter coat. And in the evenings we would read aloud to each other from our favourite authors before I returned to my rooms.

Among much else, we read Aldous's new poem *Leda*, which he

sent us when I wrote to him about our engagement, and in our euphoric state must have missed its point, for when Juliette wrote a note of glowing praise to Aldous, he replied with the following snub:

'22.1.19 . . . I am glad you liked Leda – though I fear your critical faculty may have been a little warped by your personal feelings! For you seem hardly conscious of the profound and painful irony which is the thread on which all its beauty is strung. You must read it again later. It is certainly very good! – but perhaps not so good as your feelings.

Yours, Aldous.'

And then, back in London in the cold January of 1918, I had to decide on my future.

I went down to Oxford and was offered a fellowship in Zoology at New College; I was taking the place of my erstwhile tutor, Geoffrey Smith, whose brilliant career was cut short when he was killed on the Somme. I was so firm with Professor Goodrich, by now Head of the Zoology department, that he agreed to give me £500 as Senior Demonstrator, so making up my total income to the £750 I had enjoyed at the Rice Institute, quite enough for a couple to live on in those days.

Juliette and I didn't want a long engagement, so fixed the wedding for the end of March. (As I write these words, we are about to celebrate our golden wedding – we can't believe that half a century has passed since that auspicious day. But it has, and I shall later have much to say of these fifty years of our joint life and many travels.) Though I was not a believer, nor was Juliette (perhaps because she had been brought up as a strict Calvinist!), we decided to be married in St Martin-in-the-Fields in Trafalgar Square, by my clerical cousin Gordon Selwyn, later Dean of Winchester. Aldous was best man and Juliette was given away by her uncle-by-marriage, Richard Howlett, Groom of the Chambers to George V. As I was dressing for the ceremony I found that, in my long absence, my pin-striped trousers had been gnawed by mice. I had hastily to borrow a spare pair from my father, and we reached the church just in time, in the middle of a snowstorm.

For the first part of our honeymoon, we went to the Trevelyans' cottage, Robin Ghyll, in Upper Langdale. Juliette wore slacks and an amusing black and white sweater with matching cap, and we scrambled happily over the fells, long loved by me, gazing awe-struck into the depths of Dungeon Glyll, and enjoying the snowy panorama from the crest.

Our most ambitious effort was to walk over Styhead Pass, struggling through snow up to our middles, with Angle Tarn beside us, covered with great sheets of pack ice, and Bow Fell's cliff above merging with the clouds. It was a frozen and awesome world, apart and utterly lonely: we two, who had been somewhat diffident of each other in this fresh adventure of marriage, shared the joy of being together in overcoming these external difficulties. It remains one of the most wonderful memories of our joint life.

Over the pass, on the river Duddon, we were rewarded by sun-shine and a swarm of daffodils, like those Wordsworth immor-talized on Ullswater, 'tossing their heads in sprightly dance'. Next day we walked back on the outskirts of the mountains via Coniston, and I have to confess that Juliette (perhaps owing to her Swiss background) outwalked me, arriving at Langdale much less tired than I.

But our most important pilgrimage was to Fox How. Built on the banks of the Rotha between Ambleside and Rydal as a holiday retreat by my great-grandfather, Thomas Arnold of Rugby, it was now inhabited by his only surviving child, Frances, always affec-tionately called Aunt Fan by all the Arnold brood, and indeed by most of her neighbours.

She was a tall, strong-minded woman in a lace bonnet, with a white wool shawl over her black bombasine dress. On our child-hood visits she had been the subject of many giggles by Trev and myself, because of her resemblance to Charley's Aunt in the famous Oxford farce.

The place was alive with memories of my childhood. She had rhyming rebukes for breaches of table manners. 'Pudding *and* Pie – Oh my, Oh my!' when I had clamoured for both; and once, when I said I *loved* chicken: 'You may love a screeching owl, but only *like* a roasted fowl!' – delivered in a stern voice but with a twinkle in her eye. . . .

There was the fascinating fact of a spring *inside* the house, welling up in the slate-floored cellar and emerging as a tiny brook, fern-bordered, flowing between green lawns – where my father had introduced me to the rudiments of cricket, and I had seen my first pied fly-catcher – past a miniature tree-crowned knoll, into the little river. And at that very spot I had once lost my precious toy yacht, which was swept down to Windermere.

The dining-room still had a plate-glass window directly above the fireplace, a phenomenon which had puzzled my childish brain; and from the drawing-room, with its compartmented box of tropical shells, delightfully Victorian, we looked right up Rydal coombe to Fairfield (*field*, as my father explained to me, was a corruption of the Norse *fjeld*, the high fell). When I was only eleven, he had taken me right up to Fairfield's 2,800-foot summit. I was so tired that he had given me my first nip of brandy there on the panoramic top – adding to my sense of pride at such a manly achievement.

Aunt Fan remembered Wordsworth and told me how, after a visit to Fox How, he had written a sonnet on the view of Wansfell from its south window. I took Juliette to his final abode, Rydal Mount, just round the corner, and showed her the stepping stones across the Rotha on the short cut to Ambleside, remembering how precarious their passage had seemed to me as a child. Juliette was fascinated by Aunt Fan, and the whole atmosphere of the place, and she in her turn approved of Juliette.

The second half of our honeymoon we spent in Frensham village, at a little house called Cherry Tree Cottage, which still stands with the same cherry tree blooming after fifty springs. I was anxious to follow up my studies of the great crested grebe, and rigged up a small hide on the south-east corner of Frensham Great Pond. Juliette always maintains that I spent the week absorbed in the love-making of grebes, while she had to wait outside the hide in the bitter April winds, without any practical study of human love-making. I am afraid there is some truth in this: I was too keen to get on with my scientific studies of bird display. We did, however, have a lovely time bicycling round the country, visiting all my favourite haunts in my beloved south-west Surrey, which Juliette came to enjoy as much as I did.

All too soon the honeymoon period was over, and we had to betake ourselves to Oxford to start on my work. Gradually, trouble developed – not with Juliette, but in my own mind. The optimism with which I had been filled since my engagement began to give way, and I found that I had forgotten a great deal of the zoology I was supposed to teach. Things came to a head while I was giving a demonstration: I found myself unable to answer the undergraduates' questions, and collapsed on the floor in a semi-faint. I remember Pip Blacker, one of my more brilliant students, later a well-known medical man, saying, 'Poor chap, poor chap', and arranging for me to be taken back to our lodgings. I am afraid it was a great shock to Juliette. There could be no doubt about it; I was having another breakdown.

It was decided that we should go to Switzerland, first to stay with Juliette's mother in Neuchâtel, and then to Lausanne to be treated by Dr Vittoz, recommended by Lady Ottoline. We set off with heavy hearts. Juliette had never even heard of a nervous breakdown, and was bewildered and frightened; and I was in that calamitous state when any mental effort, and any attempt to reach a decision, even in trivial matters, becomes a source of anguish. I knew the burden I was putting on her, yet could do nothing to lighten it.

She took me to Dr Vittoz and I began the treatment. His method was to propose some simple subject on which to concentrate, such as visualizing a circle or a square, or solving an easy mathematical problem, and to test the validity of my efforts with the side of his hand on my forehead, whereby he claimed that he could feel and estimate the special brain-pulse accompanying genuine concentration. Gradually more complex subjects for concentration were propounded and the exercises became easier to carry out. I thus got a little more control over my depression, but it was a dreary summer for us all.

On our return to Neuchâtel, Juliette took me on walks in the lovely Jura mountains, but I was still feeling weak and everything was an effort, often tinged with suicidal fantasies. However, the change of scene and the treatment had done me considerable good, and we were able to return to Oxford in time for the autumn term.

To prepare for my teaching work, I appealed to my friend and colleague James Gray of King's College, Cambridge, who generously lent me his notes on experimental zoology and embryology, courses which I now had to undertake. With these, and various textbooks, I was able to plan and deliver a reasonable set of lectures, and to regain my intellectual footing and my control over my inner life and feelings.

Later that year we moved to our first real home, Postmaster's Hall in Merton Street, a lovely, small Tudor house, inhabited by the famous antiquary Anthony Wood in the seventeenth century. It had two panelled rooms, one of which had been painted white; we improved it after the Garsingtonian fashion by gilding the borders of the panels and putting soft orange curtains in the windows. The house was a great joy to us both. So were the good friends we made in post-war Oxford. Among these, most specially, were Dr and Mrs J. S. Haldane, and their children, Jack and Naomi, just married to Dick Mitchison, lawyer and later M.P. There were wonderful parties at their rambling house on the Cherwell, mostly Nebuchadnezzar charades and romping picnics on the river.

I had a few advanced pupils, brilliantly original men who all made their mark: C. P. Blacker, Gavin de Beer, Charles Elton, A. C. Hardy, John Baker and Bernard Tucker among them – and I began to enjoy my tutorials with them. I think they equally enjoyed the essays I set them and the discussions which ensued.

Meanwhile I began to think of research work for myself. I had read of Gudernatch's experiments with frogs, in which he induced premature metamorphosis of tadpoles into froglets by feeding them on thyroid gland; and I wondered what would happen if I gave the same diet to axolotls. The axolotl is a strange tailed amphibian from Mexico, often kept in aquaria, for it normally lives permanently as a tadpole or eft, with moist skin, external gills to breathe with, and a broad swimming fin round its long tail. In the autumn, I started feeding some axolotls on thyroid, bought from the local butcher. Juliette complained that I was much more interested in them than in her welfare and that of our first child, born on December 2, 1920. He was christened Anthony Julian in New College Chapel by Warden Spooner himself. The ceremony was carried out faultlessly by the remarkable old gentleman, though we had been secretly a little nervous that he might spoonerize the child's name.

Anthony grew up in an Oxford atmosphere, learning French from his mother as well as English. He loved the gardens of New College, and often referred to them as 'mon New College'. Probably it was here that he first developed the love of flowers that eventually led him to become editor of a gardening magazine, and to publish some very successful floral guide-books.

Meanwhile the axolotl experiments worked. The gills shrank, the membrane round the tail became resorbed, and the aquatic efts turned into large salamander-like creatures with dry skin, adapted to air. It really was exciting to have recreated a land animal which had not existed, except in tadpole form, for many thousands of years.

By chance, the publication of my results in the scientific weekly *Nature*, roused the attention of the popular press. The *Daily Mail* went so far as to assert that 'young Huxley has discovered the Elixir of Life'! Some of my friends, including Jack Haldane, warned me that I was losing my standing as a reputable scientist and would end by being taken for a quack. In spite of my innocence in the matter, I was naturally concerned about the extravagant statements appearing in the papers, and welcomed the opportunity of writing an article clearing up the facts. This also gave me the first money – ten guineas! – that I earned with my pen, and set me off on the popular and semi-popular writing on science, behaviour (human as well as animal) and sociology which occupied much of my later life.

It is curious to reflect that, owing to the breakdown of scientific communication during the war, I had failed to discover that my results had been anticipated on the Continent. If I had known I should, in all probability, never have embarked on this interesting experiment, and become such a successful popularizer of science that I was awarded the Kalinga Prize for this activity; but more of that later.

A much less pleasant consequence was that I was bombarded with letters from cranks and sufferers from all over the world. One pathetic writer from India lamented that he possessed 'an under-sized and under-developed male organ' and demanded to know whether it could be 'at least doubled in dimensions' by this miraculous thyroid treatment, and if so, where – 'Here, or there before you?' I spent much more than my ten guineas on stamps and secretarial help in answering them.

In the meantime we moved again, to Juliette's great sorrow, as Merton College required Postmaster's Hall for one of its own Fellows. This time we went to No 8 Holywell, not so beautiful but in many ways more convenient, as it was just opposite the north gate of New College and had a pleasant garden at the back.

CHAPTER X

Spitsbergen

THE next important event in my life was the Oxford University Expedition to Spitsbergen.

Its origin was curiously accidental. An ornithologically inclined undergraduate called Paget-Wilkes kept pestering me to go with him to study Arctic birds, and had set his heart on Greenland. He was so persistent that, in the end, I agreed to see what could be done. I discussed the problem with my zoological colleague Alec Carr-Saunders and the Rev. F. C. R. Jourdain, a local vicar and excellent ornithologist (though also, I regret to say, an avid egg-collector), and decided to organize an all-round scientific expedition to the Arctic, but chose Spitsbergen as an easier target.

We got support from various Government departments and commercial firms, and set about building up our party. One day I was at work in the lab when in walked a rather short man with a red beard, who looked like the rumbustious Captain Kettle of schoolboy fiction. My surprise turned to delight when I discovered that it was Dr Tom Longstaff, then holder of the world's altitude record for his climbs in the Himalayas. He would act as our medical adviser and loved tough assignments: needless to say, I at once accepted his offer to join the party.

We secured Summerhayes and Walton as botanists; an Australian geographer called Frazer; N. E. Odell as geologist; my pupil Charles Elton as ecologist, even though he had not yet taken his Finals; Seton-Gordon, an authority on Highland birds, as second ornithologist besides Paget-Wilkes, and a cheerful undergraduate, George Binney, to act as quartermaster.

Our selection paid off. Summerhayes rose rapidly in the Kew

XIII/XIV Juliette Baillot, below, in 1917, two years before her engagement to Julian Huxley. Right, Lady Ottoline Morrell, at whose house, Garsington, they met, taken at Bedford Square about 1912 *by permission of her daughter, Julian Vinogradof*

XV Julian Huxley in 1922, when Fellow of New College, Oxford

hierarchy; Walton obtained a professorship at an early age; Binney became so enamoured of the Arctic that he himself led two further expeditions to Spitsbergen (he was the first to use aeroplanes in Polar exploration, and almost lost his life when his plane came down in the sea) he later became a Director of the Hudson's Bay Company; Elton, largely as a result of his experience in Spitsbergen, started the detailed analysis of biological communities which led to his election to the Royal Society, and the periodic fluctuations in numbers of animals like lemmings, ending up as director of the Bureau of Animal Ecology at Oxford; Jourdain obtained some new eggs for his collection; while Carr-Saunders and I had our geographical and biological horizons much enlarged by our acquaintance with the Arctic world.

In early June, we set off by steamer for Tromsö, with its goats cropping the turf-covered roofs in the midnight sun. Here we boarded the 60-ton sealer we had chartered and set off for Spitsbergen by way of Bear Island, a dreary place, but interesting because north-temperate and arctic sea-birds overlap on its cliffs. Here Tom Longstaff made use of his fishing-rod, which he never had occasion to put together in Spitsbergen. He made a noose at the end of its line, and was able to snare a number of guillemots, whose fishy-flavoured breasts the members of the expedition later consumed. Meanwhile Jourdain had gone mad about Brunnich's guillemot, of which he had no egg in his collection; he managed to secure a series, which he blew with great pains. Longstaff, however, who had a mischievous sense of humour, pointed out that it was impossible to tell the eggs of Brunnich's guillemot from those of the common, more southern species, which nested on the same ledges. So, being a conscientious scientist, Jourdain scrapped the lot.

Longstaff was naughty in another way. I had told him how Sir Ray Lankester, the fat old professor of Zoology, noted for his rudeness as well as for his remarkable researches in comparative anatomy, had reacted to someone calling egg-collection *oölogy*. Oölogy, he had grunted: that would imply a science, while actually, when the so-called oölogist had got hold of his precious egg-shell, all he had for his pains was a coloured fart! This story

Longstaff persisted in reciting within the hearing of poor Jourdain.

As we neared Spitsbergen, Tom Longstaff and I climbed into the crow's-nest to enjoy the first sight of our promised land. The view was indeed beautiful; blue sea with glittering patches of drift-ice, and, straight ahead, the mountains after which Spitsbergen is named, sharp-pointed peaks with snow on their upper flanks, rather as if the top four thousand feet of the Alps had been cut off and transplanted to the Arctic Ocean.

Our first destination was Cape Boheman in Storrfjord, where coal had recently been found. Somewhere near here had been a real town called Smeerenberg or 'Blubbertown' in the seventeenth century during the heyday of the Dutch exploitation of the 'Greenland' whale fishery, with streets and men ringing handbells to advertise suet muffins and hot drinks. Even in 1921, with all the slaughter of whales, Spitsbergen was still a small whaling base, and we saw arctic skuas pecking at the putrid remains of a whale carcass on the beach.

On the way to the Beardsmore Glacier at the canyon-like head of the fjord, which was calving off little icebergs into the sea – a remarkable sight – Odell and I were much struck by the so-called stone polygons which cover much of the flatter landscape. They consist, as we found by excavation, of a series of polygonal enclosures, generally hexagonal, with a border of extruded stones marking them out, while the central part was made of finer material, sometimes just mud, and always slightly bulged up in the middle. We showed that this strange form of surface marking was due to a special sort of solifluction or soil-creep, brought about by alternate freezing and thawing. The freezing pushes the stones outwards and up-ends them, while the thawing softens the central part, later bulged up by frost. We wrote a short paper on this curious phenomenon.

One day we went up into the hills to look for fossils, in beds of carboniferous age. It was hard going and we got rather tired: but the fossils – and the coal – were proof that this arctic island had once enjoyed a warm steamy climate – very different from today. No one seems certain of the cause of this – tilting of the earth's axis, continental drift, or a world-wide spell of warmth.

We saw only a few arctic foxes. They must always be pretty ravenous: when the exploring party went off across the central range to North-east Land on the far side of the island – the first to make proper charts of the area – they made a cache of some geological specimens they didn't want to lug along. When they returned, they found that foxes had actually eaten some of the gummed labels they had left on their collections.

Their sense of smell must be prodigious. In winter, they sniff out ptarmigan sheltering deep under the snow and feeding on the remains of berries, and, as the winter guardian of the coal mine told us, are able to detect the scent of dried ptarmigan flesh in a trap, from over a mile away.

The rest of us turned northwards, leaving me and three others on the elongated island, Prince Charles's Foreland, off the west coast. We camped on the shores of Richard Lagoon, and watched the seals playing, obviously enjoying the exciting sport of holding their own against the tidal rush at the entrance, so strong that we could scarcely row against it. Living in the summer's perpetual daylight seemed to agree with them, but I began to feel a bit queer, and we all had to force ourselves to keep regular hours.

> So by excess of light I learnt to treasure
> Light's enemy and light's own proper measure

as I wrote in a little poem, composed in the shelter of my tent.

All arctic explorers suffer from this excess of summer light (and still more from excess of darkness in the six months' polar night).

Several pairs of red-throated divers nested on the edge of the lagoon. Some were incredibly tame (one I had to push aside with my boot when I wanted to see her eggs), and I was able to study their courtship behaviour without bothering to build hides. I was delighted to find that my observations corroborated much that I had seen in the great crested grebe. The sexes were alike in their handsome breeding plumage, and here again played interchangeable roles in ritualized display. One ceremony I christened the plesiosaurus-race: the birds raced along in parallel, one slightly in the lead, with necks arched and most of the body submerged. Up to four birds might take part in the 'race', uttering a peculiar rolling growl.

Most remarkable was the emergence ceremony. As in the grebes, one bird dives with a splash while the other splutters a few feet away. Then the diving bird emerges with vertical neck, the bill bent down along it and the body erect, gradually settling down to face its mate.

At the north end of the island we visited a great colony of cliff-birds. On our way, the arctic skuas showed their resentment by swooping at our heads with outraged screams, while others were pursuing gulls and compelling them to disgorge their fishy prey. The cliff itself was an unbelievable sight, with its thousands of little auks, puffins, Brunnich's guillemots (no common guillemots so far north), razorbills and swarms of gulls and terns, the air crowded with wings and a crashing chorus of screams and calls, outdoing the din of the Zoo's parrot house. It was interesting to find that the herbage below the cliff was much taller than elsewhere, fertilized by the rain of guano from the birds above. Over most of the low-lands it was confined to creeping willow and dwarf birch, with a few saxifrages and buttercups.

I couldn't face the long journey back to base without a rest, and actually slept for an hour, without extra covering, only 600 miles from the North Pole.

Other interesting birds that I saw for the first time were grey phalaropes and purple sandpipers; grey phalaropes like their Iceland cousins the red-necked phalarope have lobed toes for swimming (like those of grebes and moorhens), and with their aid twirl around in boggy pools to stir up the tiny shrimps and snails and insect larvae on which they feed. And they show the strange distinction of reversal of roles between the sexes – the hen is brighter coloured and takes the initiative in courtship and sexual display, while the protectively coloured male broods the eggs and looks after the young chicks.

The purple sandpiper shows the same reversal of roles as regards breeding and caring for chicks though the sexes are alike in appearance – both protectively coloured.

My suggestion for this state of affairs was that the laying of four eggs of the larger size needed to give the chick a good start before it has to migrate south in the autumn was such a strain on the hen that she could not manage the arduous job of brooding the eggs and looking after the young, and that in phalaropes the reversal of roles extended to courtship; and I still think that this is the correct explanation.

The purple sandpiper was remarkable for another habit – it lured intruders or enemies away from its nest and young in the most extraordinary way, much more spectacular than the 'luring' displays of so many ground-nesting birds. It shuffled away from the nest with outspread wings, looking more like a large mouse than a bird and so doubtless provoking the arctic foxes to follow it as possible prey. But when the nest was well behind it, it became a bird again and flew out of reach.

From the top of the island I had an interesting geographical experience. In the clear air, I saw the 4,000-foot mountains of the mainland disappearing hull down both to south and north – a wonderful demonstration of the earth's curvature. I still retain a vivid memory of the harsh beauty of that strange land, and understand the fascination of the Arctic, which draws so many explorers to its wilds – icy, yet teeming with life, even bumble-bees.

We went back to Tromsö and Bergen. There I left the party and proceeded to Denmark, where I purchased a copy of Wegener's newly-published book on continental drift. I was fascinated by his idea that the continents were rafts of the earth's crust, floating on the molten interior like slices of toast on treacle, which had in the coal age been conjoined in a single mass; but, separated by submarine rifts like that which constitutes the Red Sea, had slowly drifted apart, always westwards, owing to the earth's rotation. I greeted the idea with enthusiasm, as it explained so many peculiarities of animal and plant distribution, such as the existence of those beautiful flowers the Proteas in Australia and South America, as well as in South Africa, and of marsupial mammals in South

America and Australia. But it was much attacked by conservative geophysicists. Today however, Wegener's views have won general acceptance: we even know the rate at which North America is drifting away from Europe – a mere three centimetres a year. But three centimetres over 350 million years is quite a distance – just about the gap between the Old World and the New.

Thence into eastern Germany. It was strange to be among people with whom we had so recently been at war. I detected a vague sense of resentment and was often embarrassed by their poverty compared with my relative affluence. Eventually I managed to get home, but absolutely broke, having taken advantage of the collapse of the mark to become what the Germans called a *Valutaschwein,* a dirty dog profiting by the low exchange rate to buy a charming coloured lithograph of a parrot on a bowl of flowers with my last few pounds. Juliette had to pay for my taxi and my clothes were so fruity with long wearing and no washing that they all had to be burnt.

The printed results of the expedition were all bound together and published as *Spitsbergen Papers.* I believe they more than justified our efforts, as well as leading to the foundation of the Oxford Exploration Society, the first of the British university exploration clubs, which are now so numerous and so useful, both to their participants and for the knowledge they bring back.

CHAPTER XI

Oxford Research and Oxford Characters

So here I was, back in the old groove. Oxford was still full of 'characters'. The most notable was Spooner, Warden of my own college, whose peculiar verbal affliction made him a legendary figure and even earned him a place in *The Concise Oxford Dictionary* in his own lifetime. What he did was to transpose initial syllables, and sometimes employ wrong words by some curious slip in association. He was well aware of his reputation as word-twister. Once, at a college gaudy in Hall, he ended an amiable little speech with the words, 'And now I think I ought to sit down, or else I might be saying – er – one of those things.' The applause and laughter nearly took the roof off.

'Kinkering kongs their tatles tike' seems to be the only well-authenticated spoonerism. However, this did not deter the Oxford dons, including Fellows of his own college, from inventing a whole series of imaginary ones. Thus, when his hat blew off in Long Wall Street, he is supposed to have trotted after it, saying: 'Please, will nobody pat my hiccup?' And when a cat (or, as some preferred to allege, a housemaid) fell out of a window in the Warden's Lodgings, he reassured his audience by saying: 'She popped on her drawers and away she went.' Some of my favourites are, finding his seat in chapel taken, and asking, Who is occupewing my pie?'; 'the Minx by spoonlight', for the most remarkable sight in Egypt; 'erotic blacks' (erratic blocks), brought back from the Alps; a visit to the optician to purchase 'a signifying glass' – and when the optician politely said he had none in stock, Spooner declared, 'It doesn't magnify'; and many others.

135

I had one or two experiences of his slips of the tongue. After a discussion about our expedition to Spitsbergen, in which I had stressed its easy accessibility in spite of its high latitude, he remarked to his wife: 'My dear, Mr Huxley assures me it is no further from the north coast of Spitsbergen to the North Pole than it is from Land's End to John of Gaunt.' Mrs Spooner, a large and majestic woman, fixed me with a stony look: I didn't even smile.

On another occasion I was accompanying him on his so-called 'Progress' to inspect the College's estates (the fourteenth-century Fellow had to go with the Warden to make sure he wasn't embezzling the rents: today he merely helps to assure his comfort). As we crossed Bayswater Brook, which I knew quite well from my walks, he said: 'You know, my dear Huxley, this place is called Piccadilly . . .'

His other peculiarity was in being an albino. He was also very small and had a curious unctuous voice, as if butter were actually melting in his mouth. In spite of these various handicaps, he became a worthy and respected Warden, and successfully administered the College's affairs for many years.

Phelps, the Provost of Oriel, was another Oxford character. He embellished legendary jokes in a way peculiarly his own, stroking his long beard and repeating the end of his story. He loved walking, and did it very fast. Cyril Bailey saw him one day striding along the tow-path, with a couple of undergraduates tagging behind him. 'How are you, Provost?' said Cyril, to which Phelps flung back the cryptic remark: 'Waiting for the end, Bailey, waiting for the end.' The Oriel undergraduates used to gather in front of his rooms in the early mornings to hear his self-encouraging mutterings before taking his cold bath: 'Now Phelps – come on–be a man Phelps – now Phelps' – and then a splash and a gasp.

J. A. Smith went on worrying his grey head about whether there was such a subject as 'Metapheesics', even though he was paid £1,000 a year to expound it! And, as his friends sadly anticipated, his great philosophical work never got written. Schiller of Corpus incurred the wrath of all other philosophers by proclaiming himself a pragmatist – something very brash and American, and certainly (in those days) un-Oxonian.

One of our most frequent visitors was Jack Haldane, he too a Fellow of New College, teaching physiology, though he had taken a First in Greats. He was another odd character. He dropped in whenever he liked – which was usually at tea-time – and devoured plates of biscuits, protesting that he couldn't eat a crumb, while reciting Shelley and Milton and any other poet you chose, by the yard. He had a fantastic memory and knowledge of the classics, and enjoyed displaying them. Once he went on reciting Homer so long that I had to escort him, spouting Greek all the time, downstairs to the front door. When at last the flow stopped: 'What a rotten memory I have got,' he said, and lumbered off.

When my axolotl experiment came off and captured the popular press, he expostulated with me, as I wrote before. Then, in 1924, it was his turn: he gave a paper to the Heretics Society in Cambridge on the future of biological discovery, including the possibility of ectogenesis, or birth outside the body. This was published by Kegan Paul under the title of *Daedalus, Science of the Future*, and shook the public in a big way.[1]

His father, old Dr Haldane, was deeply pained. Oxford was talking of nothing else, and the family became the butt of donnish jokes and quips, so much so that Jack's mother wrote me the following letter:

Cherwell, Oxford

Dear Julian

I find the S.P. [she always called her husband the Senior Partner] is frightfully upset about *Daedalus*. Will you abstain altogether from poking fun at him on account of it? and if you can do so, keep people off the subject altogether when he is about?

---

[1] The first steps towards this have now been taken, both in lower mammals and man, and early embryos have been made by fertilizing ova with sperm in a test-tube. But it is unlikely that they can ever reach full term, and many abnormalities occur as they develop. Meanwhile the outcry against 'test-tube' babies and interfering with God's laws continues, though the method opens up immense eugenic possibilities.

I knew he'd object, but had no idea till to-day how really unhappy he is – odd people these Liberals and no accounting for them!

But an' you love me, keep people off him, or he'll hate you all! (which is not only sad for him but extremely inconvenient for me.)

Yours aff:
LKH.

Dr Haldane called himself an organicist, which implied being anti-mechanist and yet not a mystic vitalist – I never quite grasped what he really meant. At any rate it led to some passages at arms. As I was describing some experiment which demanded a mechanistic explanation, he burst out with, 'But it's a norganism, my dear young fellow, a norganism.'

Mrs Haldane was endlessly kind to Juliette and gave her a great deal of help and advice about our young baby. Like all young mothers, Juliette was often worried about the little creature and found immense comfort in being able to discuss her problems with such a wise and experienced friend.

Through my devotion to bird-watching I met Warde-Fowler, a classical don at Lincoln College, and a keen ornithologist. I made many happy visits to him in his country cottage. He was a modern Gilbert White, grey-haired and shaggy-browed, who wrote the natural history of his beloved village of Kingham, just as Gilbert White had done for Selborne.

He lived with his sister, both of them musical but extremely deaf. It was a touching sight to see them playing classical duets on their old piano, while I wondered if they could hear what they were playing: probably, like Beethoven in his old age, they heard with the inner ear of imagination, while enjoying the physical activity of striking the familiar keys.

His deafness also interfered with his enjoyment of bird-song, about which he had written such charming essays. I had great arguments with him about tree-creepers, which he asserted sang but rarely, while I knew that they sang regularly, and had even been woken by them at Prior's Field. Once I heard one singing on a tree in his front garden, and called him out to listen, but he refused to be convinced, for the song was too high-pitched for his old ears. I remember my father, who after sixty could no longer hear the high squeaks of bats.

Warde-Fowler had discovered one of the few haunts of the rare marsh-warbler in Britain and took me to it. He asked me to describe the bird's song. The reed-bed could well have harboured sedge-warblers or reed-warblers', but the song, I told him, was not harshly repetitive like the reed-warblers, and much more melodious than the sedge-warbler's chatter, with some notes equal to a nightingale's. Ah, he said, then it *is* my marsh-warbler – and so it was. A new bird-species for my list, and a triumph for the old birdwatcher, who enjoyed the song even at second hand.

I corresponded with him for years. I have just found a letter from him, where he writes: 'I agree with you that foreign nightingales don't sing as well as ours. Probably the climate is too dry for them. All birds seem to sing better in our moist climate than anywhere else: they need some damp to wet their whistles.'

When he died, in the early twenties, I wrote his obituary notice for *British Birds*, stressing the value to ornithology of gifted amateurs like him, and the literary charm of his *Essays on Bird Life*.

I renewed my acquaintance with Gilbert Murray, and brought Juliette to meet Lady Mary at Boars' Hill. She was very kind, though with a rather intimidating manner; a strict teetotaller, she had helped pour the family wines at Castle Howard down the drains. After Francis' birth she asked what we proposed to call him; when Juliette said Francis John Heathorn she exploded, saying that three Christian names were excessive and we had no right to saddle the child with such a rigmarole. However, she lent us her cottage in the grounds of the Murray house, and we spent a happy month there with Anthony and our new baby.

Gilbert Murray had a telepathic gift, especially in connection with his lovely daughter Rosalind, and we once attended a séance at his home. Rosalind was put in a remote part of the house, while Gilbert and his guests were seated in the front drawing-room. Rosalind thought of some passage in English poetry and, almost invariably, Gilbert could detect the author and often quote some of it. It was the best proof of the existence of telepathy I have ever known, better even than the experiments with drawings where the 'percipients' often draw something *connected* with the 'sender's' subjects but rarely the subject itself.

Other members of the Boars' Hill group were John Masefield, the future Poet Laureate, and Robert Bridges. Masefield was friendly, gave many parties, and often produced his own plays with the aid of local talent. We were both in the cast when he did *Jesus the King*. Lillah MacCarthy (Lady Keeble), wife of the Professor of Botany, was to have been the Madonna but failed at the last moment through illness. Juliette was put in to replace her, and, draped in blue robes, gave a creditable performance in spite of well-justified nervousness.

The Masefields kept goats, believing that their milk was free from T.B. The nannies were all right but the billy was wild and fierce, and its habit of escaping at least once a week led Masefield to invoke the old legend that it spent that day with the devil. The creature's looks fully justified this opinion.

Bridges was a strange and fascinating person, of few words, but whose brusqueness concealed real friendliness. In his poetry he strove after a rather archaic style: I remember Robert Nichols telling me that when, as a budding poet, he sought Bridges' advice, he was told to use the word *nith*. It means *without*, he was told, and is shorter and more expressive. . . .

He was always interested in what his visitors had to say about nature, and ready to utilize their experience in his work. I didn't know this at the time, but thanks to the courtesy of his son, Sir Edward Bridges, I have been shown a letter of his making it clear that he was fascinated by what I had told him of the marvels of bird song and courtship displays. He had read Selous' works on the subject and my own essay on bird mind, entitled '*Ils n'ont que de l'âme*' in my second book, *Essays of a Biologist*.

Perhaps I may quote a couple of passages from his *Testament of Beauty* (2nd edn., pp. 4–5, lines 87–118), showing how he had drawn on Selous' and my experience.

'Now since the thoughtless birds not only act and enjoy/this music, but to their offsprings teach it with care,/handing on those small folk-songs from father to son/in such faithful tradition that they are familiar/unchanging to the changeful generations of men/ – and year by year, listening to himself the nightingale/as amorous of his art as of his brooding mate/practiseth every phrase of his espousal lay,/and still provoketh envy of the lesser songsters/with the same notes that woke poetic eloquence/alike in Sophocles and the sick heart of Keats/– see then how deeply seated is the urgence whereto/Bach and Mozart obey'd, or those other minstrels/who pioneered for us on the marches of heav'n/and paid no heed to wars that swept the world around,/nor in their homes wer more troubled by cannon-roar/than late the small birds wer, that nested and carol'd/upon the devastated battlefield of France.

Birds of all animals are most like men/for that they take delight in both music and dance,/and gracefully schooling leisure to enliven life/ were the earlier artists: moreover in their airy flight/(which in its swiftness symboleth man's soaring thought)/they hav no rival but man, and easily surpass/in their free voyaging his most desperate daring;

(then compares the planes he is hearing to)

. . . a migratory flock of birds/that rustle southward from the cold fall of the year/in order'd phalanx –'

Of course we had bicycles, and also a great deal of energy. We rode once all the way to Nailsworth in Gloucestershire, where Donald Leney, one of my early pupils, had settled down to run a trout farm. It was hard getting there, but the scenery was beautiful. There I saw a surprising thing, a piscivorous wren coming to the edge of the fish-trough and picking out young trout to feed its brood. Some such wren may well have been the ancestor of our modern dipper.

Later I bought a two-stroke motor-bicycle from Carr-Saunders. I am afraid it wasn't a very good bargain; whether Juliette was riding pillion or not, I had to get off at every hill and push the wretched thing. But it enabled us to get further afield.

Francis, our second son, was born in 1923 at 8 Holywell. He too turned out to be very able – perhaps not so scientifically precise as

Anthony, but with a more embracing imagination, which led him into out-of-the-way corners of human activity – investigating the vanishing rituals of South American Indians; Haitian voodoo; the effects of drugs on the human mind; psychiatry and the interaction of mind and body, and paranormal happenings like telepathy.

I have mentioned Robert Nichols: he was a poet, with some good war (and other) poems to his credit; a tall, thin man full of interesting ideas, though often over-intense. We later spent many week-ends with him and his wife at their charming house at Winchelsea. Looking down from its windows we could see the green marsh which, surprisingly, had accommodated the whole English fleet in mediaeval times, before the shingle had piled up and blocked it from the sea.

Once when the sea threatened to break in on to these accumulated flats, Robert organized the locals into a protection force, directing where trenches had to be dug or barriers put up. Always literary, he said he was following the example of Goethe's *Faust*, who ended his career by draining a marsh.

He was a really good talker, gay but bewildering, always hurrying from one subject to another. He had some grievance against the Sitwell family, and spent much time writing an enormous satire on them and their habits, which was finally published under the title of *Phisbo*. He was immensely disappointed not to be challenged to a duel – verbal or otherwise – by the Sitwells and their friends; but the truth was that they never even read the book.

I enjoyed the tutorials with my students, but lecturing was another matter. Goodrich was Professor and gave all the Honours lectures; so I had to deliver the prelim. lectures and conduct the demonstrations, which all those going in for medicine and biology had to take. I am sure it was good for me and taught me a great deal, but it was drudgery at the start. However, I soon learnt to be reasonably fluent and made a number of friends among my pupils, including Eric Strauss and Russell Brain, later the country's leading brain surgeon.

Following Richard Hertwig's proof that delayed fertilization in frogs resulted in a preponderance of males, I tried the same experiment with trout eggs, as well as repeating it on frogs. Trout had already been used by Mrsič in Hertwig's laboratory, with similar results. Unfortunately, my figures did not show any significant deviation from equality. I am at a loss to account for this, though perhaps the fact that Mrsič had worked with rainbow trout, while I used brown trout, may have had something to do with it. I was away in Spitsbergen during some of the experimental period; and this meant that Juliette had to go round in the dark at the Museum, then only dimly lit with gas-jets, to see that all was well. Her most unpleasant task was to separate the pairs of copulating frogs and place the males in another tank. She never forgot the slightly gruesome experience.

Many interesting experiments followed, mostly on growth and differentiation, some with colleagues like Carr-Saunders, visiting students like P. D. F. Murray of Australia, and my ex-pupils, E. B. Ford and Francis Ratcliffe. Our results were duly published and led to further contacts and a constant widening of my scientific horizon. It was a germinating period – we all worked hard and enjoyed life.

Soon after returning from Spitsbergen, I wanted to show Juliette what camping was like. We took a train to Brockenhurst and proceeded on our bicycles to a lovely glade in the New Forest, with all our equipment in rucksacks on our backs.

I had brought a red beard back from my Arctic spell, and also rode a green bicycle. This made me a winning target for the game then in fashion called 'Beaver'. The rules of this rather foolish game were that if several people were out together, whenever one of them sighted a man with a beard, he shouted 'Beaver'. One beard counted one, a red beard ten, and a red-bearded man on a green bicycle one hundred (and game). It had a very short vogue in the early 1920s, but while it was on, our trips were enlivened by too much public attention, so we had to find secret retreats in that amazing forest. This was easy, for in those days the giant groves were deserted, and one was soon lost in a magical world.

My ex-pupil, A. C. Hardy, was by now official naturalist to the Fisheries section of the Ministry of Agriculture and Fisheries. He had been studying the first link in the marine food-chain, the microscopic animals and plants called plankton – the floating meadows of the sea – by the aid of a gadget of his own invention, a constantly uncoiling sheet of fine gauze at the entry to his tow-nets, which gave a continuous record of the different species netted during a long transit through different regions and levels of the sea. Now, in 1924, he wanted to study the atmospheric plankton of minute insects, spiders, pollen and plant spores carried up by warm air-currents. From a balloon he trailed gauze funnels ending in a bottle, very like those normally used at sea, but without arrangements for continuous recording. He found that aerial plankton was much more abundant than was then expected, and accounted for the widespread dispersion of many species.

He told me of the joys and surprises of ballooning – and I was delighted when he invited me to accompany him on a balloon-trip to France.

On a Saturday evening, we met at the famous cricket ground, the Oval in south London, where there were special pipes for filling balloons with gas; but it turned out that here we ran the risk of colliding with a spectator stand, so we drove off to the Welsh Harp at Hendon and inflated the balloon from a stand-pipe there. In the great days of ballooning, in mid-Victorian times, London was encircled with three service stations for balloons. It would be interesting to know what other cities made similar provision for aeronauts.

It was a delicious sensation, floating noiselessly through the air over London. The chief drawback was the strong smell of coal-gas, which also made smoking impermissible. Another was the lack of steering facilities. We drifted over Wembley, illuminated by searchlights from the great Empire Exhibition being held there; and after an uneasy sleep in the corners of the basket-work car while we drifted slowly over Surrey, we woke to see the woods of the Weald gleaming in the dawn. It was much more beautiful than a view from a plane because there was no noise and we were only a few hundred feet up. But we found that we were losing height much too fast. We were busily engaged in throwing out sacks of ballast, when we landed in a country churchyard, just in time for the assembling congregation to see us bump among the graves, and, now lightened, disappear again into the clouds – messengers from heaven who had delivered no message. . . . Then the wind failed altogether, and we had to come down, using a long trail-rope to regulate our height and skip over tall trees. With no time to choose a convenient landing spot, our gas leaked out and we found ourselves dropping into a meadow with a large inquisitive bull in it. We wondered, cowering, what to do. However, the farmer appeared, walked up to the bull, put his arm round its neck and quietly led it away. We never got to France, but the trip made me realize the fascination of ballooning as well as its impredictability.

In the spring vacation of 1926, Juliette and I rented Robin Ghyll, the Trevelyans' cottage in Upper Langdale where we had spent our honeymoon, and took Charles Elton and his young bride as guests. One sunny day we climbed Rosset Ghyll, from the top of which there was a wonderful view of Angle Tarn and the surrounding mountains, very different from the icy landscape we had ploughed through in 1919.

On the way back, as I prided myself on my downhill running, I leapt down the stony track as fast as I could. But pride had a fall – I crashed among the jagged rocks and Juliette discovered me groaning, flat on my face, with a dislocated and excruciatingly painful shoulder. She and Elton helped me back to the car and the cottage. A local doctor, a self-important fellow with a high stick-up collar, with Elton's help pulled my shoulder back into place in a most primitive fashion, anaesthetizing me simply by pouring chloroform on a piece of cotton-wool in a dusty old jam-jar. The ache in my shoulder gradually ceased, and I was soon all right again, a little bit wiser – perhaps! But I still enjoyed running down hill whenever I went into mountain country.

It was the lambing season, and Juliette thought it would be a good occasion to explain some of the 'facts of life' to the children. Francis was a bit young to take anything in, but Anthony, rising six, was much impressed. After a pause for reflection, he said:

'Mummy, I don't think I shall ever get married. I am sure it hurts' . . . which shows how difficult it is to combine tact and clarity in such matters. Actually, he married during the war and produced three charming granddaughters for us.

That summer we took a trip down the Danube and on the way visited Ljubljana. There the professor of Biology gave me two specimens of the blind albino amphibian *Proteus*. We had seen this slender creature living as a large water-breathing eft in the huge underground caves of Postumia in Carinthia. I wanted to find out whether, like axolotls, they could be metamorphosed into the adult salamander stage by thyroid or by thyroxin, the concentrated secretion of the thyroid gland. We transported them all the way home in a Thermos flask, tenderly looked after by Juliette. She left them overnight to exercise themselves in her wash-basin in our hotel rooms – to the horrified fascination of the maids. Unfortunately, the poor *Proteus* came to a sad end. Having, after many vicissitudes, got them safely back to my lab, I was just preparing my experiment when my assistant came to confess that he had carelessly let them slip out into the sink while changing the water, and they had gone down the plug-hole into the sewer. As a matter of fact, later work on the Continent showed that they were so closely adapted to their way of life in the Carinthian caves that their own thyroid gland had become vestigial. They remained permanently blind, aquatic, and insensitive even to large doses of thyroxin. It would have been a biological disadvantage to turn into a land salamander when the dry limestone country outside the caves was so barren.

Steaming down the Danube took about five days, and proved somewhat monotonous. The banks were hilly and interesting, sometimes indeed beautiful, as far as Linz, with small rock-perched castles dominating the river. But the landscape soon flattened out to high reeds fringing endless plains. We stopped at every landing place and people came and went. On one occasion we saw a most extraordinary German. He had a round, brachycephalic head with not a hair upon it, and his false teeth were of an undivided strip of silvery metal. He looked like a product of the *Brave New World*, later hatched in Aldous' active brain.

On our return we met Aldous and Maria at Venice: Venice enchanting as ever, and Aldous indefatigable. In spite of his poor eye-sight he had examined all the paintings in the galleries before we were half-way through. He unerringly stopped before the best paintings and used a monocular pocket telescope to notice details which most of us passed over. But then Aldous's eye-sight had ever been a mystery, and we were always amazed by his extraordinary perceptiveness, as well as his wide knowledge of painting. He never failed to visit any collection, and always absorbed the best in it. Much later, when he had a house at Sanary in the south of France, he himself spent happy hours in painting, and some of his gouaches were outstanding. But the strain on his eyes was too great and he had regretfully to give it up after he moved to California in 1937.

From Venice, where we both bought enormous felt hats, we all went up to Cortina d'Ampezzo, where the Aldouses had taken lodgings for their son Matthew's health. Maria drove a small Citroën at full speed round the hair-raising bends of the mountain road, while Aldous had charge of the horn, which he tooted faithfully all through the trip.

Meanwhile, in the autumn of 1925, I had succeeded Professor Dendy as Professor of Zoology at King's College, London. My salary was £1,000 – the first time that a four-figure income had been given to a biologist in Britain. We bought a house in the mock-Tudor Holly Lodge estate in Highgate (Tudorific was our nickname for its style) and I went to and fro by car or tram. The house was conveniently close to Hampstead Heath, and we made regular use of it, the boys bicycling up and down its paths, while we walked, and sometimes bathed in the excellent outdoor swimming pool.

I had been daunted by the prospect of giving the elementary lectures in zoology for the pre-medical students who formed the majority of the classes, for they had, I had been told, a reputation for disorderly conduct. Certainly they turned the lectures of my botanical colleague Professor Ruggles Gates into a pandemonium, but, to my agreeable surprise, they sat docilely through mine, I think because they found them interesting. When I was told by my physiological colleague that I had been chosen not on account of my research work but mainly because I had a good reputation as a lecturer, I felt rather hurt – but my experience with the pre-medical students made me realize how important it was to keep them in order by holding their attention.

In London we had many new friends old and new. Lady Ottoline Morrell had now left Garsington and was living in Gower Street. As always, she had the gift of inspiring her guests, and I still remember the delight her parties were. She did not, like Lady Colefax, specialize in 'lions', but generously extended her circle to young people who had taken her fancy, and was endlessly kind to the lonely. There has recently been a smear campaign against her, which my wife and I deplore as malicious and unjust. I hope that some loyal friend will soon write her Life, showing her as the great personality that she was, original and fearless in her taste and ideas, generous in understanding, and forgiving of human foibles.

Among her guests were many Bloomsburyites from the old days at Garsington – Lytton Strachey, Virginia Woolf, Mark Gertler, Clive and Vanessa Bell, Mary Hutchinson and others ceaselessly entangled in quarrels and reconciliations. One of the most amusing was James Stephens, a leprechaun figure with a leprechaun poetic charm, enchanting us with his imaginative world of beasts and plants and legendary elves. Another frequent visitor was Kotelianski – Kot as he was called by his chosen friends – with a shock of hair like a halo on his striking head, booming like an Old Testament prophet. His favourite description for people he mistrusted or disliked (and they were many) was 'a crrriminal stink'. His particular strength was an inflexible integrity and loyalty, a rare and precious quality. W. B. Yeats and Gogarty always called at Gower Street when they were in London and so did many other literary and artistic figures. We remember Ottoline with admiration and love. She died just before the Second World War.

Through Aldous I met the eccentric poetaster millionaire Evan Morgan, Lord Tredegar. Once while lecturing in Wales I was invited to dinner at his big house in the Rhondda district. In the drawing-room later, while inspecting the Tsarevitch's bed-table, made of a single slab of onyx, I was suddenly roused by a sharp nip. One of Evan's pet macaws was using my leg as a ladder for claws and beak, to climb up to the sofa.

Evan had a predilection for exotic creatures. Soon afterwards a groom arrived in haste to say that his pet baboon had escaped from its stall and was roaming the stables in a threatening manner. Evan merely said to me: 'You know about animals, come along,' picked up a torch, and off we went. The baboon was certainly alarming, snarling and showing its teeth. But we coaxed it into a corner, and Evan caressed it until it calmed down. And so we returned, the baboon in excited nakedness, perching on Evan's dinner-jacketed shoulder and contentedly munching a carnation it had snatched from his button-hole. A strange sight in that luxurious drawing-room; it made me think of decadent Roman emperors indulging in slightly obscene masquerades.

And so I could go on, remembering the dinners given by Sybil Colefax, Enid Bagnold (by now wife of Sir Roderick Jones, head of Reuter's English branch), Mary Spears, Margot Asquith, Violet Hammersley, Osbert Sitwell, Arnold Bennett, H. G. Wells. . . . It is an era gone for ever, with its gaiety and irony, its bitter contrasts of wealth, poverty, luxury, and unemployment, and its blind onrush to the Second World War, which was to create so many fundamental changes.

It was about this time that I read my old colleague Carr-Saunders' remarkable book on population, in which he showed that primitive people all over the world had deliberately adopted some method of regulating their numbers. This made me think hard. It was another case of relative growth,[1] of man's numbers relative to his resources. It was clear that unlimited multiplication at any positive rate of compound interest, however small, would lead to deforestation, shortage of food, gross overcrowding and other

[1] See p. 215.

troubles. Malthus had arrived at the same conclusion, but believed that excessive numbers could only be kept down by continence or disease. I became deeply interested in the problem and, ever since, I have campaigned for family planning. In the late twenties I wrote various articles stressing the need for birth-control, including sterilization after a certain number of children had been born. As a result I was asked to give evidence to the World Conference of Anglican Bishops at Lambeth Palace in 1930, one group of which was discussing sex and marriage, and eventually reported favourably as regards family planning, stressing the dangers of over-population, and leaving the practice of birth-control to the conscience of the individuals concerned.

I corresponded on the subject with my friend William Temple, recently made Archbishop of York. Perhaps I may quote from a reply of his, dated December 7th, 1930:

. . . when you get home let me know, so that I may again arrange for you to meet the Bp of Winchester, who was Chairman of the relevant Committee at the Lambeth Conference. The question of sterilization was raised and squashed in that Committee and never reached the Conference at all.

My impression (it is no more) of what happened is that when the subject was mentioned the American bps vehemently resisted any allusion to it, on the ground that it would be a fearful shock to their constituents – not on the ground that the experiments had proved it a mistake – but that it was not worth while to administer so great a shock for the sake of so tentative a reference.

Further *my impression* is that those who wanted to include the reference were ready to give way rather than pile up antagonisms against their Report when it was already rendered precarious by its attitude to birth-control.

By the way, you say that the one objection that you have to the Report on that subject is the use of the word 'unnatural'. But I cannot find it! I should cordially agree with you that birth-control is just as much and just as little 'unnatural' as a pocket-handkerchief or false teeth – and that anyhow this has, and can have, nothing to do with the moral issue.

> *Yours affectly*
> *William Ebor.*'

I had advocated birth-control in a broadcast. This infuriated the puritanical Director of the BBC, Sir John Reith, who summoned me to his formidable presence and abused me for having profaned 'his' ether with such disgusting ideas. I am not sure that he did not add 'wicked' to his condemnation. He must have been disagreeably surprised by the Lambeth Conference's Report.

It is interesting to know that the Conference thought their approval of birth-control put them in a difficult position; and also that the more enlightened bishops, like Temple, found artificial birth-control by no means 'unnatural' – like the late Pope John, but unlike his successor Pope Paul. I should add that sterilization, especially male sterilization by vasectomy, is today widely used in countries like India (though not for eugenic purposes, as I had hoped)[1] and that even abortion, under strict control, is now legally permitted in Britain and other Western nations. Moreover, the practice of birth-control is rapidly spreading, new methods like the Pill have been devised, and it seems possible that many Roman Catholics will give way on the subject, despite the Papal Encyclical of 1968. But the threat of over-population still looms large, and it will be long before we achieve stability, let alone any reduction in world numbers.

In 1956 I was honoured by the presentation of the Lasker Award of the Planned Parenthood Federation in America, at a banquet celebrating the fiftieth anniversary of the foundation, by Margaret Sanger, of the first birth-control clinic in the world. When she started, let us remember, birth-control was a crime under New York State law; she was arrested and had to spend a night in the cells before she came up for trial. The persecution continued. Even to advertise her clinic by circular was to use the US mail service for 'pornographic' purposes, and therefore a criminal offence.

In the mid-twenties she came over to Europe to gain support for her cause, and saw me as well as H. G. Wells and other sympathizers. I was only too ready to give her my name, and was quite

---

[1] I have just read that Indians who are vasectomized are given portable transistor radios, so that any decrease in Indian numbers will be accompanied by an increase in Indian noise.

won over by her combination of ardent zeal and common sense. One result of her visit was the foundation of the first birth-control clinic in England, by Marie Stopes, who by this time had obtained a degree of nullity of marriage against her husband, Professor Gates, my old colleague at King's College.

So far the emphasis had been on the need to help individual women to avoid the misery of unwanted pregnancies, and the burden of large families. But now, under pressure from myself and many others, the birth-control movement, still with Margaret Sanger at the helm, began to lay increasing stress on the dangers of over-population. She organized a World Population Conference at Geneva in 1927, and again enlisted my help. I well remember her face – the face of a martyr lined with suffering, but burning with zeal and hope. She never flagged. She managed to get the laws against birth-control repealed in many States of the US, set up a Population Reference Council as a study group and a powerful lobbying agency in Washington, and eventually, in 1952, helped to found the International Planned Parenthood Federation, which now has branches all over the world.

I later saw her at the birth-control conference in Delhi, in 1959: she had persuaded the Ford Foundation to give large sums for birth-control work in India and other under-developed countries. Later in the year, she was guest of honour at the banquet in New York commemorating the jubilee of her work, which I have already mentioned. She was by then a frail old woman, much shrunken but still full of fire, only a few months before she died.

I am proud to have known her, and to have contributed something to the crusade she started – a crusade *against* woman's sufferings and *for* greater human fulfilment – individual, national and global.

I had long been a member of the Rationalist Press Association, but found their attitude too rational and materialistic, too much concerned with attacking existing churches and picking holes in religious dogmas, while discounting the value of any religious or mystical experience.

My nervous breakdown in 1912, due to my unresolved conflicts about sex, had inflicted on me 'the dark night of the soul', in
which all sense of fruitful communion, in human love, or with
natural and man-made beauty, and even in fruitful moral or
intelligent co-operation, went overboard. The essentially religious
feeling of oneness with nature, with art and my fellow-beings, was
lost. Even the consolation of work was denied to me.

I gradually recovered my normality while in Texas, and renewed my enjoyment of work and natural beauty, and of human
company. And then, while in Colorado Springs Hospital, I read
the essays of Lord Morley, where he affirmed (as Renan had done
before, but I didn't know it) that 'the next great task of science
will be to create a religion for humanity'. He stressed that writers
and artists as well as scientists could play their part in this transformation.

Earlier my aunt Mary Ward's book, *Robert Elsmere,* had made a
deep impression on me, and helped to convert me to what I must
call a religious humanism, but without belief in any personal God.

In 1927, this book, in combination with Morley's words,
prompted me to undertake a book on religion in general: its
origin in magic and sacrificial rites; its dangerous tendency to
fossilize into intellectual or moral dogmatism; the growth of substitute religions such as Marxism; the role of ritual in heightening
the sense of awe, that mixture of fear, wonder and admiration
which is at the heart of every religion; and the uplifting sense of
transcendence which can arise from contemplation, from natural
beauty or great art.

In the introductory chapter, 'Personalia', I wrote:

'In spite of all my intellectual hostility to orthodox Christian dogma, the
Chapel services [at Eton] gave me something valuable, and something
which I obtained nowhere else in precisely the same way. . . . In-
dubitably what I received from the services in that beautiful Chapel of
Henry VI was not merely beauty, but something which must be called
specifically religious. But once the magic doors were opened, and my
adolescence became aware of literature and art, and indeed the whole
emotional richness of the world, pure lyric poetry could arouse in me

much intenser and more mystical feelings than anything in the church service; a Beethoven concerto would make the highest flights of the organ seem pale and one-sided, and other buildings were found more beautiful than the Chapel.

It was none of the purely aesthetic emotions which were aroused, or not only they, but a special feeling. The mysteries which surround all the unknowns of existence were, however, dimly contained in it, and the whole was predominantly flavoured with the sense of awe and reverence.'

I worked furiously on the book, mostly in the little Cottage-on-the-Common at Cuttmill which we had rented for the summer. It was published in December, under the title *Religion without Revelation*. It met with immediate success, and has been twice reprinted and revised, so it looks as if I had contributed something of value in this vital field of human feeling and behaviour.

CHAPTER XII

'The Science of Life'

IN 1926 I met H. G. Wells. He had just finished the publication, in weekly instalments, of *The Outline of History*. Though infuriating to many professional historians, it was deservedly a great public success. The first attempt to present history on a world-wide scale, it was also the first undertaking of the sort to be accomplished by a group of professionals working under the direction of an amateur. I had been greatly impressed by it, and when H.G.W. invited me to participate with him and his son G. P. Wells (then a young zoologist at University College, London) in a similar encyclopedic work on biology, to be called *The Science of Life*, I was deeply interested. Yet, returning from early discussions about the machinery of collaboration, I could not help thinking: 'What am I doing with this little philistine?' But the next minute, recalling the compulsive enthusiasm, the convincing certainty which one recognizes in men of great achievements, I would say to myself: 'Yes, but what a genius he is!' (Lenin made identical remarks when H.G. visited him in Russia).

So I finally accepted to work with him and Gip (as H.G.'s son was always called). This time H.G. was not an amateur director. He had taken a course in biology under my grandfather T. H. Huxley at the Imperial College of Science, acquiring a great admiration for his teacher, and a deep interest in what he taught. (His choice of me as collaborator had something to do with his feeling for T.H.H.) He had for some years taught biology as assistant master in a private school. It was only after a serious illness that he started writing his novels and wonderful science-fiction books, and gave up teaching for this much more lucrative activity. However, he had forgotten much of his biology and what he remembered was by now old-fashioned – pre-Mendelian, with little study of animal behaviour or ecology. Thus the bulk of the scientific work would fall on my shoulders, though Gip would be able to contribute a good deal on various modern developments. H.G. would make all the business arrangements, and guide and control the output, as well as collate the material. Financially, he hoped that each of us stood to make at least £10,000 out of it, but, as he wrote in 1927, 'We must give good value for this'. Actually I received rather less than £10,000, but, what with translation rights, my total eventually came pretty near it.

This extract from his *Experiment in Autobiography* gives his idea of the scheme:

'I exerted myself to create a real text-book of biology for the reading and use of intelligent people. I got Julian Huxley and my eldest son Gip, both very sound and aggressive teachers of biology, to combine with me in setting down as plainly and clearly as we could everything that an educated man – to be an educated man – ought to know about biological science. This is *The Science of Life*. It really does cover the ground of the subject, and I believe that to have it read properly, to control its reading by test writing and examination, would come much nearer to the effective teaching in general biology which is necessary for any intelligent approach to the world, than anything of the sort that is so far done by any university.'

We started work in spring 1927, and I realized that I could not expect to keep my chair at King's College and also write my stint for *The Science of Life*. I soon discovered that H.G. demanded every ounce of my knowledge and called upon a gift I had never fully exerted before – that of synthesizing a multitude of facts into a manageable whole, aware of the trees yet seeing the pattern of the forest, and drawing conclusions which gave the whole work vitality. This, I may add, did not come easily.

Accordingly, I resigned my professorship, though staying on as (unpaid) lecturer and still conducting my own and my graduate students' research work, besides attending scientific meetings and giving occasional external lectures. I engaged two secretaries to help with the necessary research, the selection of illustrations and the mounting load of script to be typed.

H.G. was a hard and determined taskmaster – no doubt exasperated by my extraneous occupations – and bombarded me with letters:

Easton Glebe,
14. VII. 27

My dear Huxley,

Now about the book. Let us go right on with it. Time slips by and the mass of the work ought to exist by the beginning of December next. It will not do so unless we get right ahead now.

In my folder I have now

The Introductory part – written

The first Chapter of Part I – partly written

I want to get copy as soon as possible of *Parts Three, Four and Five* from you.

Will you go ahead and deliver duplicated typed copy to me and Gip as it is done.

Now that you are free from your professional incumbrances I want to urge upon you the need for a steady *drive* to produce copy and get illustrations ready. You do not know, as I do, how these things crumple up at the end if the bulk of the work is not done swiftly and furiously *soon*: The eleventh hour is the time for revision and fitting together, and you can have no idea how much work that will mean and how much time it will take. It is imperative to have the main bulk already there by October or November; then we can really polish, fill in and refine. But for God's sake don't let us be like a company of bad actors who say, 'It's all smooth, my dear boy. It will be *All right on the night*.'

The time for hurry is at the beginning.

Yours
H. G.

Another letter dated 6. VIII. 27., less than four weeks later:

Dear Huxley,

I do want to have this *Science of Life* job getting on. Nothing material seems to be getting done about the illustrations or indeed about anything. . . . And the work has to be done well. If a satisfactory mass of material does not show up by Jan 1st 1928 then I shall cancel the whole thing, return Doran [the American publisher] his money and wash my hands of the project. I can't cluck after you and Gip like an old hen after ducklings. I thought the thing was good enough for both of you to work hard and do your best. I find that holidays, research, the Leeds gathering [of the British Association], a summer holiday, any little thing of that sort, is sufficient to put off work on the *Science of Life*.

Well, that means scrapping it and the sooner it is scrapped the less it will cost us to get out of it.

Yours, H. G.

Then, on December 22nd of the same year, another blast:

My dear Huxley,

I have just had a visit from Doran here. He is very anxious to see the *Science of Life* taking shape. He tells me that up to date you have only written 20,000 words: this I am sure is not correct. You told me in October, did you not, that you were doing 1,000 words a day? Anyhow I think we must get copy in hand faster than this – even if you have to make notes and then dictate from them. I had hoped for 100,000 words at least at the turn of the year and a good bale of material for illustration.

After all, nothing else you can do is likely to be nearly so profitable as the enterprise *if it is well done.*

The Outline of History brought me in over £60,000, and this is, or should be, more interesting and far-reaching. But you must do it as your big job and not in the interstices of little text-books, odd lectures and going to and fro. It has to be got into shape and the bulk has to be fairly written and in type well ahead of delivery, because we cannot foresee what remodelling, polishing, pointing and so on, may be needed to get it into its most effective form. A hastily mulled eleventh-hour performance is fairly sure to slump – and great will be the slump thereof.

Forgive my anxieties. I had imagined that things were going on fast and strong, and that when I got back in March the best part of the first half would at least be in typed existence.

Yours ever
H. G. Wells

During that autumn of 1927 we went down to H.G.'s country

place at Easton Glebe in Essex for week-ends of correction and discussion. Since H.G. demanded an impossible rate of progress, the atmosphere was apt to become stormy, and Juliette generally came along to lighten the tension. Yet after work he was a charming host. Supercharged and as if indestructible, H.G. worked, talked and played with a sort of fury. He had guests to meet us, with whom we played tennis and charades, and the famous Barn Game. This was a special ball-game played in the Long Barn when the weather was wet. The rules seemed to be made up by H.G. as we went along, but there was tremendous enthusiasm and plenty of exercise, a good game that left no post-mortems. Meals were gay with witty quips – H.G. never repeated a comic story – and his retorts were sharp, quick and very funny (also, alas, elusive – I could never remember them).

In the evenings, when other visitors had gone, we played bridge. On one occasion, after some gross overbidding by H.G. and myself, Gip threw down his hand and shouted 'Bastard' at his father. After a shocked silence, H.G. replied in his squeaky voice: 'In the old days, God would have thought nothing of striking you dead for less than that.'

H.G.'s curious, atonic, thin voice remains physiologically inexplicable. No eunuch was he for sure. Equally uncharacteristic was his small, neat and undemonstrative handwriting. Small and witty drawings often accompanied his notes, like a shorthand comic strip. His figure was not impressive, more in the tubby line, with small hands and feet. Though he had a remarkable brain, his head was several sizes smaller than most of his friends'. I have an amusing snapshot of him wearing David Low's 'diplomatic' hat, which enveloped him to the ears, while David's cranium looks as if buttoned by H.G.'s headgear.

H.G.'s wife Jane, a wonderful person, died late in 1927 after a long spell of suffering. In spite of her illness she had insisted that all H.G.'s activities should proceed as usual. To his letter of July 7th, he added:

'Jane is very plucky and patient and sane. We have had some good days, half-happy days and there are more to come yet. . . .'

159

I am sure that part of his petulance with me was due to his worries over her.

We went to her funeral with very sad hearts. I remember her, small and fragile, but full of enduring courage and wisdom, humour and understanding. He loved her dearly. She had accepted his tumultuous infidelities, and in her own exquisite manner had created for him and their two boys a home of great beauty, a place of refuge from the noisy public world.

Finding myself still a target of invitations to lectures and social engagements, I decided to get right away, to concentrate on finishing my part of the *S.o.L.* So we took a chalet at Diablerets for the winter, *Les Arolles*. It was large enough to accommodate us and to induce Aldous and Maria, with their boy Matthew and a governess, to join us. There was even room for visitors. Soon D. H. Lawrence and his wife Frieda were ensconced in another chalet near by and we all began a cheerful three months together. Aldous and I wrote hard till lunch, while Juliette was busy typing my script and Maria that of *Lady Chatterley's Lover,* for Lawrence. In the afternoons we set off on skis and were joined for picnics by Lawrence and Frieda; sometimes they came for tea and talks. Lawrence often exploded with a snort of impotent rage when we talked about scientific matters. Aldous and I discussed evolutionary and physiological ideas, including the possibility of mankind's genetic improvement. This particularly infuriated Lawrence, who believed that more power exercised by 'the dark loins of man', greater freedom for our instincts and our intuitions, would solve the world's troubles. His anger was specially directed against myself, as a professional scientist. I learnt to disregard his outbursts of fury, but we had many a stormy passage.

Our evenings were spent reading aloud. Aldous and I taking turns, we got through the whole of *The Pickwick Papers*. It was a happy time, the white landscape soothing and protective, and much work was done.

H.G. was spending the winter at Grasse, from where he continued to prod me:

Lou Pidou, St Mattieu, Grasse   Feb. 12. 1928

My dear Huxley,

How goes the work? Shall we have 120,000 words from you and Gip (or more), *beautifully typed* and ready for editorial treatment (& after that delivery) before the month of March? I hope so. So far as the *Science of Life* goes I have been marking time, merely. But I have done nearly half of my fantastic pseudo boys' adventure-story which will be my *Candide*, my *Peer Gynt*, my *Gulliver*.

Tell me the work is all right. My warmest good wishes to you both and to Aldous and Mrs Aldous also.

Yours ever
H. G.

P.S. You don't mean to be *too* Behaviourist, do you? I found Watson [the American founder of this ultra-mechanistic movement] very repellent (intellectually), no gentleman, and he seems to me to ignore the physical element in aptitude and disposition. No amount of conditioning or deconditioning reflexes will produce a specially sensitive hand, a thin skin, a large or small stomach, exceptionally weak or exceptionally strong footwork in boxing etc. etc.

This friendly letter was followed by further notes:

614 St Ermins'
Westminster   Feb 23rd. [1928]

Dear Julian,

Gip has no right to afterthoughts which wreck the whole argument of Book IV. I am against any further alterations of that Bateson paragraph. I know the man. My last talk with him was with Morgan in N.Y. and he has a schoolboy pleasure in making trouble and a Samuel Butler-like hatred for Darwin.[1] Any fool can play the negative game and no doubt some of the young fools will go on with it.

I do hope you will come (with Juliette) to Easton for Easter, and please get on with Book VI and keep the illustrations lively.

Yours ever
H. G.

[1] This was not strictly true. In his early work Bateson had over-rated large mutations as cause of immediate evolutionary change, but he eventually, under R. A. Fisher's influence, came to accept a Darwinian position – natural selection by the slow selection of favourable genetic combinations, including occasional mutations, mostly of minor scale.

I was now working hard, yet he kept up – perhaps with some justification – and wrote in March:

My dear Huxley,

I don't see much good in 'discussing the time question'. We've undertaken obligations to these people, we've got them to put down huge sums of money, and we're honourably bound to try to meet the requirements.

If you will press on, the work can be done, but you must press on. If side-shows like Geneva, the Royal Institution, holidays, other works, etc., are to scoop out your time and energy, obviously we shall make a mess of the job. What we want now is steady systematic writing, not discussions.

And while I am writing, I wish you would leave the editorial job to me and just do your writing with Chapter and Section headings on the uniform lines laid down at the beginning. If you have ideas for 'vivid' headings put them in the margin, but please do not start a lot of sub-sectional headings, cross-heads and so forth for your part, independently of what is done in other parts of the work. This to and fro, to and fro, putting things in, cutting them out again, wastes an inordinate amount of time and nerves. What is wanted from you and Gip is to get right on with writing, each going ahead. . . .

Write: that's what has to be done and please write your earlier parts first.

I suggest you should scrap your engagements for Easter and put in time at the *Science of Life*.

Do you remember that originally you proposed to break the back of the work before Xmas 1927? And here we are!

Yours ever
H. G.

Pushed on by such strong blasts, I sailed forth at full speed, reading everything available on the subject, checking and writing at a terrific rate. This brought another storm upon my head:

Easton Glebe, Dunmow   Oct. 29th. 1928

My dear Huxley,

You will know that Brown [Curtis Brown, Doran's literary agent] has turned down part of Book III as boring. He objects to the evolution of the Horse being done in such detail. I have now re-read Book III.

He is wrong about that section, but he is right about objecting to Book III as it stands. The only interest of that horse stuff lies in its controversial value, and Book III begins so lazily, loosely and slackly that only the initiated will grasp the bearing of this horse material. Accordingly I have written a final Chapter I for Book III and recast the contents. Miss S. will copy and clean the MS and return it to you *in order that you may see what is to be done.*

Will you look it over and send it on to Brown at once please. *Don't, I implore you, alter it again.* There is no time.

I have cut out the section I return you herewith. Manifestly it overlaps the *History of Life* in Book Five.

Now about Book Four. *Brown is pressing for the copy.* But Gip tells me you have at present only a monster of 150,000 words ready.[1] This is hopelessly impossible. The maximum length of this book is to be 60,000 words and a vast undigested mass of stuff is no good at all. What is to be done? It is surely your job to produce the Book at something like its proper length. Can you rewrite it rapidly? What has happened to cause this frightful distention? I don't see how one can *cut* 150,000 to 60,000. Shall Gip and I take over this accumulation as raw material, as note-book, and write a Book IV to shape and scale? Or can you do anything promptly, to produce a decently typed and slender and sinewy Book IV? I am amazed and distressed by this news. I counted on getting Books IV and V by this time and here we are with only raw material! All summer gone!

It seems more than ever plain that I shall have to come back to London after Christmas and set down to write this *Science of Life*, from your accumulations, part by part as the printers wait.

I can't do any other work. I might just as well be writing the whole bloody thing with Gip myself.

Can't you get in stenographers, take your distended Book IV in hand, re-dictate it to proper dimensions, send the stenographs to a competent typing office and then let us have the good clean copy of 50,000 to 60,000 words we have a right to expect, for us to do our share upon.

Look at this letter! If it was an article I could get 1500 dollars for it. Look at the waste of time and attention, Oh my collaborator!

Yrs ever

H. G.

[1] This was the section on insect behaviour.

However, the storm abated. His next letter was from London:

My dear Huxley,
    Yes, let's say no more about it for two months. You've taken my comments charmingly and I'm glad I'd written the letter if for no other reason because it has produced so frank, friendly and good-tempered a reply. . . .
                                                    Yours ever
                                                    H. G.

VIII ought to contain good moral teaching – fumatory habits – obsession – . . . and so forth. Boil down the Ants and Bees.

    I had indeed been so carried away by my interest in social insects that I had produced this 'monster' of 150,000 words, but it clearly had to be cut: and cut I did, though it was a painful operation. I utilized the surplus portions to produce a little book on *Ants and Termites.*
    H.G.'s sharp monetary sense now suggested that our shares should be altered:

'You suggested 40:30:30 for yourself, Gip and H.G. My own feeling is that 40:35:25 better represents the toil of the enterprise and anyhow there are excellent fiscal reasons for throwing my profits into Gip's hands at once. Then I think we can look to him when VII is cleared to take up at least a part of VIII. There is a growing trouble in my mind about VIII, I value Jung's work very highly and I think a lot of mental science hangs on to the evolutionary conception of social origins. VIII is I think about our most important book. What do you think of making VIII deal with animal behaviour only? taking IX, social biology, next and then hang a Book X on the human mind. I don't like this but I throw it out as a sort of point of departure for a rearrangement.
                                                    Yours ever
                                                    H. G.'

About the same time, the following note arrived:

THOUGHTS IN THE NIGHT

Note to go to my esteemed collaborators one after the other.

The reader for whom you write
   is just as intelligent as you are but
does not possess *your* store of knowledge,
   he is not to be offended by a recital
in Technical language of things known to him
   (e.g. telling him the position of the heart and lungs and backbone)
   He is not a student preparing for
an examination & *he does not want to be
encumbered with technical terms,*
   his sense of literary form & his sense of humour is probably
greater than yours.
   Shakespeare, Milton, Plato, Dickens, Meredith, T. H. Huxley,
Darwin wrote for him. None of them are known to have talked
of putting in 'popular stuff' & 'treating him to pretty bits'
or alluded to matters as being 'too complicated to discuss
here'. If they were, they didn't discuss them there and *that
was the end of it.*

This job is an important job; your own researches and your professional
career are *less important.*
Note also: it is easier to expand than cut down.
   Get all the ground covered first.

Don't leave God the Father[1] to look up facts. It is not his *forte*. The
conversion of millimetres into inches or of degrees C° into degrees F° is
not his job. And don't send him in bad, dirty, patchy typing. You are
getting enough out of the job to get the typewriting properly done &
in time.

H.G. now suggested that Juliette and I should join him in the
spring at his villa, Lou Pidou, near Grasse. (Lou Pidou was local
dialect for *Le Petit Dieu*, Odette's nickname for him.) He had built
the house for his mistress Odette Keun, and on the mantelpiece

----

[1] Gip often called H.G. 'God the Father'.

were inscribed these words: TWO LOVERS BUILT THIS HOUSE. This proved unfortunate, as they eventually separated, H.G. being unable to cope with her.

Never before were two such bouncing lovers contained under one roof. The impact on outsiders was instantaneous, and left us staggering. Their relations with each other generated a fantastic atmosphere, abrasive quarrels alternating with passionate reconciliations, which both of them relished – for a limited period.

Odette was no nymphette, but the most articulate, unreticent, explosive female that ever was. She was then in her early middle age; her face had more character than beauty, her carriage more style than grace. There was a dubious charge by the British Government that she had done some spying for a foreign power during the First World War, and she was therefore *persona non grata* in Britain. This suited H.G. perfectly, as he could always retire from the field when he had had enough.

But Odette was not at all content; she wanted a London triumph. On one occasion we were at Lou Pidou when Sir William Joynson-Hicks proposed a visit. He was then Home Secretary, and in his power lay the possibility of a British visa for Odette. He had been recently involved in the banning of Radclyffe Hall's lesbian novel, *The Well of Loneliness*, as an obscene publication, and Odette announced that, in view of this illiberal action, it was her duty to be rude to 'Jix', as he was nicknamed. With some asperity, H.G. desired her to behave decently to his guest, which she reluctantly promised to do. She put on her best dress and smile and welcomed the party most affably, saying to Joynson-Hicks: 'Do let me show you the garden, Jix. I want you to do me a small favour – give me a visa for England. If you refuse, I will dig a little Well of Loneliness for you and drrrrop you in it!' Shocked but polite, he bowed and followed her. They soon returned in ominous silence; there was no prospect of a visa.

The party went in to tea; there were quite a few people, including Mrs Hanbury Williams, Jix's hostess, his son and some smart girl friends, as well as ourselves. Odette was roused by this very British atmosphere, which her Levantine temperament naturally disliked. She forgot her promise to H.G. and, suddenly turning to Jix, asked him in ringing tones why it was worse for a woman to sleep with another woman than with a man. There was no answer from Jix's frigid lips, and she turned to me: 'You, Huxley, you are a biologist – *you* tell me why.' There was a shocked and frozen silence, which even H.G. could not cope with. The party broke up, sheltering its outraged feelings under banalities. Odette floated over the aftermath with disarming surprise. 'Did I do anything wrong?'

Between these stormy occasions, *The Science of Life* went on. Blue-pencilled pages emerged to be laboriously rewritten. H.G. lost and recovered his temper, and so did I, but on the whole, the atmosphere was gay and friendly. After strenuous mornings of work, H.G. took us for drives; we visited the strange mountain village of Les Baux, and sped along the beautiful cliff road, the Corniche, and even had a shot of gambling at Monte Carlo, where Juliette won on her first stake. 'Beginner's luck', said H.G., and swept her away before she lost it all.

Back to London, more research and intense writing. In the summer, Juliette took the family for a holiday at Port Blanc in Brittany, where I joined them for three weeks, shortening my piece about social insects and doing other revisions.

We had fun too. Port Blanc was then a small village with a sandy foreshore full of huge granite blocks. I remember a night of full moon when the sand-eels came up from their burrows, and we joined the entire local population in forking them up with sickles. It was a wonderful sight, everyone armed with lanterns to spot the burrows, busily scooping out the silvery fish, which were delicious when cooked.

We drove to Douarnenez in Pierre Chevrillon's Bébé Peugeot, passing a religious procession or *Pardon* on the way, with peasants in their beautiful traditional Breton dress, a carved Celtic *calvaire* as their goal. They stood there to pray until the tall candles they held were burnt out.

But our most memorable visit was to the huge beech Forêt du Cranou, where we found a family making sabots by hand, skilfully carving out the rough blocks with a curved blade attached to a bench. They lived in huts made of branches, with the most primitive camping equipment – strange survivors of mediaeval craftsmanship, refugees from the encroachments of technology.

We also visited Alexis Carrel, the noted physiologist, who lived on an island opposite Port Blanc. I had met him in his big Medical Institute in New York, where he showed me through room after room full of the latest apparatus, attended by rows of female assistants and secretaries all garbed in white, and mostly very pretty. He was rather vain, but gave me some useful tit-bits for our section on Man.

During our time at Port Blanc H.G. and Odette descended on us. This created quite a problem; we were staying close to our old friends the Chevrillons (André was a Membre de l'Institut, a famous writer and friend of my aunt Mary Ward), and his son Pierre had lodged with us for a year when he was studying English at Oxford. André and his wife were naturally keen to meet H. G. Wells. But when they heard that he was accompanied by his mistress, they decided they could not receive him. So we had a discreet picnic with H.G. and Odette on the beautiful shore, and they departed in a cloud of dust and a shower of admonitions concerning my work.

In my papers about the *S.o.L.* I find the following letter from myself with marginal notes by H.G.:

Feb. 10 1930

Dear H. G.,

I have been looking through the galleys of Bk IX in connection with the illustrations. I find Section 5 of Chapt 2, The Breeding of Mankind, still unsatisfactory in certain definite ways. I think I must have been so exhausted last Aug. that I let you and/or Gip triumph unopposed by me!

As they stand, the remarks about different social classes are to me untenable. You make sweeping assertions about the absence of difference between them which I really can't pass. I am quite willing to let you cut out my 'sweeping assertions' about the positive difference *Agreed, we say* between them, but let us point out the problem. To be sure I wasn't *that now.* biased, I wrote to Carr-Saunders about the point, and he writes a long letter back which boils down to what I also had in mind – that the present state of affairs may be eugenically neutral, cannot be eugenically good, and probably is slightly eugenically bad.

This concerns the main bulk of the nation. As these differences will I hope soon be wiped out by birth-control, I agree to passing it over with a v. slight reference. On the other hand, I have again been reading *Don't talk of submerged tenth.* the Mental Defective Rept, & it is really quite alarmist (considering what a conservative body the C'ttee was) about the 'submerged tenth' problem. And this is untouchable by birth-control. Every birth-control worker I meet tells the same thing.

I really think we ought to say something on this point. It comes to this, that the evils of slum-life are largely due to the slums, but to a *It could be. I pray you not to do it.* definite extent *caused* by the type of people who inevitably gravitate down, and will make a slum for themselves if not prevented.

I have written suggested insertions. Will you please look over it and see what you think. If we don't have some changes in the text, I feel I shall be reduced to a minority footnote, which would be a pity, as the Trinity has hitherto been unanimous. I am sending a copy to G.P.W.

By the way, you will be interested to hear that my old pupil, J. R. Baker of Oxford, working for the Birth Control Investigation C'ttee has discovered a practically ideal chemical contraceptive – cheap, easy *Yes, but I want some for Odette's sister.* and harmless! We are just looking into the best way of preventing the discovery from being exploited, before announcing it.

Yrs ever

Julian Huxley

H. G. answered my letter on its margin: 'Forgive me returning your letter, but it is the quickest way of getting the points you discuss. God bless you both. *H. G.*'

This formidable work was finally done; the manuscript was delivered to the publishers, and the original collection of separate fascicules appeared in three bound volumes late in 1930. They had a well-merited success, and it was unfortunate that the Second World War prevented their reprinting.

The work was indeed an important achievement, bringing the facts and implications of biology, including human biology and psychology, before a public already bewitched by physico-chemical science and its technical results. It is now out of print, except in translation, but its effects are still manifest in the increased space allotted to biology in the educational curriculum, and the greater interest of the general public in biological facts and their consequences.

I had the major burden of writing it and finding suitable illustrations, and was extremely tired when the work was ready for publication. But I had learnt a great deal about my own subject, and also, under H.G.'s stern guidance, about the popularization of difficult ideas and recondite facts, which stood me in good stead in my later career.

I have just looked at my original copy of *The Science of Life* and am astonished at its range. Beginning with human anatomy and physiology, it went on to the variety of animal and plant types, their adaptations to different habitats and modes of life, and their evolution in time (Jack Haldane told me that my graphic representation of evolution and extinction was the most telling he had ever seen). There were special sections on reproduction and disease, animal and human, and a long chapter on animal and human behaviour, including normal and abnormal psychology. I expanded my little book on *Individuality* to cover parasitism, symbiosis and various types of colony-formation, and we ended with a section on human cultural evolution – the results of technical advance, good and bad, the problems of urban life and the possibilities of eugenic improvement (where, as is clear from my letter of February 1930, I found myself in disagreement with H.G.). And the illustrations, copious and abundant, really did illuminate the text: their selection involved very hard work, mainly by my two secretaries and myself.

We took a well-earned holiday that summer in Switzerland, in a chalet on top of Chaumont, the Jura mountain that towers up three thousand feet above Juliette's home town, Neuchâtel. There were lovely walks along the ridge and down through the woods, full of wild strawberries and strange fungi, many of them edible. In a village church nestling on the slopes, we found a memorable euphemism for adultery engraved on the wall among the Ten Commandments: '*Tu ne paillarderas point*' – no romping in the hay!

Juliette enjoyed showing us all the treasures of her childhood environment, and the boys began their life-long appreciation of the Jura.

Before embarking further, I want to round off the memories we have of H.G.

In 1930 he gave up Easton Glebe and moved to a large flat in Chiltern Court, where he gave numerous parties. One, in November 1933, must have been outstanding. I was away lecturing in America, but Juliette wrote me a long letter about it. The party was too large for the flat so they dined at the *Quo Vadis* restaurant, and (I quote from Juliette's letter):

'therefrom to return to Chiltern Court, where the Countess Benckendorf, sister-in-law of H.G.'s close friend, Moura Budberg, would play the harp for our pleasure.

The company was as varied as distinguished. H.G., smiling, comfortable, amused, benevolently received the generous outpouring of good wishes. [It must have been his birthday.] There was Lady Keeble in red velvet, skittishly ladling out admiration. Christabel McLaren, faithfully loved, faithfully loving. Lady Cunard in ermine, almost invisible under pearls and diamonds, scenting out the lions. Lady Lavery, shrouded in the glorious vestiges of her mortal beauty, white as a wraith, gaudy in purple and scarlet. Enid Bagnold, now Lady Jones, suffering from nettle-rash on her face, brazening it out under a scarlet visière from which depended an orange veil – un peu Homme-au-masque-de-fer, but intriguing and romantic. Myself, in my new black velvet coat with ermine collar and ermine tails at the back of the neck, and round white buttons all the way down to my feet; David and Madeline Low, Harold Nicolson, Baron Stuttenheim, Will Irwin, Francis Meynell, Gip and Frank [Wells], both with their wives, Moura Budberg, Maurice Baring, Max Beerbohm, Violet Ford and many others whose names I didn't catch or forgot. Horse-shoe table filled the room. H.G. in the centre, rosily smiling: all the guests talking at once, an appalling cacophony. All the guests behind their façade, dressed-up, and Lady Jones behind her double one, carefully inserting her food below the little curtain, lighting her cigarette at the end of a long holder.

I sit between David Low and Will Irwin. David Low talks of

spiritualism, survival, escapes, tortures. He is honest and solid. Irwin, I gather, writes in the U.S.A. He is old, a struggler and sincere. Across the table, Francis Meynell talks of his job of advertising, and Violet Ford ruminates gloomily on her great thwarted love for Ford Madox Ford. The heat of the room grows with the human generators, and the noise rises with food and drink. H.G., urbane host and provider, scrapes his chair and gets up, suggests adjourning back to the flat where champagne awaits us, and music. So in small groups and with a variety of transport we make our way back to Chiltern Court. In the lift I find Lady Keeble and Lady Lavery both much agitated and distressed – Lady Lavery is certain she has been poisoned by the foreign food at the *Quo Vadis*: Lady Keeble asks me if I have ever eaten there before, and if so, did I survive it?

We flutter up to the flat, and arrange ourselves for the rest of the evening. But alas, Countess Benckendorf is taken ill, the music is cancelled: there is nothing we can do but drink the champagne and look at the harp the Countess did not play. It was not a good party.'

Earlier, on October 14th, Juliette wrote in her diary:

'Driving home with Julian after seeing Francis at Abinger [both the boys went to Abinger Hill Prep. School, but by 1934 Anthony had gone on to Dauntsey's, the public school in Wiltshire] we got talking of how funny H.G. had been at his dinner-party last Thursday, and how one should remember those things . . . Even now, only a few days later, we just couldn't tell what it was that had convulsed us with laughter: Julian & Christabel, Sir Frederick Gowland Hopkins and Eileen Power, and Dr and Mrs Brierley. H. G. anyway, was having one of those dinners to discuss a magnificent idea he has, to unite science to save the world against all its growing dangers: Fascism, Communism, Japanism, Americanism and Journalism. Christabel, for ever tentatively beautiful, was listening to her own preciously articulated words, asking the questions that Socrates got poisoned for. H.G., benevolent as ever, was answering them with a pinch of salt in the tail, which set the rather slow and ponderous Dr Brierley [of Reading University] thinking and talking. Julian, who thinks twice as fast and gets to the point, acted as catalyst. Eileen Power refused to be drawn in. Sir Frederick, wise, genuine, profound and so humanly interesting, would have had much to say had he been given a chance by Dr Brierley. H.G. "chaired" the meeting in his squeaky voice, which becomes quite a handicap in such circumstances. Nothing was decided, naturally, except the *need for something*, and H.G. will go on giving dinner-parties to discuss saving the world . . .'[1]

When the war broke out, H.G. went to live in Hanover Place, Regent's Park. He was suffering from diabetes, and had to follow a tiresome diet. His family and friends begged him to leave London for some safe retreat in the country, but he stubbornly refused to move: 'Only rats leave the sinking ship,' he said. He was also beginning to feel the bitterness of seeing his gods, Science and Reason, brought down by human violence and stupidity.

In 1941 there came a break in our happy relationship. I was chairing a meeting of the British Association, and had been instructed to allow only twenty minutes to each speaker, so providing time for general discussion at the end. H.G. had submitted a special paper, summarizing his book on *The New World Order*, concerned with his deep anxiety about the fate of mankind, and taking over forty minutes to unfold. This, I was obliged to tell him beforehand, was unfair to the other speakers, and he would have to limit himself to the allotted twenty minutes. It was the last straw. He had gone so far in seeking for the solution of human perversities, he held the key in his hand; and here I was, measuring his time when crucial words could be spoken before disaster overtook us all. An angry correspondence and protest followed, but when the time came, I had to ask him to cut short his discourse. He never forgave me.

At the outset of the Zoo crisis, to which I shall come later, when I was away in America, Juliette enlisted him as one of my supporters, and he offered his flat as a meeting-place for the informal protest committee which she had called together. However, during the night preceding the meeting, he was reminded of that aborted paper of his at the British Association, for which he held me responsible. He cancelled his offer at the last minute, and

---

[1] The outcome of such confabulations was probably H.G.'s *The Shape of Things to Come*, or possibly *The New World Order*, published in the first year of the Second World War.

Juliette had to find another venue for her meeting within a few hours of its scheduled time. She had a large amount of trouble arranging this, and collecting the members – and he had his revenge.

I never saw him again – but during the last years of his life, when he became too ill to do more than sit in his armchair, Juliette often dropped in to visit him. He looked shrunk, she said, his face curiously altered, concentrated around an elongated and pensive nose. Visitors were not encouraged, as they tired him out, and he seemed very lonely. His tea was carefully measured and a piece of cake weighed, to balance his diabetes. A tall Buddha, extending his blessing, stood on the mantelpiece, 'He knows a thing or two,' murmured H.G.

We were away from London when his illness entered its terminal stage in 1946. One of his last visitors, a serious young man seeking some guidance from the old prophet, received this snub: 'Oh, be quiet. Can't you see I'm busy dying . . .'

Juliette and I cherish his memory – a truly extraordinary person, omnivorous of knowledge, prodigal of ideas, yet with strange gaps in appreciation; gay but not malicious, never weary of embarking on some new panacea, some new adventure of mind or body, but quick to anger at the slightest obstacle to his projects, or bruise to his concept of himself, his dedication to a high ideal.

Early in 1928, I joined the Society for Psychical Research. There was much talk then about curious phenomena such as ectoplasm, telepathy, communication with the dead, extra-sensory perception, levitation, and so forth, and I became interested in the subject. I don't really know what I expected, but I went to several meetings and read some of the literature, only to find that the whole subject was in a state of confusion. I was therefore delighted when Juliette and I were invited by one of the daily newspapers to take part in an investigation of spiritualism.

The team included a couple of our medico-psychological friends, Eric Strauss and C. P. Blacker, several members of the S.P.R., some sceptical of the spiritualists' wilder claims, others inclined to credit them, and a sprinkling of devotees who regularly attended séances and firmly believed that they were put in communication with departed friends and relatives.

Lord Charles Hope was our link between the network of organized séances and our group, and arranged for us to appear under an alias (the name Huxley would have made the mediums and their followers suspicious). We were thus able to investigate some half-dozen professional mediums and the manifestations at their seances. I must say at once that, although we approached these with an absolutely open mind, we were never satisfied that any of them could not be explained, either by natural causes or, more usually, by fraud.

One in particular I remember: the medium was called Evans, and claimed to be in contact with St Teresa – though, when questioned, he was not clear whether it was St Teresa of Avila or of Lisieux. The routine was similar to that at most other séances. We sat in a circle holding hands, in the dark, while a phonograph played hymns loudly in the background, effectively drowning any sound made by the medium's movements. We were warned on no account to touch the medium in trance, and to obey his directions without question. Evans did allow himself to be searched beforehand, but the room was not investigated – was it because our host was a believer? Evans was a small man with tiny hands and feet; he was expertly roped to his chair (by a deep-sea fisherman), and the séance began. Soon his loud breathing announced that he was 'in trance' and we prepared ourselves for some extraordinary happening. Suddenly above our heads came the sound of trumpet and tambourine, and a ghostly bit of pale drapery seemed to float in the air. 'It *is* St Teresa,' said the believers; 'she has come . . .' The 'manifestation' bestowed moist kisses on the forehead of the ladies with its blessing, and answered questions to 'departed' relatives in a falsetto voice, always saying that 'things were wonderful over here' or similar reassuring messages, but quite unable to give concrete information about conditions in the 'other world' or any proof that the voices were those of the particular spirits who had been 'summoned' from the hereafter.

The whole thing was clearly a fraud, and we decided to expose it. Our group obtained a further séance, before which it was agreed that, at a given signal, the person nearest the switch should rush to turn on the lights. The performance was even more nauseating than the former one, with a pretended infant's voice telling 'Mummy' how happy she was in her heavenly 'crèche' among the 'flowwers'. At this the signal was given and one of us switched on the lights.

'St Teresa' was revealed as Evans draped in cheese-cloth and trying to hide a phosphorescent plate, which had conveniently reflected the folds of the drapery and given him a ghostly appearance. He had got out of the fisherman's knots by squeezing his small body out of his jacket and the ropes, and had been happily padding round the circle in his socks. 'You have killed him!' shouted the believers, as Evans was found lying prostrate in an apparent faint – light being (rightly!) considered lethal to 'embodied' spirits. However the two doctors, Strauss and Blacker, pronounced him perfectly fit, and told him to stop fooling and join us all in the next room for a discussion. Evans signed a confession, which was published next day, admitting his fraud. Three weeks later he was repeating the performance at Liverpool, where another paper published an enthusiastic report, signed by various notabilities, among them Rosita Forbes, the well-known but rather credulous traveller. Needless to say, the 'true believers' were not in the least bothered by our proof of Evans' fraudulence, and went on believing just as before.

On another occasion we went to a house in Putney where a Miss Lewis was the medium. She recited people's telephone numbers and several surprising snippets of private knowledge: for instance, she told Juliette, quite correctly, that she had been worried about a piece of coral-wood for carving, which should have been delivered earlier; Juliette had that very morning telephoned the firm about it. She also promised flowers from Paradise. These did not 'materialize' during the séance, but inside our car as we were driving Miss Lewis home, a small bunch of early violets fell into Juliette's lap, tied with an orange thread. How easy to flick them out of a pocket! Soon

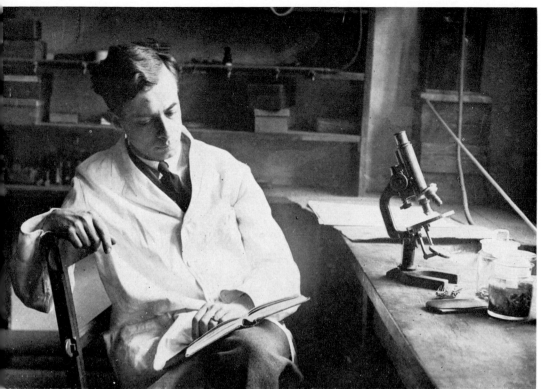

XVI Julian Huxley in his lab. at Oxford, about 1922

XVII H. G. Wells, his Son Gip, and Julian Huxley, working on *The Science of Life* at Easton Glebe, Wells's home, in 1927

XVIII Juliette in 1932 (*Dorothy Wilding*)

after, we discovered that Miss Lewis was a telephone operator and had fruitfully tapped messages but, though the earthly florist was traced, we never found out who gave away our anonymity.

Comic relief was provided by two women mediums from Scotland, who claimed to summon up the spirits of departed dogs in bodily form. The séance took place in total darkness, and the audience were not allowed to hold the mediums' hands or even to sit near them. The elder medium asked if any of the audience had owned a dog which had recently 'passed over', to which a lady novelist said, 'Yes'. Within seconds there was a swishing noise, as of a handkerchief being flicked back and forth on the floor, and the elder medium exclaimed, in a strong Glasgow accent: 'Aye, there he is, waggin' his tail.' The lady novelist said, alas, that it couldn't be her dog, which was a pug whose tail had been docked, but that it might be a friend's peke. Someone mischievously added that it was a very unusual peke, with a splash of yellow on the back 'as if someone had spilt an egg on it'. The younger medium, who claimed to see in the dark, at once confirmed the presence of a peke with an eggy patch on it, thereby giving us our money's worth – and another confirmation of mediumistic fraud.

We had great hopes of 'Stella', who was said to levitate objects, but we sat with her for long spells of trance and never an atom was lifted.

The only abnormal phenomenon noted by any of us was a curious feeling, as of a band of cold air creeping up the arm, which I experienced at a session with Rudi Schneider. Spiritualists say that it is a frequent phenomenon at séances – presumably a psychosomatic reaction, caused by the anticipation of something mysterious or frightening, like shivering at strange nocturnal noises.

We found no proof of any communication with departed spirits, but plenty of evidence of trickery, sometimes physical mumbo-jumbo, but mostly by suggestion, ingeniously contrived to take in the gullible. But it always followed a general pattern, as if most mediums had been to the same school, depending for their success on the poignant need of their victims to be reassured and comforted.

On the other hand, the existence of telepathy between living persons seems to be well-attested, but our knowledge of its mechanism and of the conditions which favour it is still in a very limited and fragmentary state. There was no evidence for its occurrence at any of our séances.

CHAPTER XIII

First Voyage to Africa

As a member of the Colonial Office Committee on Education, I was asked to go to East Africa to report on the role of biological science in African education, and also on the value of nature conservation in the area. This was a great opportunity, and I accepted. Leaving the family on top of Chaumont, I set off in mid-August of 1929, armed with field-glasses, my old box-camera with lots of plates, and a cine-camera for my own use, as well as a projector and some nature films to show in African schools. Juliette was to drive the children back to London with their grand-mother, and join me later in Africa.

The boat trip from Southampton to Dar-es-Salaam was un-remarkable, except for four facts: the appalling heat of the Red Sea, where the ship often had to turn to get a breath of northerly air; the presence of a very attractive American girl, with whom I fear I flirted (she took it much more seriously than I); a set of poems I wrote in spite of the heat, entitled *A Freudian Faustulus*, in which I tried to set down in verse my own state of mind, and my relations with nature and other people; and the squalor of the French boat, a relic of pre-war days, with such an abundance of rats that they gnawed holes in one of the English passenger's trousers – I shall always remember him brandishing them irately in the face of the bearded little French captain.

Considering this voyage now in the light of my further experiences, I realize that it was one of the most important turning-points in my life. Both Juliette, in her *Wild Lives of Africa*, and I, in my *Africa View*, have written about our journey and our impressions of the region, its human problems and its wonderful wild life and scenery, so I will only touch on the highlights of our trip.

We were particularly lucky to have our first taste of wild Africa in the comparatively early days before jeeps and planes had opened up the country. The mixed blessings of civilization had not penetrated to the remote communities of that timeless world, before technology became the dominant force that it is today. Populations of all sorts of animals and plants co-existed in a harmony forged by compulsive necessity into a self-regulating system, adjusting itself to droughts and floods, to disease and over-multiplication.

At the tsetse research station in Tanganyika I learnt a great deal about the tsetse fly. As they have to penetrate the hide of buffaloes, large antelopes and even hippos, their proboscis is amazingly powerful. This I discovered for myself when my buttocks were bitten through the seat of a deck chair and my khaki trousers: it was like the prick of a hot needle, luckily in a trypanosome-free area. The tsetse is commonly regarded as the scourge of Africa, since it injects trypanosomes into horses, cattle and man, causing serious and often fatal illness, but the wild game have acquired immunity to the disease and are not affected. Accordingly, while man and his intrusions of domestic animals died or fled the affected areas, the magnificent hierarchy of the original wild creatures remained in full vigour, able to take advantage of the extended resources of the land, which they earlier had to share with human beings. These so-called 'restricted areas' became the first game reserves and national parks, where visitors could be safeguarded by anti-trypanosome serum and fly-nets over their beds. They are now in fact the nearest image we can get of what the African world was like before the white man's advent.

It was inevitable that he should trigger off an unending series of explosions affecting practically everything in Africa. The most obvious was the massacre of great herds of wild animals, regarded as reservoirs for trypanosomes, and the taking of virgin land to make room for cities, farms, railroads, dams and more and more human beings, black as well as white. In the last hundred years, it is estimated that 90 per cent of the wild life of Africa has been destroyed, and much of the land ruined by ecological misuse, such as over-grazing and deforestation (these often due to the Africans' lack of forethought), coupled with lack of fertilizers.

Thanks to the tsetse, vast tracts of land were put 'out of bounds' to human settlement, and devoted to preserving nature and wild life. Is it therefore absurd to suggest that a monument should be erected to that insect, as the saviour of unspoilt Africa and its unique fauna?

In the weeks before Juliette joined me I worked hard on my educational mission, visiting schools and colleges, talking to teachers and doctors, administrators and missionaries, and showing my films in many schools – to boys only, as no girls were yet admitted to school.

One film was of sea-animals in the Plymouth Aquarium, while another showed the speeded-up growth of plants, and the methods by which they are fertilized. The boys were then asked to write essays on what they had seen. Here is an extract from one of them: 'At five o'clock all the headmasters, teachers and even workers followed behind us, on account of good singing, good drums and very nice clothes of boys washed well . . . so we reached house-cinema . . . But the first picture is about fruit and flowers. Ah!, I wonder for these nice English people how they can draw a picture plant, how it grows, how we get good flowers, and how the bees got into flowers to take something from flowers. I was pleased indeed when I saw these bees do so.'

One must remember that these boys had only a year's training in English. The essential thing, the headmaster assured me, was the degree of interest and understanding manifested. This was the first time films had been shown in Africa as an adjunct to formal education, and I am glad to say that the practice is now widespread.

The general emphasis on education, however, was then much too much on unpractical subjects like history and literature, turning out a surplus of would-be clerks, but few agriculturists, doctors, or engineers to fill the rising demand. Makerere High School in

Uganda had the most all-round curriculum and the best teaching, and I prophesied (rightly) that it would soon achieve university status. I incorporated all this in my official report, but little came of it for many years.[1]

Though my official duties took most of my time and energy, I managed to see a good deal of the country. In Tanganyika I took two days off to climb up to the moorland zone of Kilimanjaro, with elephants crashing away in the forest – only to find that the snow-covered volcanic peak, soaring to 19,000 feet in the clear African blue, seemed just as far off as it had from the plains 8,000 feet below. I was awed by the thought of the long sequence of eruptions that had thrown up this vast mass of lava and ash, the highest as well as the most extensive volcano in the Old World.

In the train between Kenya and Uganda I had my first sight of the great African Rift. This is a remarkable phenomenon: volcanic action has caused faulting and the dropping of the floor between the two steep fault-scarps, and a number of volcanoes are contained in the valley. Ever since I first read about the African Rift Valley in Gregory's book (he was the first geologist to explore the rift, well before 1900), it had filled me with a strange excitement. To see it for the first time was a wonderful moment, but it is a sight I have never tired of. Time and again I have flown, walked or driven across the Rift, and always this vast fissure, cleaving a continent and extending right up through the Red Sea and the Holy Land to Syria and the Turkish border, has given me a feeling that the earth is alive under its mantle of soil and vegetation, recreating its features. Wegener was right: these fissures, notably those on the ocean floor, have made it possible for the continents to drift slowly apart during the billion years of their existence.

At the time of my visit, Nairobi as a city was rapidly emerging from a collection of mud huts, tin shacks, Indian shops and a few

---

[1] The educational situation in East Africa is now much better, though naturally many Africans of both sexes accept grants from various international and national bodies to pursue postgraduate study in technically more advanced countries. The only serious danger is that national rivalries between these three ex-colonies, Kenya, Uganda and Tanzania, may fragment the unified system of higher academic and technical education that was set up after the Second World War.

official villas built along an earth road. Nairobi was originally little more than a name on the map, with a few Kikuyu huts beside an unmade track. It began its career towards being the capital of Kenya with the laying of the railway from Mombasa, which even by 1901 reached into Uganda, bringing in a quantity of Indian skilled labourers and shopkeepers. The plains close to the settlement then swarmed with every sort of wild animal. All that is left of them today is in the Nairobi National Park, created soon after my visit by Mervyn Cowie on the outskirts of the modern metropolis.

But this was 1928; now there were rumbles of discontent among the Kikuyu, precursors of the later Mau-Mau revolt. The Kikuyu were not unnaturally indignant at having their best lands given to the white settlers; yet it seemed clear that, if not strictly confined to their reserves, they would have cut down all the trees for firewood and reduced the whole fertile uplands to an eroded 'desert', useless for intensive agriculture. On the other hand, their high reproduction rate overcrowded the reserves, and forced thousands of Kikuyu into a squalid existence in Nairobi and other northern towns, where the girls too often became prostitutes – and often into areas inhabited by their hereditary enemies, the ferocious nomadic Masai.

The Kikuyu were also having trouble with missionaries who rightly wanted to stop the barbarous and cruel practice of female circumcision at puberty, which can render birth both difficult and dangerous. Unfortunately the Bible, translated into Kikuyu, refers to the Virgin Mary by a word meaning a girl who had not only undergone circumcision, but was permitted and even encouraged to practise a modified form of sexual intercourse, so long as no babies resulted! Here, as elsewhere in Africa, the Tower of Babel was putting difficulties in the way of mutual understanding between blacks and whites.

The Wakamba Hills to the south were already a desert. Almost the only trees left were sacred ones on the hill-tops, reminiscent of the sacred groves of Baal, against which the Old Testament Jews were always protesting – and doubtless, like them, once used as places of bloody sacrifice.

Africa has little written history, but Louis Leakey, then a young paleontologist, was exploring its pre-history. He had chosen a site at Elmenteita, near Nairobi, where he showed me a cave piled high with ashes, human and animal bones and vast quantities of obsidian tools, of late Aurignacian type – which in Europe were dated about 70,000 B.C. but here may be much later, associated with bones characteristic of modern Hamitic types. These were so sharp that a disbelieving lady visitor was able to use one to cut thin slices of bread and butter for our tea.

On the plateau were implements of the cruder Mousterian type, associated in Europe with Neanderthal man, stooping, low-browed, with less developed brains. The more intelligent Aurignacians had apparently ousted their more primitive Neanderthaloid forebears from the caves and forced them out on to the open plains, where they later died out as more and more 'modern' men, *Homo sapiens* irrupted into sub-Saharan Africa from the north and north-east.

Leakey was convinced that early man had evolved in Africa, and ceaselessly continued his researches. Thirty years later, in the cliffs of Olduvai Gorge in Tanzania, he confirmed his belief by discovering the remains of a much earlier humanoid type, earlier even than the ape-man unearthed by Broom in South Africa, a primitive ape-like being, yet capable of walking almost upright, which he called Zinjanthropus. When I first met him at Elmenteita his infectious enthusiasm and energy fascinated me, and I have followed his hard-working and many-sided career with the greatest interest. He has now been Director of the Coryndon Museum at Nairobi for many years, and was responsible for initiating the admirable studies of wild chimpanzees by Jane Goodall, and of gorillas by George Schaller and, with even more extraordinary results, by Dian Fosse.

At last Juliette joined me at Jinja, then the terminus of the railway from Mombasa. She stepped out of the train, a fragile-looking figure in white, and we drove happily back to Entebbe on the shores of Lake Victoria, where we were staying with the Governor, Sir William Gowers. It was the Hindu New Year at the beginning of November, the villages we passed through were lit by small lamps carried from hut to hut by long-robed Indians[1] celebrating their festival, and under the canopy of high trees fire-flies flitted endlessly. It was a magical velvet night.

Entebbe had an excellent botanical garden, with enormous lianas hanging from forest trees, looking like bell-ropes to summon the splendid black-and-white Colobus monkeys that leapt about their branches. And nearby we visited a sacred crocodile, named Lutembe by the local tribe, ancient survivor of an ancient cult, who came to the call of his attendant priest and devoured his offering of fish only a few feet from my cautiously held camera.

Only a few years ago, Lutembe had been used as a 'judge' in local cases involving theft or personal violence. All the Africans involved were forced by their headman to parade in front of the huge reptile, presenting their left arm in front of his great snout. If Lutembe took no notice, the man was innocent, but if he bit the arm, this was proof of guilt. The missionaries tried to shoot Lutembe as a relic of barbarous habits, but luckily they missed. Lutembe was officially preserved, though no longer allowed to carry out the trials by ordeal. When we were at Entebbe a quarter of a century ago, he had become a tourist attraction – no one knew how old he was, but it was probably over a hundred years.

Reptile worship is not uncommon in Africa. Earlier, in Tanzania, I had climbed an isolated rock pinnacle to get a better view, only to find that it was inhabited by a huge and aged monitor lizard, nearly five feet long, hissing violently at me.

I managed to bring it down, and then noticed that the approach to the rock had been crudely barred with sticks. It was clear that the monitor was the tutelary spirit of the locality, a kind of living totem. I let him wander off into the bush, a bit worried about the villagers' reaction when they found him missing.

[1] Today (1969) the Hindus and Pakistanis, who were the chief shopkeepers and minor officials in East Africa, are being 'Kenyanized' out of their jobs, and under severe restrictions as to exporting their savings. It is a poor reward for over sixty years of hard work, helping the then colonies towards a viable independence.

While I am on biological topics, I might mention that I was struck by the abundance of scarlet flowers in East Africa – red-hot pokers, Strelitzia, flame trees (Erythryna) red lilies, red hibiscus, Leontodon and scarlet-flowered gigantic dead-nettles. Why all this scarlet brilliance? I asked myself – when suddenly I realized that sun-birds are common here, and that birds can see red, unlike non-primate mammals which have no colour-vision, and bees, which are insensitive to red but can detect blue and even ultra-violet. And these and other small birds are the chief pollinators of red day-flowering plants (and white flowers in the twilight). Our temperate red flowers are rarely, if ever, pure scarlet – they have a tinge of pink or purple, or, if red, have non-red markings on the petals. This link between red flowers and small tropical birds is now a commonplace.

Kampala was then the most civilized capital in East Africa, its African inhabitants the most intelligent, with a well-developed parliamentary system of their own. And the women were beautiful in their bare-shouldered robes of bark-cloth, flowered cotton or even silk and velvet, proudly walking with their purchases, even little ones like match-boxes, on their heads.

My official duties done, and my note-books packed in readiness for the report I was to write, we decided that the next eight weeks should be devoted to the adventure of a safari right up country, into the newly created Parc National Albert in the Belgian Congo. Opened in 1928, it was then the only national park in East and Central Africa, though the Kruger Park in South Africa had been founded somewhat earlier. John Russell, a very nice fellow from the Uganda Education Department, was assigned to us as our protector and planner of the expedition.

We drove out from Kampala in his little Morris Cowley, all three of us squashed in front, thrilled and expectant. The first two hundred miles were through lush green country, still with tall women in their draped beauty. But as we got into the hills, the draperies were replaced by shorter tunics of poorer material, and by the time we reached Kabale, the end of the motor road, the Africans of both sexes were dressed in scanty bits of skin.

We stayed on the way with Temple Perkins at M'barara, who showed us our first lion, and indeed the only one we saw (though we heard plenty) during that first trip. The lion was dead. It had been preying on goats and calves, and deserved its death. The whole population of M'barara crowded round the lorry containing the limp body of their enemy, with murmurs of awe.

At Kabale, we stayed with Tracy Phillips, the D.C. of the frontier district. Here our camping gear, sent by lorry, was awaiting us. We now collected men for our foot-safari: a cook and servant boys, nearly fifty carriers, and a military Askari sergeant, to keep them in order. He knew only four words of English: John Russell luckily had a fair command of Swahili, East Africa's lingua franca.

This was the most wonderful journey we ever made. I had already seen much of East Africa and its ebony-eyed people, black Negroes and dark-brown Hamites, a few wild animals and many miraculous birds, as well as fine scenery, and lakes swarming with flamingoes: Lake Elmenteita very like the south end of Lake Windermere, but with pink flamingoes instead of water-lilies, and later, from the heights of Menengai, Lake Nakuru shining blue with a coral border all round its shores – a border of flamingoes. I estimated roughly that there were over a million of these lovely creatures on this lake – strange ones too, the only vertebrates to feed with their bodies upright and their heads upside-down.

Among other notable bird sights was the communal mating dance of the beautiful crested cranes, and its transmutation into human terms by a group of girls in Uganda. Nor must I forget our first sight of wild ostriches, one male outrunning our jeep, another in the ecstasies of display, alternately flapping his rudimentary black and white wings and careering wildly in all directions, his naked thighs flushed a rosy pink with excitement.

So I could go on – with tales of a pair of shrikes singing a duet, and of huge kori bustards puffing themselves out in display till they looked like gigantic feathered chrysanthemums: but I must restrain my ornithological enthusiasm, and merely say that East Africa's birds are just as spectacular as its large mammals. But nothing we had seen before compared with the fascination of our safari. Whether it was the feeling of having done my work and being now free to enjoy myself, or the delight we experienced at all the strange things we saw, allied with the fact that we now were *walking* over the red earth, pacing the miles – it all added up to an inspiring experience.

Setting off at early dawn at the head of our long line of fifty porters, winding along narrow paths which led us past lakes edged with water-lilies and swamps frothy with papyrus, up and down friendly little hills hiding thatched villages in their folds, right to the frontier post at Kigesi, and on to Ruchuru, in the Belgian Congo, we felt we were discovering a wonderful Africa for ourselves. In spite of minor mishaps and occasional hardships, there remains this imperishable memory, the awareness of unspoilt nature, magnificent and cruel, generous and ruthless.

We changed porters every day, after a palaver with the chief and our Askari, paying every man the princely sum of threepence for carrying our loads on their heads. It was amusing to see them scramble for the smallest loads: but the smallest of all was hastily rejected – it contained the mass of copper coins for paying the porters and buying food for ourselves. The cook and tent-boys remained with us all through, for better or for worse.

The plains south of Lake Edward were dotted everywhere with herds of antelope, zebra and buffalo which we watched through binoculars. Our scent made it impossible to get near the creatures, a serious handicap which we had not foreseen. In fact, though we heard elephant and lion, sometimes very close, we never saw a single one. They vanished into the bamboo and high bush forests or the tall grass of the plains. Today, of course, one goes everywhere by car or jeep, and human scent is masked by the non-alarming smell of gasoline – or perhaps the animals believe the machine to be a new and harmless kind of herbivore. Years later, we motored to within feet of lions and a few yards from elephants.

Across the border, Ruchuru, the District HQ, was also the administrative centre of the Parc National Albert, as it was then named (today they call it Parc National du Congo). To the north is a vast plain, partly in Uganda, partly in the Congo, reaching right up to Lakes Edward and Albert; on the south, the Park climbs the high flanks of volcanoes, covered with tropical rain-forest and, westward, takes in the foothills of Ruwenzori. When we emerged on the Rift scarp we were gripped by a magnificent sight, the whole chain of the Virunga volcanoes, extending right across the rift floor: 13,000-foot Muhavura, then Mahinga, Sabinio the Father of Teeth, Visoke, and, still further east, on either side of a depression in the mountain wall, Karissimbi, almost as high as Mont Blanc, and craggy Mikeno, sometimes called the Matterhorn of East Africa, followed by two still active volcanoes, Nyiragongo and Nyamlagira. There can be few places in the world which present such a spectacle.

An ancient track led us between foot-hills, pleasantly meandering along gentle slopes.

Russell and I started to climb Muhavura, but only he achieved the summit; I gave up, slightly mountain-sick, at about 11,500 feet. But the exercise prepared me for the later ascent of Karissimbi.

Next day we rejoined the party a further stage westward. This meant that Juliette was left in charge. When the time came to leave, the porters were squabbling noisily over the loads and were reluctant to start. In this quandary Juliette took up her stick and started walking. This initiative by a solitary memsahib so tickled the porters' fancy that they roared with laughter, picked up their loads, and gaily followed her.

After two days at the Catholic mission at Lulenga, we started to climb Karissimbi, in search of gorillas. The torrential rains had made the steep track, strewn with scented waxy flowers dropped from the forest trees above, treacherous and exhausting; but we plodded on till we pitched camp at nearly 10,000 feet. We were up at dawn and off again, taking a steep path along the side of a splendid gorge. Here we had our first sight of Africa's strange Alpine vegetation: lovely epiphytic orchids, tree-heathers (Hagenia), tree-groundsels, tree-lobelias, not to mention the giant parsley which is one of the gorilla's chief food-plants, and giant nettles with a formidable sting.

We saw gorilla footprints and came across several sleeping-nests. They were built among the buttress-roots of big trees instead of up in the branches, like those of chimpanzees and gorillas in lowland areas. But alas, the animals we never saw, much to our disappointment. I had to console myself with taking a picture of Juliette sitting, disapprovingly, in a vacant and rather dirty nest.

Eventually we emerged on the grassy plateau which lies at 12,000 feet, between the wicked-looking peak of Mikeno and the gentler slopes of Karissimbi, catching a magical glimpse of Lake Kivu, blue in the southern distance.

We set about exploring the plateau and paying homage to the tomb of Akeley, the American naturalist and explorer. The Parc National Albert was the result of his endeavours, for he had been so deeply impressed with the grandeur of the range and its strange anthropoid inhabitants, as well as the richness of the plains beyond in all manner of large mammals and lovely birds, that he made urgent representations to the Belgian Government, who finally declared the region a National Park. He died of fever and dysentery on the slopes of Karissimbi, and was buried on the mountain he loved so well.

After our descent from Karissimbi, Russell and I wanted to look into the crater of Nyamlagira (a wonderful sight, as we now know from the splendid colour film of its molten rivers of lava taken by Tcherchieff); but there were miles of abrasive lava to cross, our boots began to split, it poured with rain and we had to bivouac under a poorly-erected tent (no way of fixing a pole in the lava); and Russell sprained his ankle. So we returned ragged and exhausted to the White Fathers Mission at Lulenga. Juliette meanwhile had been staying at the Nuns Mission, and hearing of our sad return, came over the mile to visit us – heralded by violent screams and banging of tin drums to keep off leopards, emanating from her escort of young African postulants, slim, bare-breasted and very un-nunlike girls.

On the Sunday we attended mass in the open thatched church. African men on one side, women on the other, often suckling their babies or gliding out to perform the African equivalent of changing their nappies, naked black children crawling between the seats, and black choirboys in white frilled shirts and scarlet gowns – what a scene for a painter!

From there we went in the Mission lorry through pouring rain to Ruchuru, dumped our surplus gear there and set off for Lake Edward, accompanied by the Park Curator, Monsieur Hemmeleer. After the cold and the rain of the mountain forest, it was stiflingly hot on the bare sandy plain. Here we saw masses of game, including topi, Uganda kob, hartebeest, cavorting wildebeest, graceful reed-buck and a few eland, largest of all antelopes. I was again impressed by the beauty and strangeness of these wild creatures, and more than ever determined to fight for their preservation, their right to live free in their own environment, and the right of man to enjoy the sight of them.

We camped on the bare plain and took several perilous trips on nearby Lake Edward. Perilous because, as in Edward Lear's non-sense poem, we 'went to sea in a sieve'. For lack of big trees to make dug-outs, the local canoes were made of strips of bark sewn together with bast fibres, and our seats were the skulls of hippos. We all had to take a hand in bailing, while two skin-clad Africans punted the craft among vast herds of hippos disporting themselves all round us in a rich soupy liquid of mud and droppings – taking care not to get too close to mothers with young, or to jealous old two-ton bulls, who can snap a canoe in half if they feel threatened.

Steering for the shallow estuary of the Ruendi, we were suddenly confronted by an incredible multitude of water-birds: flamingoes, pelicans, jacanas, marabouts, terns, darters, tiny jewel-like Malochite kingfishers, white-throated cormorants, purple gallinules looking like imperial moorhens, stilts, herons, egrets, jabiru storks, and even sandpipers, recalling the Scottish moors from whence they had migrated. As soon as they saw us the alarm was given, and they all flew off (except the darters, who just dropped into the water) in a fantastic darkening of the sky, each uttering its own cry, a deafening chorus of protest. This was certainly one of the high points of our safari, and together with my experiences in Kenya, Uganda and Tanganyika, made me determined to include birds in any scheme for African wild-life preservation.

We returned to Ruchuru and sadly retraced our steps to Kabale and Entebbe. Thirty years later we returned to Kabale and, this time in a car, re-lived our journey to the foot of Karissimbi and up into the gorilla forest. As Juliette wrote in her *Wild Lives of Africa*, 'it had now become a sort of double journey, a counterpoint of inner and outer landscapes, of remembered and new visions. More and more landmarks fell into place, recalling our young selves walking like ghosts across our present'. But again we saw no gorillas, only heard them crashing off at our approach.

The lake trip had taken more time than we expected, and we were forced to make a double march from Ruchuru to reach Mucho at the north end of Lake Bunyoni if we were to get back to Entebbe in time. We set off at our best pace. After a few miles we were overtaken by a native runner with a cleft stick containing a note for us. There were but few travellers on our route and it was a dead cert that he would eventually catch up with us, but we marvelled all the same. We rewarded the messenger, who took himself cheerfully back as if all this running about in the wilderness to deliver a scrap of paper or even a verbal message was quite a normal affair – which of course it was in earlier days in Africa, and in all of pre-conquest America.

At the halt we lunched while the local chief hastily collected a new set of porters to take us on. They came running in, with their wives bringing them little bags of food for the journey. We noticed that they were laughing, and asked our Askari what it was all about. They are laughing, he said, because the white men say they are going to reach Mucho tonight – and they think that is very funny.

The porters' doubts were justified, but it wasn't funny. It started to rain as we toiled up to the edge of the forest; the sun went down and it was dark before we had gone half-way. We had to cross a bamboo jungle full of fresh elephant droppings; then a nasty swamp, followed by high forest. The porters seemed to vanish and the guide finally announced that he had lost his way. This was a situation which called for certain gifts to cope with it, gifts of survival one might call them, which none of us had had any call to use. We had a flashlight and a map, but, as we had not the slightest

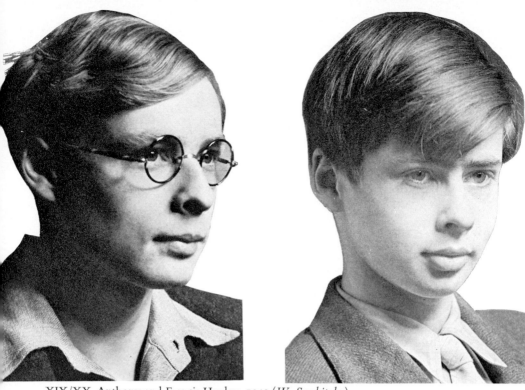

XIX/XX Anthony and Francis Huxley, 1940 (*W. Suschitzky*)

XXI Dr Julian Huxley, Professor Gilbert Murray and Sir William Beveridge during a Brains Trust broadcast in 1942

XXII Julian Huxley on the National Parks Commission in the summer of 1945, somewhere near the White Horse of Uffington on the Berkshire Downs

idea of where we were, neither was any use to us. Never had we felt so city-bred. The prospect of spending the night huddled together in the forest without food or shelter was far from enticing. How long, I found myself thinking, could white people of our sort survive if left to themselves in this environment?

And then the miracle happened. An old man appeared as if out of the ground before us. When we said *Mucho*, he nodded knowingly. Our hopes leapt up and we put ourselves unconditionally in his hands. He made us retrace our steps, then found a slope, steeply descending in the pitch dark. Our eyes, by now attuned to the dark, were just able to discern his moving shadow before us. After a mile or so the old man, never wavering an inch from his invisible path, surprised us by suddenly calling out in a sing-song voice, a forlorn and, as we thought, ridiculous communication into an empty wilderness. We stopped in our single file to listen to a possible echo. But it wasn't an echo which answered, it was a far-away ululation of syllables, to which our god-sent guide answered with another high-pitched call. We then learnt what these hill-dwellers had always known, that certain modulations of the human voice can penetrate to great distances in this silent world. The voice in the far-away night went on, a tenuous and improbable emanation. Our guide replied, 'Make everything ready, white men are coming', translated Russell. We continued our descent, for what must have been well over a thousand feet. Suddenly out of the darkness a flickering flame leapt up in the distance and we discerned small match-stick figures throwing wood on a fire. It stimulated our weary legs, and twenty minutes later we found ourselves sitting on mats in front of a blazing heart-and-body warming fire, with our supper in the making.

The porters were wonderful. In spite of wet bodies and miserable pay, they struggled on with their loads, like us guided by voice and fire, and one by one rejoined us. It would have been so easy for them to leave our baggage in the forest and make for home without more ado. One even walked in after a lonely night in the open, as we were having breakfast. He made us laugh, for he was carrying a live hen for our previous day's supper on top of his load.

Next day was sunny and relaxing. We enjoyed a delicious rest while being paddled in dug-out canoes along the length of Lake Bunyoni, between the banks of water-lilies at the foot of the brilliant tropical green of the hills.

An exciting trip to one of the Sese Islands on Lake Victoria ended our first voyage in Africa. We were guided there by Captain Pitman, Uganda's chief game warden, who borrowed two government launches for the occasion. His aim was to show us a curious type of antelope, the Sitatunga, which had developed long splayed-out hooves in direct relation to the swampy nature of its normal environment, enabling it to get a foothold on the marsh reeds; but here, on a rocky island, the long hooves, he said, had been worn down to normal shape and size, showing that their length was not genetically determined, but merely the result of growth unchecked by abrasion.

After a good look at these graceful creatures, we retired for the night to our tents, enchanted with the peace and beauty of this desert island. But a sudden and violent thunderstorm woke us up. The wind wrenched the anchors out of the sandy bottom of the lake, and the two launches were soon drifting towards the rocky shore, where they smashed to driftwood in less than ten minutes. So there we were, marooned some sixty miles from Entebbe, with our steamer home scheduled to leave Mombasa in four days.

Luckily for us, Captain Pitman had found four men illegally fishing on the island, which was out of bounds because of tsetse fly. He had confiscated their canoes and planned to imprison or fine the men on our return. However, our emergency was great, so the men were released and sent off next morning, which was brilliantly still and fine, to make their way to Entebbe with an sos. It would take them at least two days paddling, all things being equal, and another day at least before rescue could be organized. Tied up for three days, we had enough food and time, to try out our dream of a romantic island life, but worried by thoughts of our further journey.

The shore was littered with the shreds of our poor launches. The engines were still sticking in the hulls, and were salvaged with some difficulty. The rest was left to drift around, to remind us of the fragility of ships and plans when nature shows her spirit.

Next night, after an early bed, we were woken by the noise of drums and singing on the lake. Soon a large canoe, laden with friendly and inquisitive people from the neighbouring island, landed on our shore. Later, more canoes arrived, for somehow the news had percolated to all these little lost outposts, and more and more black people, all in high spirits, scrambled up from the little sandy cove. They had brought their drums and refreshments, even their dancing girls, and set out to entertain us with dancing and singing. Pitman explained that their songs were ballads telling the tale of our shipwreck. The girls danced with swaying hips and bellies, their downcast eyes modest yet lascivious.

The company then settled down to sleep on the shore, which looked almost like Margate on a bank holiday.

We had a short night, for at six-thirty next morning we heard the sound of a tug. In no time at all we were on board, eating a welcome breakfast, and soon steamed away, leaving the islands shrouded in several new storms and water-spouts. Our poacher-messengers had apparently met with a government patrol. They had been anxious and our SOS had been speedily delivered. The Governor had been worried lest we had lost all our equipment and food, and was relieved to hear we had suffered so little. The question of the two wrecked launches was left unprobed, though they represented two-thirds of Uganda's navy.

Two days later, after just catching our train while it was already in Jinja station, Juliette and I were safely embarked on the French boat the *Grand Didier*, and landed home in January 1930.

We were, I realize with deep conviction, immensely lucky to have had this experience of Africa in 1929. We saw a continent which had hardly changed in the last five hundred years, but was about to experience the mixed blessings of technological and educational 'progress', political independence, and drastic changes in its economic and social set-up.

As soon as I got back, I began my book, *Africa View*, in which I wrote my impressions of our journey and also my hopes for future developments. I also presented my report to the Colonial Secretary, Sydney Webb, the noted socialist theoretician. He was a small man with a huge head, and tiny feet dangling from his office chair. I found him warmly sympathetic to my findings, particularly in favour of more and better secular education in the colonies. But when I pleaded with him for more Game Reserves, he became negative. *Game*, for him, with his socialist sympathies, meant something for landlords to shoot, and *Reserves* meant *Preserves* where mammals and birds were kept safe for rich men's sport. However, I explained the real position, my report went into the files, and within a few years National Parks were established in all three East African territories. I am proud of having done something for the preservation of East African wild life, though of course, others later contributed much more, both in the way of money and effort. My only fear is that over-population and commercial development may eventually override all other considerations, and lead to the whittling down or even abolition of the Parks. However, I am still hopeful that the ever-increasing revenue from tourists, anxious to see this unique assemblage of wild life in its natural setting, will keep the Parks safe for at least a century – perhaps for ever?

As a result of my report, I was asked to serve on the Committee advising on Lord Hailey's monumental *African Survey*, which was to make a comparative study of all the problems confronting sub-Saharan Africa.

The Committee, which contained many distinguished men and women experts in African affairs, met for five years from 1933 to 1938; but the really hard work began in 1935 when I had just been appointed Secretary of the Zoo. My undertaking of this laborious outside commitment was one of the Zoo Council's sources of resentment against me.

Anyhow, the result of the Survey was an authoritative book of over 1,800 pages, which proved of great help to later colonial administrators.

CHAPTER XIV

First Visit to Russia

JUST before setting out to Africa I had made the acquaintance of Archibald Church, a senior official in the Colonial Office and an ardent trade unionist. While we were away, he had organized a new trade union for workers in all branches of science and technology, the Association of Scientific Workers (A.Sc.W.). On my return in 1929 he asked me to become its first President, to which I agreed, and a good deal of my time was taken up by attendance at its meetings and making speeches in various parts of the country on its behalf.

But all this committee and propaganda work, though interesting and fruitful (the A.Sc.W. has become an influential body, notably in its dealings with the Government over the status and pay of scientific Civil Servants) was honorary, and I had to make some money. Accordingly I made arrangements with Feakins, my American agent, and set off in 1930 on a lecture tour in the USA, the first of many. They are always exhausting, but well paid.

In 1924, we had taken Corliss Lamont, youngest son of the eminent banker Thomas W. Lamont, as a paying guest in our house in Oxford. And now I was invited to stay in the Lamonts' palatial New York residence, just off Park Avenue. It was an interesting experience of how the rich live. An English butler greeted me at the door, and took me upstairs in a lift lined with Chinese embroidery. My quarters included bedroom, bathroom, drawing and dining room. When the butler called me in the morning with my polished shoes and well-pressed trousers, he asked: 'Will you be taking any meals with the family today, sir?' Of course, I lunched and dined in whenever possible, and made great friends with them all.

T. W. Lamont was a remarkable man, very intelligent, and of great probity, whose advice on financial matters was often sought by the us Government. Mrs Lamont was quite charming, an amiable huntress of social lions. Corliss and I still correspond; though he was, and still is, an uncompromising anti-establishment and anti-religious humanist, he never quarrelled with his father, even if they often engaged in argumentative duels.

The household was very ample. Servants were even then hard to come by in America, but the Lamonts had eleven indoor servants, a chauffeur, and also, what I regarded as the acme of luxury, their own private car on the railway (they had to give it up in the great depression, a few years later). In spite of all their wealth they were simple and sincere, and we were always grateful for their friendship.

On this tour I renewed my acquaintance with American trains. In spite of their jolting when they got under way, jolting that would rarely be tolerated on British railways, and the inconvenience of their sleeping arrangements, I enjoyed waking in an upper berth and peering out on to the morning landscape, while listening to the deep hootings of the engine, so much more impressive than the whistle of our locomotives. The system still had the romance of a pioneering age. Today, with its fast expresses and its separate 'roomettes' for the night, it is more comfortable, but less interesting.

The transcontinental railways were also very efficient. On the southern route, one carriage was reserved for passengers wanting to visit the Grand Canyon: it was unhitched at the junction, dumped off its cargo of sightseers close to the hotel on the rim, and took them back the next day to rejoin the main line.

In 1930 I took advantage of this arrangement. I was staggered by the sight; the canyon was far more impressive than anything I had seen, even in Spitsbergen or Africa – a mile of erosion, down to the foaming brown river below. I hired a horse and rode for miles along the rim. The colours of the rocks were a striking mixture of yellow, red, ochre and brown, indicating different deposits over three hundred million years. The sight of this gigantic natural phenomenon shook me: one needed time to accept it as a fact, to take in that stupendous beauty and the wonder of its parti-coloured descent into aeons of past time. Years later I was able to take Juliette there, and we spent hours just sitting on the terrace, our minds empty of all thought except of that majestic spectacle.

The only other place I remember clearly from this tour was Leland Stanford University, a friendly campus, where I lectured to a very intelligent set of students. Afterwards I was driven up into the sierras to see that other marvel of the American West, the giant sequoia trees, up to four hundred feet tall, one of them big enough to have a road cut through it. It was a queer feeling to drive through this vegetable tunnel, over-arched by three or four thousand years of woody growth.

When I returned to England I went on with my writing and lecturing, on Africa, on evolution, and various social subjects that had begun to interest me.

In the late spring of 1931 Juliette and I went on a trip to the USSR, organized by Intourist, the official Soviet agency for dealing with foreign visitors. The object of the tour was to bring British scientists and medical men in contact with their Russian colleagues.

We set off from London Bridge, with its forest of cranes, in the Russian ship *Rudzutak*, in company with Ivy Low (who had married Litvinoff, former Soviet Ambassador to Britain); Jimmy Crowther, with whom I had collaborated in making a survey of British science and its practical application, later published under the title *Science and Social Needs*; Dr Miller (father of Jonathan Miller, the versatile medical man who is also a film producer and frequent guest on T.V. programmes); and eight or ten others. We passed through the Kattegat, with its view of Hamlet's Helsingør (Elsinore), steamed along the brackish Baltic Sea, past the grim island fortress of Kronstadt at the entry of the port, and so to Leningrad itself.

Leningrad well merited its reputation as the Venice of the North, with its canals, its prospect along the banks of the Neva, and its splendid neo-classical and baroque buildings. It bears all the marks of Czar Peter's love affair with the West. Tsarskoe Seloe, the country seat of the Imperial family, was even more magnificent with its lavishly decorated palaces set in fine parks. One of the rooms almost shocked us: it was panelled with great slabs of honey-gold amber – a reluctant gift from Frederick of Prussia to Catherine the Great, who had admired it avidly when she saw it at Sans-Souci. We felt that such regard for useless luxury, combined with apathy for her subjects' grievances, must have sown the first seeds for the bloody revolution against her successors two hundred and fifty years later.

No doubt this is exactly what the Bolsheviks wanted us to feel. They had restored the palaces and opened them up for the first time to show the public how their tyrannical rulers had lived.

We paid a memorable visit to Professor Vavilov, Head of the Agricultural Department of the Academy, and one of the Foreign Members of the Royal Society. Housed in an exquisite 'Regency' palace, he had stacked his filing cabinets all over the priceless parquet floors. They contained the most complete assortment of cereals ever collected, different strains of maize, wheat, oats, barley and guinea-corn. I remember how he pulled out drawer after drawer and let the grains run through his fingers, telling us how this type came from Peru, that from Canada, from Siberia, and so on. With his knowledge of Mendelian genetics he had made a vast study of where our cereals had originated – four cradles of primitive agriculture, in the massif of the Andes, the Caucasus, Ethiopia and, I think, Mesopotamia. He had also bred improved strains of many cereals – higher-yielding, cold-resistant, immune to fungus disease – which could markedly increase the country's food supply.

At this time he was buoyant and full of wonderful ideas, but trouble soon began. We had heard something of the serious state of genetics in the USSR through letters from my old colleague at Houston, H. J. Muller, whose sympathy with the revolutionary ideals laid down by Lenin made him believe in Soviet science, and led him, at the invitation of Vavilov, to work in Serebrovsky's laboratory in Moscow in 1932. At first all went well, but then the quack geneticist, Lysenko, emerged on the scene claiming that changes induced by treatment during an organism's lifetime were 'fixed' in its constitution after one or two generations – a ridiculous Lamarckian claim. He dismissed orthodox Mendelism and Darwin's key idea of natural selection as 'bourgeois' inventions, though still calling himself a Darwinian, in the sense of believing in some sort of evolution.

He successfully inveighed against Vavilov, who in 1940 was arrested on the trumped-up charge of being a British agent and sent the following year to Siberia. The Royal Society repeatedly wrote to the USSR Academy of Sciences inquiring about him but never got a reply; he apparently died miserably after a few years in exile.

I shall have more to say about Lysenko in the account of my second visit to Russia, in 1945 (p. 282).

Meanwhile let me quote Muller on conditions in 1937, just before he was given permission to 'go on leave' out of the country, a disillusioned man, never to return.

'The narrowness of biologists (in the USSR) on the one hand, and of most of the economic and political progressives, on the other hand, together with the inability of most people to see two things at a time, has led to a widening rift between one group, which believes in biological (genetic) improvement, and another, which believes in social betterment. There is no reason at all why these two methods should be mutually exclusive: on the contrary, each is really conducive to the other. Some people might term such an interaction 'dialectic', and I regard the antithesis that is usually set up as most unfortunate, and have done my utmost to play upon the psychology of the socially advanced group – for I expect them really to control work, or be prevented from it by the effect of the campaign of Lysenko and Prezent (crazy Lamarckists, who, however, deny being Lamarckists). . . .

The situation isn't too easy even for Vavilov, tho' appearances are kept up better with him, as he is more of a world figure. . . .

I have had no time to look at flies [*Drosophila*, the ideal subject for genetical experiment] – personally – since my return, what with the continual meetings, conferences about plans, etc. So I feel that despite our getting a new building soon [he was referring to Serebrovsky, then in charge of the Genetical Institute in Moscow], it is hardly the place, at present and probably for some years to come, where one can hope to develop genetics effectively – let alone the application of genetics to man, which I had hoped might gradually be introduced. . . .

So this time, I appealed directly to Stalin. With the letter I enclosed a copy of my book.[1]

There has been no answer (it is now 10 months) though I know that Stalin's secretary, who translated it, was much excited by it. But now I know that Stalin has been reading the book, is displeased by it, and has ordered an attack prepared against it. A fairly favourable review of it which Julius Haecker wrote for an important journal was refused publication. A reviewer was prevented from reviewing it for the "Moscow Daily News" . . . It might help your understanding of the situation to know of the attitude of the leading party people in fields connected with it. Bauman is Head of Science for the party and Yacovlev Head of Agriculture. . . . Bauman accused me of trying to carry over biological principles directly into the social level, and said we couldn't apply genetics to man that way. Yacovlev maintained that the genes of man had been changed by the environment of civilization, and therefore primitive races existing today have inferior genes. But, he said, about three generations of socialism will so change the genes as to make all races equal. Just better the conditions and you better the genes . . . If the environment didn't change the genes, how could evolution have occurred? As if this were an argument for Lamarckism! But they call their views Darwinian, and I and Vavilov are accused, even in the newspapers, of being anti-Darwinian because we believe in a high stability of the gene, and in its changes being "fortuitous". . . .

What a rotten business it is when one's mouth is gagged – what misunderstandings, minor and major, it leads to! But it isn't I who started this business of giving only one side of the facts, and my associates expect me to follow their methods. Otherwise I am quite out with them at once, and those things which I am trying to further with them will acquire a bad odour.'

---

[1] *Out Of The Night*, in which Muller advocated eugenic improvement by utilizing sperm-banks of deep-frozen sperm from men of high achievement and character. Sperm-banks have now been established in the USA and also here, but mainly in cases of infertility, not for eugenic purposes.

Muller wanted to implement his eugenic policy (see note, page 202) in practice, but when he got Serebrovsky to put forward these ideas he was rebuffed.

The Soviet authorities, under Lysenko's influence, believed that genetic improvement could be achieved by providing better conditions of life, which Muller knew to be impossible. Better education and social conditions could facilitate further realization of the individual's potentialities, but cannot possibly improve his genetic equipment – for health, strength, intellectual or artistic creativity, or indeed for any quality of mind or body.

Muller's genetical knowledge, on the other hand, rightly convinced him that selection for superior qualities would raise the level of human capacity, though he realized that the success of any eugenic measures would be slow, since each generation would show a wide range of genetic endowment, because of the recombination of the old genes, some of them deleterious, which takes place at every act of reproduction. Using sperm of high genetic quality would ensure more rapid eugenic advance, though a decreasing minority of people with neutral or even undesirable genetic equipment would still be thrown up in the process.

In spite of this drawback, Muller's method would give more assured genetic improvement than the Eugenic Society's reliance on encouraging successful and able people to marry, and discouraging large families in the so-called lower classes: though birth-control is becoming increasingly necessary for social reasons, it is more likely to be practised by successful or intelligent than by unsuccessful and stupid people.

The effects of atomic radiation must be added to the already heavy load of 'bad' genes, and after the dropping of the first atomic bomb, Muller was further encouraged to press on with his scheme for banks of 'superior' ova as well as sperm, as by then techniques for preserving ova by deep-freezing were beginning to take shape.

He goes on with an account of the factional quarrels in Russia between Lysenko's adherents and Mendelian geneticists, but these I shall recount as an eye-witness in 1945.

After Muller had left the USSR for a spell with the International Brigade in Spain, and an unsatisfactory genetic appointment in Paris, I obtained for him in 1939 a post in Crew's genetical laboratory in Edinburgh. After the war, he was able to take up an appointment at Amherst College in New England. He got a Nobel Prize in 1946 for his work showing that gene mutations could be induced artificially by radiating animals (in this case fruit-flies) with X-rays. Ever since I first met him in 1912 I realized his outstanding ability: now an official seal had been put on my faith in him.

But to come back to our journey. From Leningrad we went by train to Moscow, past banks lined with profusions of spring flowers. The Academy of Sciences was full of bearded old men in skull-caps, and we discovered the curious fact that in revolutionary Russia there was no retiring age for professors, and they could even hold several jobs at the same time. In all fairness, I must recall that a similar system prevailed in Oxford and Cambridge till the 1870s. Even in my time, an aged Provost of Queen's was still receiving a salary and living in the beautiful Provost's Lodgings, though he had done no work for decades and had outlived two pro-Provosts.

In the Hermitage picture gallery we found another English party – Lady Astor (Nancy), escorted by her son and Bernard Shaw. They passed in front of a huge painting depicting a female saint giving suck from her ample breasts to a hungry beggar. 'You couldn't do that, Nancy,' said G.B.S. to his flat-chested companion, and they passed on giggling.

We stayed at the Hotel Europa, where we breakfasted early on a mug of tea without milk or sugar, a slab of horse-meat and a slice of rye bread. We sympathized with the growing pains of the regime, but were not very enthusiastic about our breakfasts. Moreover, Intourist had inflicted on us an exhaustive and exhausting exploration of the medical, social and scientific achievements of the USSR. We were piled into buses directly after breakfast, complete with interpreter and guide, and whisked off to schools, crèches, factories, laboratories and hospitals. In one of these we were actually shown a woman just out of a brain operation, lying helpless in a cot: the Russians were very proud of their surgery and cared little that our crowd might disturb their patients.

The tours went on ruthlessly in spite of our protests and demands for lunch. Most days we sat down to our frugal 'midday' meal at four in the afternoon. . . . Famished as well as exhausted, we ate all we were offered.

Official banquets were another matter. In spite of the grievous food shortage, they were copious in the extreme – drinks and hors-d'oeuvres comprising boar's head and sucking pig, tongue, salmon and sturgeon, caviar *ad lib*, and with roasts and sweets to follow. And, of course, much wine and vodka and many toasts, so that it was after midnight before we got back to our hotel. As we left, the women interpreters shovelled the remains of their dinner into large handbags – useful perks for their hungry families.

While in Leningrad, we heard the startling news that Britain had gone off the gold standard as the result of the depression in the USA – news which did not add to our pleasure.

After the western elegance of Leningrad, we were deeply moved by the savage beauty of Moscow's Red Square. It is an immense rectangular open space with the many-cupola'd Cathedral of St Basil at its end, and the huge crenellated wall of the Kremlin on one side, surrounding the complex of palaces and chapels within. Dark official buildings framed the other two sides. It has a magic of proportion, a magnificent unity which, while it dwarfs the people wandering across it, also fills them with a sense of pride, even exaltation.

The Cathedral was then serving as an anti-war and anti-religious museum. The small chapels, each deriving directly from the onion-dome above it, were arranged to show photographs of war horrors; soldiers in defeat, pictures of denuded land and famine-stricken people, and processions led by monks and patriarchs with ikons and images of saints held aloft, obviously vainly invoked. There were many visitors there, staring at the exhibits. The chapels were dark, lit by small windows, intricately constructed to lead out of each other.

Another part of St Basil was being carefully restored; the Russians are proud of their cultural heritage, even if they repudiate its religious basis. The bulbous cupolas were covered with brightly coloured tiles; the church was built by two sixteenth-century Venetian architects, yet nothing could have been more convincingly Tartar.

The centre of the great Kremlin wall held a majestic pile of green marble containing the tomb of Lenin, with military guards at either end. It was impressive to see the crowds jostling through the gates, peasants and poor townsfolk who had waited for hours to pay homage to their saviour. We joined the procession and filed through, to see the embalmed, waxen-looking face of Lenin, lying in state with a bear-skin on his feet, serene in his immortality.

In Moscow Juliette was suddenly taken ill with some sort of fever. The hotel authorities produced a German doctor who put her on an exclusive diet of tea and *kasha* (a spongy unappetizing mess of rice), and as a fee demanded a copy of *The Science of Life*, which I duly sent him later from England.

The rest of the party went down the Volga. I couldn't leave Juliette, but had a cine-camera with me and, to my surprise, was allowed to walk about Moscow and take pictures unattended and unmolested. I took shots of the black market, where oddments of clothing were exchanged for a few onions or potatoes, and country produce was illegally sold. On a Sunday, in the Park of Culture and Rest, I snapped young people swimming, dancing and singing: their elders were still going to church, in spite of Bolshevik propaganda. I had some nice shots of babies in crèches, looking wonderfully healthy. On my return, I tried to get a producer to buy my film for a news-reel. He objected on the grounds that British people wouldn't like to see the wicked Russians enjoying themselves and looking so fit and happy! However, he did eventually take most of it, and there was no protest.

When Juliette recovered, we accepted Ivy Litvinoff's invitation to join her in Ryazan on the upper Moscow river, where she was fetching her children back from their holidays. Ryazan was an ancient fortified city, with vast numbers of cupola'd churches and empty monasteries.

For our return she booked places on the boat going down the Moscow river. This was an extraordinary contraption, just like the double-ended Mississippi paddle-steamers described by Mark Twain, except that the decks and deck-hold were crowded with Russian peasants in smocks and high boots carrying their produce to market, or just travelling around in search of jobs: every stopping place was crammed with migrating groups complete with mattresses and saucepans. One evening, we went down to the hold. Masses of peasants, crowded under the crude light of kerosene lamps, were listening to a woman singing. Her song was indescribable, full of metallic vibration, urgent and tragic. After listening to her invocation in that dark night, we often wondered what became of her, and of all those thousands who suffered for an unattainable ideal, imposed so arbitrarily on a whole nation.

Next day we tied up at a lock for a long wait. Ivy Litvinoff suggested a bathe. I objected that we had no bathing-dress, but she said no one used them anyway. We walked down a little path, plagued by flies; Ivy and I undressed (Juliette refused the doubtful pleasure) and I waded in somewhat gingerly, mud clinging to my ankles, much to Juliette's amusement, towards the ample charms revealed by Ivy. . . .

After this ordeal we went on, past the extraordinary monasteries along the river, some with pyramidal towers, others with gilded cupolas (but all now monkless), to the city itself. The walls guarding the Kremlin where it faces the river made it look more sinister in its seclusion: no outsider was then allowed to penetrate its gates. But it was also very beautiful, with its complex of pointed roofs and gilded domes.

We did gain access to the Tretiakoff Museum, which contained a collection of Impressionist pictures acquired by two rich merchants, surprisingly and prophetically aware of their beauty, long before they had become fashionable. Cézanne and van Gogh, Derain and Pissarro, and of course Picasso, are among those I remember. I believe they have since been dispersed or sold: certainly they did not conform to the standards of Socialist Realism.

In another museum we came upon masses of treasure-trove from the Danube region, the burial hoards of Scythian gold. This was a staggering revelation of a new culture (new at least to us), the so-called Animal Art which drifted to the west from the vast plains of Mongolia, figuring ibex and reindeer, wild horses and strange Saiga antelopes with bulging noses. The curious formalism of the designs, their immense vitality, and the untarnished splendour of the gold, filled us with admiration.

I was invited to a match of 'phutbol'. It was played with terrific enthusiasm but, to my eyes, less skill than shown by our British teams. At any rate, the Bolsheviks had no misgivings about importing 'bourgeois' sport.

After the game there was a reception at the big athletic stadium. Supper finished, we went out to drink coffee on the terrace, and my host, Lunacharsky, and I got into a discussion on the philosophy of art, the absoluteness or otherwise of aesthetic values and the relation of the artist to society. Radek, the arch-priest of Marxist theory, soon came up and joined us, so that I found myself pitted against two of the best all-round brains in Russia. We went at it (in the neutral ground of the German language) till midnight, surrounded by a large circle of listeners. I adduced van Gogh's painting of a chair as being both modern and realistic but was borne down in a storm of dialectical materialism. Socialist Realism was now the guiding principle in Soviet art and literature, and the inhabitants of the USSR were soon to learn the dangers of departing from its prescriptions, as well as the cramping effect it had on style and expression.

Before leaving, I went to pay my respects to Bukharin, who had been largely responsible for planning our visit. I found him in sporting attire and high boots, cleaning a rifle. He explained that he was just off on three weeks' leave, to shoot Manchurian tigers on the Amur river, two thousand miles away. Such was the size of the Russian Empire – though no one had yet accused the Soviets of imperialism. This, and the terrible purges under Stalin, were yet to come, and radically altered Russia's image in our eyes.

We were anxious to get back to the children in Switzerland, and took seats in a Russian plane going to Königsberg. This was the first flight we ever took, and might well have been our last. The plane was a veteran of the First World War, a two-seater crate with a small bay for the pilot, who was of German origin. We sat on cane chairs strapped to the floor. As we flew over vast stretches of desolate *taiga*, the coniferous and birch forest which covers so much of north-western Russia, he regaled us with stories of his prowess in the war, and of the disasters which had befallen his comrades: he was the only survivor of his squadron. What about disasters for us, we thought, as he flew just over the tree-tops for what seemed hours, and the plane bucked violently, making Juliette very sick. I don't remember seeing any human habitation until we landed, with flaming exhaust, at Königsberg, and changed there into a large non-Russian plane for Zürich.

On the whole I was favourably impressed by the developments of Russia. As I wrote in my book, *A Scientist Among the Soviets*, on my return:

'Other nations may not follow the same paths as Russia. They may be able to reorganize their disordered systems without having recourse either to open revolution or to orthodox communism. But whatever new course they pursue (and it is abundantly clear that they cannot continue on the old course) they cannot help learning much from Russia. The technique and the very idea of large-scale planning: the socialization of agriculture: the reduction of private profit and class distinction: the provision of peace-time incentives which shall on the one hand not be merely individualist, and on the other not be centred mainly on the crude worship of national power: the elevation of science and scientific method to its proper place in affairs – in these and many other ways the new Russia, even in its present embryo stage of development, is in advance of other countries: and if the rest of the world refuses to learn from the object-lesson provided by Russia, as well as profiting by her mistakes, so much the worst for the rest of the world.'

On the other hand, I was repelled by the dogmatism of its leaders, even in matters of art, and disillusioned by the lack of co-ordination between the planning schemes for different industries and regions. And the absence of free speech, which even then was apparent in all our contacts with Russians, as well as the terrific machinery of propaganda at work in schools, museums, cinemas, factories, places of relaxation, and even penetrating the people's homes with the radio, disturbed me profoundly. On my later visit in 1945 all my fears proved justified.

In the autumn, stimulated by an article written by Max Nicholson entitled 'A National Plan for Britain', in Gerald Barry's *Week-end Review*, an interested group met in Barry's office. They included Barry and Nicholson; Leonard Elmhirst (who had just started the all-round planning of Dartington, his estate in Devon); Israel Sieff, co-director of the huge, streamlined firm of Marks and Spencer; Kenneth Lindsay, a future Lib.-Lab. MP; Dennis Routh from the Ministry of Education; the financier Sir Basil Blackett; Sir Henry Bunbury, an eminent Civil Servant; Zvegintzov, who knew a great deal about international finance; Jack Pritchard, an authority on design; and myself.

It was decided to found a non-governmental planning organi-zation in London. Two questions remained – what to call it and how to finance it. After interminable discussions over its title, Pritchard proposed *Political and Economic Planning*. This was unanimously agreed; but when he added, 'PEP for short', there were some wry faces among the senior members. However, PEP has remained as its abbreviated title, and has certainly helped to establish its reputation as an organization full of pep.

At a later week-end meeting at Dartington, Sieff and Elmhirst guaranteed a handsome sum towards its formation, and appeals to various business firms provided the rest.

We rented a beautiful house in Queen Anne's Gate and held our meetings there, with specialist groups studying various subjects. PEP published their reports in full, as well as summarizing them in a series of bulletins. After the war, it moved to an office in Belgrave Square, which it shared with the Nature Conservancy, then run by Max Nicholson.

I was allotted a tiny office in the attic where, with the aid of an excellent German refugee secretary, Friedl Rothschild, I dictated my business letters and wrote a number of articles, mostly for PEP.

One ornithological result of this situation deserves mention. During the blitz, I made one of the earlier sightings of the black redstart in London. This nester in walls and empty houses had been a rare straggler in Britain before 1939, but the blitz provided so many suitable nesting sites that it became quite common in central London!

The blitz had a botanical effect too. On empty bomb-sites, even in the heart of the city, all kinds of country flowers and even trees appeared. I remember one area in St John's Wood which, by the end of the war, resembled the jungle at Angkor. In 1932, I went again to lecture in the USA.

On this trip I went to stay with my old friend Floyd Dell and his wife, always known as B. Marie, a fine woman with revolutionary tendencies. He was then writing his autobiography in his pleasant colonial-style house in New Hampshire. I shall always remember his birthday, with the fat negro cook parading round the room where Floyd was enthroned, holding aloft the birthday cake with its due number of candles and chanting a litany of praise: 'Happy birthday, Massa Dell, Massa Dell he very fine man; Massa Dell, we all loves you.' It was really very touching.

In New York I made the acquaintance of Marion Greenwood, a charming and talented artist, who lived in the Bohemian downtown area of Greenwich Village. She had been given various commissions to decorate public buildings during the New Deal period, and showed me a letter from a postmaster in the deep south saying how much her 'muriel' in his office had been admired!

Meanwhile Juliette had gone on an adventure of her own, to stay with our friends the Hubert Youngs in Baghdad, where he was British Minister. From there she travelled all over the country, right up through Kerbela, the ancient city built on its own secular ruins, to Mosul. Escorted by an armed soldier for protection against the restless Kurds, she explored this stronghold of the devil-worshippers and took photographs of the salamanders which, for legendary reasons, were part of their cult. She also went to Nebbi-Unis, the modern village by the site of Nineveh, and walked among the great sand-heaps covering the ancient ruins, frequented only by nomadic Bedouin in their black tents.

At the Youngs' she met Freya Stark, the explorer and writer, who was polishing up her Arabic in Baghdad. This was the beginning of another enduring friendship; we have just returned (July, 1968) from a visit to this learned and intrepid woman, who at the age of seventy built herself a delightful *palazzino* on a lovely hill north of Venice, and now at seventy-two has gone off on a new voyage of exploration in Afghanistan.

On my return from America I went to stay with Aldous and Maria in their villa at Sanary on the south coast of France. During this period Aldous was still doing a good deal of painting, as a change from much reading and writing. He suggested that I should try my hand and arranged a still life, with a closely-patterned cloth under a bowl of fruit. I got on fairly well until I reached the multi-coloured silk, and asked Aldous how I should deal with it. He peered at it with his poor vision, and said that all he saw was one colour! Yet in spite of this disability, or perhaps because of it, because he saw his environment only in large blocks of colour and shape, he painted a number of really good pictures, one of which hangs on my walls today.

His young son Matthew was an ardent butterfly and moth collector. One evening we went out at dusk, armed with torch and butterfly net, to search for oleander hawk-moths. It was a splendid sight to see these lepidopteran giants hovering in front of the pink oleander flowers with outstretched proboscis, showing the brilliant markings on their plump bodies. Aldous and I were as thrilled as Matthew, and reminisced about our youthful 'bug-hunting' exploits at Godalming. In 1937 Aldous left for California, partly because he loved sunshine, but also because he had heard of a Mr Bates in Los Angeles, who had had great success in remedying faulty vision (and he did help Aldous considerably). I didn't see Aldous again until during my time at UNESCO.

CHAPTER XV

1933

IN the spring of 1933 my father died.

We were on a brief holiday near Tunbridge Wells, exploring the picturesque old town with the famous Pantiles, where the rank and fashion of London used to parade when they came to drink the chalybeate waters. We picnicked among the extraordinary rock-formations near by, where the red sandstone is penetrated by caves and featured by isolated blocks, queer but friendly silent monsters.

Suddenly, on this peaceful scene, came a telegram from my stepmother announcing my father's death, and I hurried back to London. He was not very old, only seventy-two. Apparently he had had a sudden heart failure. I went into the fatal bedroom alone. It was grievous to see the familiar face distorted by the agony of his last brief moments, and I reproached myself for not having kept in closer touch with him while he was still alive. I thought of his gaiety and unfailing kindness, how he had helped me through my natural history studies, stimulated me with stories of my grandfather's career, encouraged me to read widely instead of becoming a narrow specialist. How bravely he had carried on after my mother's death! I had indeed been lucky in my parents.

With other members of the Huxley clan, we went down to Godalming for the funeral and saw him buried in the same grave in Compton cemetery that had received my mother's ashes so many years earlier – a double sadness now, yet strangely mingled with happy memories of my mother and of the beautiful countryside she had loved so much.

Years later, Professor Oliver Elton, father of my old pupil

Charles Elton, sent me the following note. It is worth quoting as a tribute to my father's character.

'. . . Many of my Oxford friends were oppressed, even bedevilled – by want of cash, or by sex and love affairs, or by uncertain ambitions, or by philosophical doubts, or by the pangs of breaking with the religion of their homes. But Leonard was born under a lucky star; he was by far the gayest of the crowd, though he seemed always to keep his head, and to be quietly thinking. He was an excellent dancer, and sometimes it seemed as if he might dance through life. Yes, he started fair, from what might seem the most auspicious home in England. Charles Eliot, who for a time knew it well, once exclaimed: "How happy these pagans are!" . . . Thus Leonard was free-born, and had none of the heart-searchings incident to parting with the Old Man Jehovah and His circle! Leonard worked hard, on the usual lines, took his two First Classes, made and kept a host of friends of both sexes, and was a favourite with his Master, the mundane Jowett. I was at his wedding with Julia Arnold, where, at the breakfast, Huxley *père* and Matthew Arnold chaffed each other in the best "Victorian" temper. I knew the bride a little, and much admired her kindliness, pluck and independence. . . .

I have some of his verses, often printed in the *Oxford Mag.* of the early eighties. They are all fresh from his heart and fancy, and redolent of the Oxford of that day.

Leonard has been dead these eleven years, but I still, at 83, cherish the image of the radiant youth with whom I walked down to his wedding ceremony.

O. Elton   6.9.44.'

Since finishing my work on *Relative Growth* in 1932, I had begun assembling material for a big book on experimental embryology. I went on working at it in collaboration with my old pupil Gavin de Beer (later Director of the Natural History Museum, and knighted for his scientific work). It was nearly as arduous as *The Science of Life*, for it meant reading and evaluating a great many English and foreign books and papers; but we persevered, and the book was published in 1934, under our joint names, with the title of *Principles of Experimental Embryology*. This proved a useful synthesis of all different aspects of the subject and was widely used in teaching and research, though now superseded by more recent work.

Furthermore, as a result of Hitler's nonsensical rantings about races and the dangers of contaminating the purity of the so-called Aryan race, I was asked by the publishing firm of Jonathan Cape to write a book on racial problems in Europe. This involved collaboration with Professor Haddon the ethnologist, my old colleague Carr-Saunders, who, as Professor of Social Studies in Liverpool, had much experience of immigrants from Ireland and the Continent, and my old friend Dr Charles Singer, who was extremely knowledgeable about ethnic migrations and cultural influences in the history of the whole Mediterranean region.

He had a charming house at Par on the south Cornish coast, close to Daphne du Maurier's big estate, and we often visited him there. It was wonderful running down to a nearby cove for a swim before breakfast, or in the afternoon, accompanied by Charles Singer carrying a long shepherd's crook. We rambled about the coast in search of rare ferns and flowers, while the evenings were taken up in talk about ancient history and the role of science and technology in cultural evolution.

The outcome of all these discussions and much reading was a book called *We Europeans*, published in 1935, in which I, with the aid of my colleagues, demonstrated conclusively that there was no such thing as a 'pure race' anywhere in the world, and that there were no unchanging racial characters, but that the qualities and achievements of each so-called race or ethnic group were determined mainly by environment and cultural history, and only to a minor extent by heredity.

It gave me particular satisfaction to put this scientific spoke into Hitler's wheel, and to do something to stop his irrational anti-Semitism from spreading into Britain under Oswald Mosley's influence – though, like all other protests, it did nothing to prevent Hitler from continuing his increasingly savage persecution of the Jews in Germany, nominally on racial grounds.

Meanwhile, thanks to an introduction from Aldous, I had got to know Gerald Heard, one of the most interesting acquaintances I ever made. He was at that time secretary to Sir Horace Plunkett, who had done so much for Irish agriculture and for international agricultural co-operation. He took me and Gerald driving in his powerful car – an alarming experience as he seemed to think that Surrey roads were as uncrowded as those in the wilds of Ireland, and generally drove on the right instead of the left. But his enthusiasm was infectious and laid the foundation for my interest in reciprocal agricultural schemes between Britain and her colonies (and later ex-colonies) in Africa.

Gerald was a strange character. Behind his secretarial efficiency there was a strong strain of mysticism, which I am sure influenced Aldous when they both went to live in California. Gerald even went so far as to found a new church with its own ritual and prayers. I later attended one of the services and found the whole thing rather ridiculous. Anyhow he gave it up, but he and Aldous remained close friends and I too found many of his ideas stimulating, though often impractical.

Among other memories dating from the early thirties was a happy holiday in early spring spent with Ronald Lockley, a great lover of birds and islands. At that time he was tenant of the solitary farmhouse on Skokholm, off Martinshaven in Pembrokeshire, an island covered with sea-birds, including vast numbers of shearwaters. This name derives from their habit of flying close to the surface of the sea, their wings nearly touching the waves as they quest for fish. They nest underground, in burrows appropriated from rabbits or puffins. Cock and hen take turns in brooding, which can be hard on the sitting bird, as its mate may be away for over a week before returning with food. The reunion is an extraordinary affair, the two birds scuffling back and forth in their burrow, greeting each other with noises I can best describe as a cross between a cock crowing and a witch laughing. It was an eerie experience to lie down with an ear to the ground and hear this jubilant cacophony a mere foot below.

At evening the returning birds gathered in great rafts on the

Sound before finding their way back to their own nests in the late dusk. Perhaps they do so by sound rather than sight, for they start calling as soon as they are over the island, and their mates answer with their own screechings. Like swifts, they cannot take off from the ground; so when they had to fly off to sea, they either waddled to the cliff-edge and threw themselves over, or scrambled their way up a large boulder which served as a launching pad. We went out with a torch one night and were fascinated by the spectacle of these bat-like creatures competing for a good take-off position.

On this isolated speck of land there were two prominent rocks, called Bread Rock and Help Rock. A fire on Bread Rock indicated that the islanders were short of food, while a fire on the other denoted an emergency – sickness or an accident – when the sufferers had to be taken off the island. Access, in the days before motor-boats, was difficult because of the severe tide-race in the intervening channel: even with an auxiliary motor, Lockley and I often got a good splashing.

Here I felt, perhaps even more than in Africa, the power and the independence of nature – nature that helps things make themselves, as Charles Kingsley wrote in *The Water Babies*. The swarms of puffins flying down from the cliffs and resting on the sea, the screeching of guillemots, the great black-backed gulls screaming and devouring the plump young shearwaters as they stumbled to the cliff-edge before attempting their first flight, yet (if they survived the predatory gull's attack) immediately at home and knowing what to do when they reached the water; the occasional gannets soaring on their wide white wings: all these manifestations of the vast interrelated web of life never ceased to provoke my interest and wonder.

On an unforgettable occasion, Lockley took me further out to the even smaller and uninhabited islet of Grassholm (the *holm* in these islands' names is a Norse word, reminder of the Viking ships that passed this way a millennium ago).

Landing here can only be achieved in good weather. Luckily it was a calm day, and we hauled our little boat up into a rocky cove. We scrambled up the kittiwake-haunted cliff and walked over the flat top, our feet often breaking through into the abandoned puffin burrows below, until we were able to look down on to the northern slope. Here we were struck dumb with amazement: the whole area, over twenty acres in extent, was white with birds and their dung. It was one of the largest breeding colonies of gannets in the world – over 8,000 pairs – and the most accessible. They were so tame that we could walk right up to the edge of the colony and even handle them, though this risked a painful peck from their large bills. There were thousands of birds brooding, their nests always close together, though just far enough to prevent their occupants being pecked by their neighbours. There is safety in numbers – robber gulls and skuas think twice before dashing down to pick up egg or chick from among a forest of sharp beaks.

We witnessed at close quarters the fantastic performance by which the young are fed. A returning bird flops down on its nest, pecked and groaned at by its neighbours; the young gannet (always a single chick), a squalid-looking creature with tufts of white down over matted grey, thrusts its head into its mother's (or father's) gullet, and the parent then, with deep heavings of its neck, regurgitates a fish from its crop into its offspring's maw. It looks almost as if the fat fledgling were being swallowed – a most uncomfortable-looking affair.

Meanwhile some of the birds were just enjoying themselves, gliding on their six-foot spread of wings, taking advantage of air-currents and rarely flapping. Beyond, others were hunting for food, dropping like plummets into the sea when they spotted a fish. They are great underwater swimmers, provided with big air-sacs to take the shock of their plunge and help them breathe while submerged.

My reaction was immediate and definite: we *must* make a film of this, I said, and Lockley warmly assented.

So, when I was back in London, I made an appointment with Alexander Korda, head of London Films. He knew nothing about birds, but because of this very ignorance was fascinated by my tales of the gannets' habits. He agreed to move into this new field, only stipulating that the film should be called *The Private Life of the Gannet,* to link it with *The Private Life of Henry VIII,* which he had just made, and was drawing huge audiences.

So in the spring of 1934 we set off with one of London Films' best cameramen, Borrodaile, all the apparatus for filming, and tents and stores for a fortnight, including a barrel of fresh water, for there was none on the island.

Everything went well. Lockley arranged for an RAF plane to take the cameraman up to film the approach to the island – first a blur of white, gradually resolving itself into thousands of separate white dots – the birds on their nests; we obtained close-ups of the feeding of the young and even of a fledgling throwing itself off the grassy cliff into the sea.

And we captured all their display habits. Whenever a bird rejoined its mate, it would present seaweed as nest material, and the pair went through an elaborate mutual ceremony, bowing their heads, preening themselves under the wing (a displacement activity, such as I had already noted in the great crested grebe), sometimes even intertwining their necks, cackling loudly and clappering their beaks. Occasionally a bird alone on the nest would be so overcome by emotion that it would perform a display all by itself.

Thanks to the constant sunshine which we were lucky to have all through our stay, the birds' dazzling whiteness shone with an almost sculptural beauty, and enormously added to the impact of our film. It had a long run in cinemas all over England and America, as well as proving useful to departments of Zoology by illustrating the breeding biology, the strange mutual displays of the birds, and their aerodynamic skill. The end of the film was supplied by my old friend John Grierson, 'father' of documentary films, who chartered a herring-boat to take close-ups of a swarm of gannets diving for fish – a beautiful sequence in slow motion.

Our enterprise was crowned with the award of an Oscar for the best documentary film of the year, which gave us a great deal of satisfaction. In any case, I had thoroughly enjoyed the making of this film, working with such keen helpers as Lockley and Borrodaile.

When we returned for a brief look at Grassholm in the summer, the gannets had all left for their oceanic feeding grounds: nothing was left of the teeming population but their empty nests in close-ranged patterns, exuding a vintage aroma of decayed vegetation, rotten fish and guano.

Meanwhile, after this remarkable natural history experience, I wanted to get back to some laboratory research in biology. Hearing from my zoological colleague, Professor Renouf of Cork University, that he ran a small laboratory on Lough Ine in south-west Ireland, we decided to take most of our summer holiday at Baltimore, the nearest village. Juliette had acquired a second-hand sports touring Hotchkiss which she christened Alexander the Great, and we packed the family in and drove by way of the Fishguard ferry. Renouf had booked lodgings for us, proudly announcing that they had the only flush lavatory in the county. We arrived tired after a long drive from Cork, to discover that the lodgings were just a few rooms in the railway station, available only because there were too few trains to warrant a resident station-master. When Juliette saw the rooms she burst into tears, and I was furious. It was a wretched place: our sitting-room looked directly on to the platform, and twice daily the window-sill became a convenient hopping-in gate for the passengers' numerous fleas. Moreover, the famous lavatory was also on the platform, and we had to get the key from the porter whenever we wanted to work that celebrated plug. There was no alternative accommodation in the small township; we just had to lump it.

However, the weather was, for a miracle, perfect, so we packed a picnic most days and disappeared from our sordid surroundings to some magical and undisturbed place. I set up my research on the reorganization of the body of the bristle-worm Sabella after amputation, and found plenty of material close at hand on the shores of Lough Ine.

And Lough Ine was beautiful. It was a salt-water pool, but filled only at high tide; one could watch the seaweed fronds in the entrance channel change direction with the ebb and flow. The tide also brought in the larvae of animals which normally inhabit the sea-bottom: close to the edge one could pick out bright red starfish, wicked-looking sea-urchins, sea-cucumbers, scallops, flat-fish and other benthic animals, including Sabella. Near by were some caves which also filled at high tide: their walls were covered with sheets of a very beautiful sea-anemone with individuals varying from white to rose-red, not to mention little green sponges and masses of brightly coloured sea-squirts. Lough Ine, indeed, was a gigantic natural aquarium.

My findings on Sabella were quite unexpected: I discovered that headless fragments of thorax would regenerate a complete thorax and abdomen, though it had been supposed that the brain and its nerves were necessary for the process; also that the transformation of thoracic to abdominal-type segments in fragments of the abdomen took place in the reverse direction to that seen in fragments of the thorax.

De Beer and I, in our *Principles of Experimental Embryology*, published later that year, could only say that in all developing organisms there seems to be a special 'organizer' region in the early embryo, from which some chemical influences spread to other regions, bringing out their potentialities, and that in regeneration the cells at the cut surface regenerate a new organizing region; but the nature of the tissues at the cut surface, and the direction in which it faces, whether headward or tailward, exerts some influence on the resultant new growth. However, the mechanism by which this influence is created remains a mystery.

Between all this regular scientific work, we were able to make many lovely excursions. We went to the beautiful lakes of Killarney where we saw some strawberry trees (*Unedo*); their name comes from their large red berries, which taste rather like faded strawberries. They are biologically interesting, since they are members of the so-called Lusitanian flora which remains in isolated spots along our mild western shores; presumably because, owing to the Gulf Stream, a few warmth-loving plants did not suffer the full cold of the last glacial epoch. They survived abundantly in south-west France, Portugal and southern Spain, but were all killed off in the colder eastern regions of Britain.

We also went with our boys, then aged thirteen and eleven, to visit one of the ladies who wrote *Reminiscences of a Country Parish* under the pseudonyms of Somerville and Ross: we had already met her at one of the spiritualist seances I have described (see page 174). Her real name was Miss Townsend and she lived with her brother, old Admiral Townsend, at Castletownsend.

The family firmly believed in the existence of the 'little folk', and gave us many instances of these fairies' and leprechauns' benevolent or malignant doings. They were also convinced that there was a kelpie in their lough, and a creature roaming their hills, half-pig and half-badger, with short legs on the left and longer ones on the right, so that when running along the side of a mountain it remained neatly fitting the angle of slope. I found it difficult to express my doubts about such a beast (what would happen if it ran the other way round?), as they took it very personally if one questioned their testimony.

Finally they produced the ultimate 'proof' of the existence of fairies – a tiny brogue shoe, of late Georgian type, beautifully made of welted leather. It had been found on the moors some decades earlier, and was kept like a relic in a special box. Juliette was fascinated, and holding the pretty object carefully on the palm of her hand, said that if real fairies hadn't made the shoe, 'fairy fingers' had certainly been at work on it. This was not well received, and she got a serious reprimand for her doubts. The little shoe was probably a travelling salesman's sample, though it was nice to think of fairies following human fashions. . . .

As we were leaving, we were asked if we had left presents for the fairies at the fairy wells we had visited. We had noticed little bits of ribbon, stumps of pencils and scraps of coloured paper hanging on the bushes surrounding some wells, but had done nothing to add to the collection. This again was sadly commented on: 'Lucky for you that fairies don't cross water, but you will surely have some bad luck after thus slighting them.'

True enough, we had some bad luck – Anthony was knocked over by a car as he was riding his bicycle at Micheldever, where we went on our way back to stay with our friends the Chances, and only by a miracle escaped with nothing worse than concussion.

We never told the Townsends. They would have been more than ever convinced of the reality of their fairies' power, even of their ability to 'cross water'. Actually it also brought us good luck, as will shortly appear.

Among happy memories are those of the further visits we paid to southern Pembrokeshire, following the stay on Skokholm which I have already described. We fell in love with that beautiful and unspoilt country and returned to it again and again. One spring we spent some time at a friend's old coastguard cottage on the shores of Linney Bay. From here we were taken on a piratical expedition by one of our hosts, Alan Best.

Alan was a young Canadian with an extraordinary gift for natural history. He knew all the birds of his native British Columbia, and on coming to England he promptly mastered those of Britain. His piercing eyes could identify a bird at great distance, which made my walks with him a mutual joy. He also had a great gift for understanding and managing children, and so we called him in to look after Anthony during his term away from school, after his accident at Micheldever. Alan had been trained as a sculptor, and we thought it would be a good idea for him to teach Anthony to handle clay and chisels. Though Anthony did not become much of a sculptor, he enjoyed learning the craft.

A more important consequence of this nasty accident was that Juliette herself discovered a hitherto unknown talent for sculpture and modelling. She learnt the rudiments from Alan, and later went to classes under John Skeaping, the well-known painter and sculptor, finding immense joy in the pursuit of this art. Her carving of a Red River hog in coral-wood was shown at the Academy and received praise and several offers to buy. But I insisted that we should keep the carving, and it still sits majestically in our front hall to greet our friends.

Close by Linney was a small cove called Ebony Bay; for, over a hundred years ago, a ship laden with ebony from Africa had been wrecked there. This wood is so rich in oil and so dense in texture that it repelled penetration by water, and remained undecayed on the bottom of the cove. So, at neap tide on a sunny afternoon, we went down to where the black logs lay wedged between the rocks. Alan and I stripped and, with a good deal of ducking and spluttering, recovered a good hundredweight of this noble wood. It was almost unaffected by its long immersion, and a number of lovely carvings were made from it by Juliette and her artist acquaintances.

Alan became a faithful and indispensable friend of the whole family: good-looking, tall and strong, his uncanny gift of understanding and taming animals served him well with human beings too. He taught the boys to ride and shoot and camp out – functions which I lacked the time and patience to perform. And when the inevitable tensions of the boys' adolescence began to be felt, he brought a relaxing sympathy to difficult situations. He later specialized in natural history, and is now a director of a zoo.

In the late autumn I paid a visit to my old friend Professor D'Arcy Thompson at his laboratory at St Andrews. He had disagreed with some of the conclusions of my book on relative growth, published in the preceding year, and I wanted to clarify my position. He was as Olympian as ever, looking like a bearded Scottish Poseidon, but he did make some alterations in the new edition of his famous book, *Growth and Form*; we agreed to collaborate in a series of essays on the subject, written by a dozen specialists, which appeared under the title of *The Measurement of Growth and Form* in 1950. They in general supported my thesis that form depended on the different growth-rates of separate parts of the body.

D'Arcy Thompson also took me bird-watching on the neighbouring mud-flats, where we saw vast numbers of waders, some of them very rare in Britain. I shall always remember the flocks changing course in mid-air, the wings reversing instantaneously like the slats of a Venetian blind.

The students and graduates still wore the scarlet gowns that my father had worn when he was assistant to Professor Lewis Campbell – wonderful splashes of colour against the grey stone of the buildings.

About this time, I had got to know Lord Horder, the physician.

I think it was our common interests, in population problems, eugenics, and euthanasia, which first brought us together. Certainly we discussed them during a delightful cruise in the Solent in Clinton Chance's yacht, just before leaving for Bel-Alp (see below).

We later visited him in his country place at Steep, under the Downs near Petersfield. He was a passionate gardener, and in order to grow heathers and other acid-loving plants in an alkaline chalk region, he constructed grooved stone balconies full of peaty soil. And when Juliette asked him how he managed to grow such splendid maples, he told her that, as President of the Cremation Society, he had obtained sackfuls of ashes from various crematoria, which provided an abundance of all the minerals he needed.

He was a wise and good friend, later a great support in the Zoo crisis, and also helped me to get over my psychological troubles afterwards.

CHAPTER XVI

The Zoo Cage

IN the summer of 1934, we called on Mrs Tyndall, the widow of my grandfather's close friend, Professor Tyndall. His large Victorian house had been the first to be built on the heathery moor of Hindhead; but as it was soon followed by others, also in quest of the pure air of those heights, Tyndall had built a huge wattle screen among his plantation of pine trees to protect his privacy. By now the pine trees had grown into a dark forest and the house felt like the bottom of a well. Here Mrs Tyndall, a frail old woman, lived with a be-bangled companion among her memories, masses of photographs of the Alpine peaks which her husband had climbed so often, and a great clutter of notes and papers which were to be the basis of her biography of him.

She suggested that we might like to spend the summer in the chalet at Bel-Alp, which the Tyndalls had built, nearly eight thousand feet up on the southern slopes of the Rhône valley, and where they used to spend every summer. We accepted enthusiastically, even when she presented Juliette with a long list of fussy instructions, the most important of which was to throw absolutely nothing away.

We departed for Switzerland on the last day of July, in order to arrive for the festive first of August, the national anniversary of Switzerland's independence. Huge beacons are lit all over the mountains, and Juliette still cherished enough patriotic feeling to wish to see the celebrations. However, we found that we had to walk all the way up from Brig to Bel-Alp, nearly four thousand feet of steep zigzags. Our baggage went on a pack-mule, but we were so exhausted on arriving that we fell straight into bed at the hotel and never saw the beacon fires. We took possession of the chalet next morning, unclasping shutters, and replacing the chimney-pot which had been taken down during the winter. The chalet was a stout construction in stone, built above the tree-line and dominating the great valley, with a splendid view of the snowy Aletschhorn and other fine peaks to the north-east. It was furnished in solid mahogany, all brought up on mule-back, and now cluttered up with an enormous variety of objects. Mrs Tyndall was one of those old ladies, like my Huxley grandmother, who couldn't bear to throw anything away. At least twenty-five years of summer copies of *The Times* were piled in the attic. The apparatus used by Tyndall for detecting bacteria in the air (even at this high altitude his flasks became infected) was still in place on the walls, and all his pencilled records (though long published) were jumbled in a drawer. While looking for kindling wood we found a small board with a note attached in Mrs Tyndall's slanting Victorian writing: 'Part of a board used by dear John when he advertised for guides', and in the incredibly full medicine cupboard, among many other potions we discovered a little bottle with a brown smear inside, bearing the words: 'A dear little medicine prescribed for John, but I know not for what or by whom.'

This last item was particularly poignant. My father told me that Tyndall suffered all his life from a stomach complaint as well as severe heart palpitations. He was given large doses for the first and very careful measured drops of something else, probably digitalin, for the second. During his last illness, he asked his wife to give him his usual dose of stomach potion, and she, scatter-brained as she was, administered a table-spoonful of the digitalin. Tyndall asked which bottle it had come from. On being told, he calmly announced: 'Then you have killed your John', and fell dead almost immediately.

She was so paralysed with guilt that, though she survived him by half a century, she just sat brooding over the accumulated material which was to be the basis of his biography, but never put pen to paper herself, nor allowed others to do so. It was only in 1945, after her death, that Professor Creesy finally wrote his *Life and Work*.

However, there we were, in that glorious summer in 1934,

perched high above the Aletsch Glacier, whose grey frozen chunks slowly churned down the valley in full view of our bedroom window. We acquired a sturdy Swiss maid called Apollonia who walked up to the chalet every morning from her parents' *alp* five hundred feet below, bringing milk and delicious butter. I started to write a science fiction story about the social effects of a mythical substance which could predetermine a baby's sex. However, like Mrs Tyndall's book on her husband, it was never finished; the press of lectures, committees, reviewing and my own serious writing and research was by now too great. But in 1926, after reading about king-worship in West Africa, I had published a science fiction tale called *The Tissue-Culture King*,[1] in which a perpetually renewed strain of royal tissue in test-tubes took the place of an embodied monarch.

There were wonderful walks, up to where the golden trollius and the great blue trumpets of the *acaulis* gentian grew; miniature climbs up the neighbouring Sparrenhorn, where we found clumps of white and pink androsace, looking like enamel brooches; and picnics by the great Aletsch Glacier, where we felt like lost ants.

My old colleague at the Rice Institute, Hermann Muller, climbed up to see us, shod only in canvas shoes; he loved the rough walking and the clear air of the heights. Our old friends David and Virginia Pye, both seasoned mountaineers, joined us in our more adventurous climbs. And before we left, Juliette and I went on a walking tour with knapsacks on our backs, up to the Grimsel Pass with its superb views of the giants of the Oberland.

Anthony and Francis throve and scrambled, as well as conducting their own experiments with Tyndall's apparatus. They claimed to be on the brink of some great discovery when sorrowfully we had to pack up and depart.

In September, after visiting Anthony at Dauntsey's School, we went on the first of several riding week-ends at Marlborough, this time accompanied by Eileen Power, the charming and learned woman who had written brilliant books on mediaeval history – especially the wool trade and its effects.

[1] Republished in *Great Science Fiction by Scientists* by Collier Books, New York, 1962.

The riding master was a strict sabbatarian, so we could ride only on Saturday afternoons and Monday mornings. The rides were glorious, over the open downs or through the unspoilt glades of Savernake Forest.

After other visits to Dauntsey's we explored the Marlborough Downs, Martinsell Hill with its vast coombe and its double street of Iron Age pit-dwellings, Tan Hill (corrupted into St Anne's Hill) with its pre-Roman earthworks, the West Wood to the north, as dark and mysterious as Meredith's Woods of Westermain and, from the crest, broad, sweeping views over what the younger Massingham had called, to my delight, 'the pinguid vale of Pewsey'.

In November I was approached by Sir Peter Chalmers-Mitchell, Secretary of the Zoological Society. He was about to retire, and asked me if I would like to apply for his job. He had previously asked me, when I returned from America during the First World War, if I would like to be Superintendent of the Zoo: but as this was mainly concerned with looking after the feeding and health of the animals, and I had no experience in such matters, I turned it down. To be Secretary was quite another matter: I would deal only with matters of general policy, and with advising and reporting to the Council. Furthermore, the salary was high for those days (£1,200 p.a.), with a comfortable flat and a big study in the Zoo offices thrown in, not to mention a couple of little rooms over the restaurant at Whipsnade, the country branch of the Zoo, with animals roving free or in large paddocks, which Chalmers-Mitchell had recently established on the windy downs near Dunstable.

So I agreed to apply, and was duly summoned before Council, which met monthly in a special room at the Zoo's offices. It was a formidable body, presided over by the aged and eccentric Duke of Bedford. Other members included Lord Onslow, pompous but kindly in a rather patronizing way; H. G. Maurice, retired head of the Fisheries Office, with a typical Civil Service outlook; Major Pam, a wealthy and able Jewish business man, who had presented to the Society a splendid collection of birds and mammals from South America, feeding them himself during the voyage; Professor McBride, the zoologist (and my scientific enemy, because I had publicly attacked his belief in the inheritance of acquired characters); Alfred Ezra, another rich Jew, a friendly person, who found relaxation from his financial affairs by keeping humming-birds, which he used to let out to fly in his London rooms and even in the open air in the country. Altogether a curious assemblage, largely of wealthy amateurs, self-perpetuating and autocratic.

After some questioning which established my reputation as a zoologist, and the fact of my wide travels and contacts, my appointment was ratified. I took Juliette round our new premises, and when we reached the study we found that Chalmers-Mitchell had created an entirely black setting for himself – black walls, black carpet, black curtains and even a black ceiling. 'My goodness,' she said, 'the man must have a womb complex!' The study and the flat were redecorated, and we settled in. During the early summer of 1935, I began my strangely miscellaneous duties.

Next year (1936) I was sent on a tour of Continental zoos, including Vincennes in Paris, Liège, Bremen, Frankfurt and Munich. I also met Jean Delacour (later a member of the Zoo Council), who lived at Claire, near Dieppe; this remarkable man had a private zoo in the wide park of his château and let several of his animals completely free in the grounds. There were parakeets screeching in the trees, and gibbons swinging from branch to branch. These would come down at Delacour's call and advance on their hind feet, balancing themselves with their upraised arms, to be caressed and given titbits. He also showed me his flamingoes stalking about in their beautiful pink plumage, due to the B vitamin in their diet of shrimps. His free-roving gibbons gave me the idea of the gibbon island at Whipsnade, and his flamingoes the plan for the flamingo island in view of the restaurant.

This wonderful park was completely destroyed in the Second World War and the château burnt to the ground. Poor Delacour was only just able to escape to the US with a few of his precious birds; however, he went gallantly to work again, advising a Californian zoo and collaborating in a splendid monograph on the world's water-fowl.

At Bremen, the Director, one of the Hagenbeck brothers, proudly showed me what he described as '*ein synthetischer Auerochs*', a reconstruction of the original wild bull or aurochs of the German forests by means of a series of crosses between different breeds of domestic cattle. The aurochs was famed in early times as the most dangerous of all wild animals. The synthetic animal was not so fierce, though he looked very grand.

At Frankfurt they were starting an imaginative new policy, fully realized after the war – creating beautiful scenery *inside* the buildings and giving the utmost liberty to their occupants. Tropical birds of all kinds flew among the visitors and perched in the exotic foliage, confined to their aviary simply by a fringed curtain at the exit. This was an important step for non-dangerous captive creatures, hitherto narrowly confined. It is now widely extended to zoos and private collections, relying on mutual trust between animals and men. The recently-built tropical house at Chester Zoo, for instance, is planned in a similar way to the bird-room at Frankfurt: both have little waterfalls trickling through tropical foliage, with birds flitting free from branch to branch.

Perhaps this is the place to say a few words about zoos in general, in the light of my own experience. First, is it right to deprive animals of their liberty and make a public spectacle of them? This to my mind depends on the type of animals and on the accommodation provided. I see nothing wrong in confining invertebrates, fish, amphibians, and reptiles, even huge creatures like crocodiles, pythons and giant tortoises. Nor do I find it wicked to confine birds and mammals, but with the important proviso that they have enough space for exercise and opportunities to enjoy themselves.

Here I think the London Zoo was at fault, especially in regard to the larger predatory birds and most mammals. The cages were too small, there were not enough opportunities for play and exercise, and visitors were encouraged to feed their favourite animals, often with serious effects on their digestion. It was tragic to see the splendid giant gorilla moping and solitary in his little cage, and the lions and tigers reduced to endless and aimless pacing up and down. Today this has been partially rectified – the young chimps obviously enjoy demonstrating a natural buffoonery at their tea-parties, and some gibbons have full scope for their acrobatic gifts in an open-air enclosure.

A large open-air aviary has been constructed, but many of the birds in it seem to prefer standing around to free flying. The humming-bird house is the only place where the visitor can be sure of enjoying birds flying round his head, but is still too small for my liking.

The London Zoo has always tried to assemble the largest possible variety of species. This policy is scientifically important, as evidenced by the value of the prosector's findings on the cause of death in zoo animals, by the Secretary's and curators' reports on the habits and development of their charges, and more recently by the success of its new laboratories of Comparative Pathology in assisting medical progress. It is also educationally valuable to the public as a living museum, demonstrating the extraordinary variety of animal types and their remarkable adaptations. On the other hand, it has the disadvantage of reducing the space available for each species.

Zoos enjoy another advantage. In housing their animals, they can experiment with new and striking architectural designs, too advanced for general acceptance outside. Thus I am sure that Lubetkin's beautiful penguin pool, with its intersecting spiral ramps, has encouraged various exciting plans for public buildings.

On balance, I am *for* zoos, always provided that they are properly run, under a liberal-minded and scientifically competent council, that the animals are kept healthy and given enough space to avoid claustrophobia, and finally, that full advantage should be taken of educating visitors in the scientific interest of the exhibits. (This has now been done in London, by introducing press-button records, which explain the habits and distribution of specially interesting animals.)

I used to walk round the Zoo grounds every week-day after breakfast, making contact with my colleagues and the keepers (a fine lot of men), and inspecting the animals in various houses. The Superintendent, Geoffrey Vevers, became a close friend; he had abandoned a medical career for this post at the Zoo, and had to travel a good deal to arrange for exchanges of animals with foreign zoological gardens. We still visit him in his retirement at Whipsnade, where he lives in a bungalow built with his own hands.

Our greatest pleasure was to spend the week-end on the job at Whipsnade. A part of the grounds was not utilized for animals, and in summer we used to camp there, first in tents and later in a couple of shacks. In winter, we slept comfortably in the flat, and bought food from the restaurant for picnics, looking at the magnificent view across the valley to Ivinghoe Beacon. We bought a couple of Iceland ponies, Thor and Odin, which we and the boys used to ride round the park before the gates were open to the public, or after they were closed. The tigers stalked them with grim if vain purpose, the polar bears scared them, and the ponies were all too anxious to get on. Elsewhere, however, they trotted happily, enjoying the exercise as much as we did. Sometimes we went across the valley near Ashridge and rode full-size horses through the beautiful park, which I had often explored on foot or bicycle when staying at Stocks.

The boys were given a .22 rifle and enjoyed stalking the numerous rabbits (this was before the myxomatosis epidemic). Under Alan Best's guidance, they got quite good at providing their own supper and cooking it, a valuable training in self-sufficiency.

After London and the formal parties, the responsibilities and the telephone calls, we always looked forward to these week-ends of relaxation and simple games, with songs round a bonfire. And so did our friends, who happily joined in whatever we were doing, riding, cooking, playing deck-quoits or just gardening. Juliette had always longed for a garden, which was denied her in the London Zoo, and had coaxed a small plot into cultivation. I remember a visit from Paul Rotha, the film expert, which coincided with the delivery of elephant-dung for some apple trees. He gallantly helped to spread the opulent manure, which soon demonstrated the inefficiency of proboscidean digestion by giving rise to a rich crop of oats and barley . . .

Meanwhile things went smoothly enough at council meetings,

but the old Duke of Bedford was a difficult man. He had been one of those who had introduced the American grey squirrel into England, which resulted in our more beautiful red species being ousted from most of its British haunts. He ran a private zoo at Woburn Abbey, which included some European bison, the increasingly rare survivors of the animals painted by prehistoric man on the cave-walls at Altamira and Lascaux. He also possessed the world's only herd of Père David's deer from China, with antlers quite different from those of any other species of deer, surviving in monastery gardens until the Boxer rebellion, when all those left in China were slaughtered. The council were concerned at this state of affairs. They felt that the future of these two rare species should be assured by breeding more of them in the London Zoo or at Whipsnade, so I was sent to Woburn Abbey to broach the subject to the Duke.

It was an extraordinary experience, reminiscent of eighteenth-century England. At the lodge I was confronted by a top-hatted porter in uniform, who sent me on half-way up the mile-long drive to a sentry-box, where another porter in similar rig had been warned of my coming by telephone. He again checked my bona fides, and rang up the mansion, so that I was greeted on the door-step by a butler and two uniformed footmen. I was then led along corridors adorned with ancestral portraits, to await His Grace's pleasure in the Guardi room, whose walls were plastered with the Venetian's brilliant paintings of life in his native city – more of them than in any public gallery!

Finally the Duke arrived, and we set out to see the park and its animals in an old car, very high-sprung to go easily over the bumps. At each enclosure we stopped; the Duke handed a bunch of keys to a footman in the back; the footman unlocked the gate and the car passed through; the gate was relocked; and the footman handed the keys back to his master. Again I felt transported back in time.

I did my best to persuade the Duke, but he was adamant; in spite of the risk of disease breaking out in the Père David herd and wiping the whole species off the face of the earth, he insisted on keeping them all at Woburn. As regards the European bison, he allowed the Zoo to have one female, but refused a bull from which we could raise a herd. The Zoo had to wait until after his death to obtain more of these precious animals.

I wanted to make the most of the scientific opportunities provided by the Zoo and got permission for Professor Honigman, a refugee from Nazi Germany, to work in the Zoo laboratory. I suggested that he should study the digestion of sloths by using coloured grains in their food. He found that it took about three weeks for these grains to reappear in the faeces, so proving the sloth's digestive processes to be as sluggish as its movements.

There are no mammals so slow of movement as the sloths. I suppose they get away with it because they are safe from predators while hanging upside down in the branches of tall forest trees, and are inoffensive, feeding only on leaves and fruits. However, this does not explain the slowness of their digestive processes, which I confess surprised and fascinated me. I don't know if anyone will ever come up with an answer to this peculiar slow-motion way of life.

I was also approached by another refugee, Ludwig Koch, who specialized in sound recording. I gave him permission to record the sounds produced by the zoo animals in London and Whipsnade, and in 1938 we published a joint book, with text by me, sound recordings by Ludwig, and splendid photographs by Ylla, called *Animal Language*. His enthusiasm for his subject knew no bounds: he would rush into my study and demonstrate the uncouth noises made by a mother camel and her young, or the difference he swore he could detect in the sea-lions' 'vocabulary', which seemed to me merely a succession of grunting barks.

He had already, with Max Nicholson's text, published a similar 'sound book' on the songs of British birds and two sets of recordings, often obtained at the cost of long hours of chilly waiting, which formed the basis of the BBC Sound Recording Library, of great value both to scientists, especially ornithologists, and BBC producers.

Meanwhile, in London, I was busy nearly every evening in my study, preparing a book on evolution. This was to cover not only variation and natural selection, but every topic bearing on the subject, from the biochemical basis of heredity to the evolution of consciousness, with its effects on human cultural development, and the problem of defining evolutionary progress. It was a vast task, but I forged steadily ahead and completed it in 1941, after five years of slogging. I got into trouble with my publishers for making so many alterations in proof; but it finally came out under the title *Evolution, the Modern Synthesis*, in 1942, just after I left the Zoo.

It seems to have been useful, for it continued to sell both in Europe and North America, and in 1964 was republished with an introduction summarizing new studies published in the intervening twenty-two years. It is perhaps the work I am most proud to have achieved.

Stimulated by the controversies over classification which I came across while writing it, I took a leading part in founding a new body, the Systematics Association, which led to fruitful discussions on the principles of classification of animals and plants, on the Latin names to be retained or rejected, on evolutionary trends, etc. Partly due to its work, largely under the guidance of my friend Francis Hemming (p. 261) the scientific nomenclature of animals has become reasonably stabilized, though that of plants has remained more confused, probably because new types formed by hybridization are much more common in plants.

As a result of these discussions, I introduced a new term, the *cline*, to denote a series of forms grading between one distinctive type and another. This rapidly came into general use and much confusion has been cleared away as to whether one should call closely related forms true species, sub-species, or mere varieties, each with their own Latin names.

The Council meetings continued, with their rather boring agenda. We used to give lunch to the members beforehand, and on one occasion had invited Sir John Ellerman to join us. He was no mean naturalist, specializing in rodents, and had prepared the official check-list of the group for the Natural History Museum. (Some people said that he was only interested in mammals which were small, nocturnal, ugly or neglected by the general public!) He was also very rich, having inherited the Ellerman Line and many other valuable assets.

He soon was co-opted to the Council and later agreed to give money for a special house for nocturnal animals, mostly rodents, to be illuminated by infra-red light. Maxwell Fry was to be the architect. He had already built the charming shelter with undulating roof at the Zoo's north entrance. I warned him that Ellerman would be much more interested in the comfort of the animals than in the design of the buildings. This proved to be true: when our discussion was over, Max said to me: 'The rat indeed has a friend!'

However, the war put a stop to Fry's elegant plans. All building at the Zoo came to an end, revenue from visitors slumped, and moreover Sir John announced that, what with paying nineteen shillings and sixpence in the pound in income tax (although I calculated that this would leave him with about £40,000 a year tax-free!), he simply could not underwrite the Rodent House, or help in any more direct way. (Today, thanks to Charles Clore, a much finer house for small mammals has been constructed, with bats and badgers, armadilloes and bush-babies, as well as rodents, in its nocturnal section.)

The Children's Zoo was another pet scheme of mine. I got permission from the Crown Commissioners to take in a narrow strip of Regent's Park, and some of my friends enjoyed working out what animals should be shown and how to accommodate parents who wanted to see how their offspring were behaving. This was approved by the Council in principle, but again war prevented the project from being carried out as planned. A modified version of the Children's Zoo was created on another site and was an immediate success. I was asked to show it and the rest of the Zoo to the present Queen and her sister. I was delighted to find that they behaved like all other children in the tunnels, running and shouting through them, and again like all other children, delighting in petting the ponies, fondling the rabbits and laughing at the baby chimps in the Children's Zoo.

Another project was not so fortunate. After seeing the success of the little news cinema at Victoria Station, and getting a promise of co-operation from its manager in obtaining programmes, I proposed building a cinema in the Zoo, which would show only films about animals, the news, and animal cartoons such as Walt Disney's Mickey Mouse and Donald Duck. I thought, and still think, that many parents, weary of tramping all over the Zoo with their children, would welcome paying a small fee to get a little rest, with entertainment thrown in.

So I arranged for a sample showing of films to the Council. The idea was not approved, mainly on the grounds that it would lower the prestige of the Zoo as a learned society, in spite of the fact that the cinema would be instructing the public about animals. The whole thing was rejected, and I still regret it.

I had obtained permission for Sir Kenneth Clark, who had become Director of the National Gallery at the early age of thirty-one, to attend our meetings as adviser on art and design. He strongly supported my suggestion that we should purchase John Skeaping's life-size mahogany carving of a horse, and this was duly erected at Whipsnade, on the round terrace overlooking the Dunstable downs. It was a grand piece of untamed vigour and beauty, and gave pleasure to many visitors. However, several members of the Council complained that it was not sufficiently realistic, that its fetlocks were not like those of a proper horse, and so on. When I left the Zoo, the Council consigned it to the rubbish-heap and let it remain there for years, untended and deteriorating. It was finally rescued and restored by the Coventry Museum, where it looks very handsome.

Eric Kennington, another of our artist friends, much admired the open-air setting of Skeaping's horse. He owned a lovely statue by Eric Gill, a nude torso on bended knees, called *Humanity*, and offered it to Whipsnade for the bare cost of its carriage.

'Humanity' was an exquisite example of Eric Gill's best work, and both Kenneth Clark and I thought it would look lovely in the little garden behind the Whipsnade restaurant. However, the Council turned it down flat: I suspect because it was a female nude, but also perhaps because they resented the manner of my proposing it as if it were a *fait accompli*. They were a tight group in love with their authority, and I never learnt, as Chalmers-Mitchell had known so well, how to play them into believing that my suggestions were really their own. The sculpture was later bought by the Tate Gallery as a notable example of modern art.

I had various other tussles with the Council over design, especially regarding a new elephant house, towards which a rich Indian maharajah had offered a large sum of money. The Council objected to Lubetkin's designs for it as too modern, too devilish ingenious, it wouldn't fit with the other buildings around it, etc. I lobbied all I could, and after endless confabulations finally got the Council's reluctant agreement. But once more the war intervened; the foundation work which had been done was left to crumble, and the project was abandoned.

After the war the new Council got Sir Hugh Casson to design the present elephant house. I admit that it is more commodious than Lubetkin's would have been, but, though I much admire Casson's buildings in general, this looks too much like a gigantic multiple oast-house for my liking.

I have already spoken of the foundation and functions of PEP, the independent organization for political and economic planning. After the war it was decided to broaden its scope, and in 1941 the Dartington Hall trustees, headed by Leonard Elmhirst and his brilliant wife Dorothy (who is, alas, now dead), widow of the rich American Willard Straight, financed a PEP inquiry into the arts, to include the visual arts (painting, craft-work and design), drama and ballet, music and documentary films. They already had an efficient arts department at Dartington which trained students in all these fields, exhibited their work, and gave music and drama festivals. Students and local residents formed the bulk of the performers, but professional talent was called in when needed. These festivals and exhibitions attracted large numbers of visitors from all over the country, and did a great deal in fostering a love of the arts among the general public in Devon.

Presumably because I had no official connection with art, I was made chairman of the Visual Arts Group in 1942, not an easy position, since the other members were all professionals – artists, designers, art critics and art historians. They included Misha Black the designer; Barnett Freedman the painter; Henry Moore, now recognized as that rare phenomenon, a great English sculptor; Sir Kenneth Clark, a director of the National Gallery and head of the Home Publicity division of the Ministry of Information during the early years of the war, which included films and war artists' paintings, trustee of the British Museum, and well-known writer on literary, dramatic and artistic history; Eric Newton the art critic; John Rothenstein, director of the Tate Gallery; Philip James, director of CEMA, the Council for the Encouragement of Music and the Arts; and one or two others. Christopher Martin, director of the Arts department at Dartington, and Peter Cox, his assistant, acted as secretaries.

Our discussions were sometimes stormy. Metropolitan personalities sometimes did not realize the importance of encouraging art outside London, while the heads of provincial galleries grumbled at their meagre financial support and their frequent lumping with archaeological collections in local museums. The traditionalists often opposed the encouragement of modern art, and it was hard to convince the Ministry of Education and local education authorities that 'art' was not just a matter of copying, and that art appreciation – through visits to galleries and notable buildings, and by way of reproductions of good pictures, old and new – should be fostered for all students, whether or not they were in special Arts departments.

However, we plugged along, and reported in 1944. We recommended that the aid given to contemporary painters under the war artists' scheme should be continued in peacetime; that the Arts Council now set up, partly as a result of our pressure, to take the place of CEMA should be an autonomous body, though financed by the government, with the Minister of Education to represent it in Parliament; that the Council of Industrial Design established early in 1944 (again largely as a result of our recommendations) should be liberally financed by the Board of Trade and should set up design centres for exhibition and training.

As regards art in schools, we had to consider two problems: the art schools themselves, and the role of art and aesthetic appreciation in general education. We recommended that art teachers should be better paid and have leisure to paint or sculpt themselves; that mere copying should be replaced by freedom for students to paint and draw as they pleased, while problems of technique should be dealt with later; and that the present rigid examination system should be replaced by reports by outside inspectors, all competent artists or critics.

We also recommended that art should play its due part in general education, by allowing all children to paint or model (with interesting results, as exhibitions of child art have proved), by introducing art as an optional subject in adult education and by familiarizing children with good painting, whether by visits to galleries or by way of colour reproductions.

This last recommendation led me, when head of UNESCO, to produce a series of colour-prints of good paintings, classical or modern, from all over the world, which were widely used in schools of many countries. The revelation of the urge to artistic expression, both in children and adults, led to UNESCO granting substantial aid to art teaching in schools and colleges of under-developed countries. Experience proved that even in areas like East Africa, where there was little indigenous art, good painting and sculpture could be achieved when proper facilities were provided.

We recommended exchange exhibitions of art and design between Britain and other countries. Such exchanges have enjoyed great success, as evidenced by the crowds drawn to foreign collections at the Royal Academy and the Tate.

And finally we recommended that art history should be included in the curriculum of schools, and greater attention paid to it in the universities.

The group certainly achieved some important results, notably in persuading the Government to set up the Arts Council and the Council for Industrial Design, with adequate financial support; but it also improved the professional art schools, and the position of the arts in the general school curriculum. It led in various ways to a better appreciation, both of classical and modern art, by the general public (though today I am beginning to wonder whether modern art isn't becoming too bizarre in its abstractions and surrealist dreams, its interest in novelty for its own sake).

Poor Chris Martin died just before the report was published. The Elmhirsts commissioned Henry Moore to carve a memorial to him: it still stands, a lovely reclining female figure, the stone now tinted with green moss, above Dartington Hall's mediaeval tilting-ground.

I was much gratified by the remarks of the Dartington Trustees in their preface to our report, in which they said that my ability to direct and synthesize the group's discussions, my sense of humour, my energy and impatience for results, were invaluable in the laborious task of collecting and analysing the mass of facts involved in the survey. But though it was hard work and I was badly overtired at the end, I learned much from the inquiry, and was able to profit largely from the experience when I was in charge of UNESCO's programme.

In August 1938 we had what was to be our last peaceful summer holiday for many years. We packed the boys and ourselves in the car, and went to stay in Switzerland, first with Juliette's mother in Neuchâtel, and then in an enchanting hill village in the Tessin, Ronco near Ascona, overlooking Lago Maggiore.

I remember that holiday with special tenderness: everything about it had an imaginative simplicity and charm. Waking up at the *Voce del Deserto*, an abandoned inn, we could reach out of the window to the delicious grapes that grew over the decaying house, grapes with a pagan taste, warmed by the early sun. And the whole magnificent panorama of mountains framing the lake rolled out beneath us, consoling and immutable. (Alas, it was not immutable; all this delightful bit of country has now been colonized by too many rich Germans.) We went to meals with Swiss friends of Juliette's near by, and explored the hidden valleys which feed the

Tessin river. The boys were happy and adventurous, climbing and swimming, discovering a new fauna and flora with stick-insects and scorpions, giant aloes and cactus. Yet Hitler was vociferating his threats too often and too loudly for us to remain undisturbed. Suddenly came the news of Munich, and Chamberlain's gesture of appeasement with its undertone of desperation. This we feared meant war, and we hastened back at once.

Anthony had already gone home by train, to be in time for the autumn term at Dauntsey's school. Francis drove back with us: we had come round Paris and were speeding along a straight *route nationale* towards Abbeville at about 80 m.p.h. when the accident happened. A little donkey-cart with three children in it suddenly swerved across the road, a bare twenty yards in front of us. I swerved and put on the brakes so sharply that a back tyre burst and swung us violently round into a tree. By a miracle we hit it not head-on but sideways, while the donkey cart, whose wheel we had just grazed, capsized on the other side of the road.

Silences occur at such moments, when shock inhibits the vital processes. We all remembered this silence, this apprehension of death. I was laid concussed and bleeding on the grass verge, where Juliette and Francis had managed to drag me, to find a jabbering crowd suddenly emerged from an apparently deserted country-side. They had heard the bursting of the tyre and the smash against the tree. A doctor arrived shouting '*Où sont les morts?*' and a priest soon after, offering to give us extreme unction. The doctor put in a few stitches where I had been cut, and when I winced, he laughed and said, '*Ah, les Boches vous feront bien plus mal que ça!*'

We sent Francis to Gordonstoun, the interesting school in Scotland founded by Kurt Hahn. We liked Hahn's system of entrusting increasing responsibility to boys, and sending them on special assignments on land or sea: out of this grew the Outward Bound movement which is now flourishing both in Britain and various ex-colonies.

For all of us in Britain, the months that followed were times of great strain and stress. 'Peace in our time', Chamberlain had said on his return from Munich. But we knew in our hearts that war was almost inevitable, that all plans had to be conditioned to that imminence, that forces beyond our control were being released. It was a twilight epoch, profoundly disturbing yet with moments of intense joy, made more poignant by the looming threat.

In the spring of 1939, I went on a yacht with some conservationist friends, Max Nicholson, James Fisher and Pip Blacker, to the remotest area in Britain, the St Kilda archipelago beyond the Hebrides.

The journey itself was interesting enough. We landed on Mull, sadly over-grazed by red deer. Here Nicholson later set up a National Nature Reserve, and proved that the deer, if properly culled, did not cause erosion and could provide revenue in the shape of venison.

In the Outer Hebrides we saw one of the few remaining 'black houses' with no windows, in which so many crofters used to live – a sad reminder of the bad old times. During our further passage, a forty-foot whale-shark came to inspect us. Peaceable and toothless, they feed like baleen whales by straining plankton through a curtain of horny filaments. I prodded the monster with a boat-hook to keep it from damaging the yacht, and with a flick of its great tail it disappeared into the depths.

On Hirta, the main island of St Kilda, the village of windowless cottages had been abandoned a few decades earlier, because the people could no longer stand their isolation – or their diet, which consisted mainly of fulmar breasts stewed in porridge, puffins and young gannets. They hardly ever went fishing, but relied almost entirely on sea-birds for their food, netting the adults and stealing the fat nestlings. Fulmars and other petrels nested in abundance on the cliff edges, providing oil for lamps and feathers for mattresses, while the bird carcasses were cold-stored in stone outhouses called *clachans*.

The ecology of the place was curious. The village house-mice had adopted the habits of field-voles and had become larger in size. The local wren had evolved into a new sub-species, bigger than our common mainland type, and with a quite distinctive song. The absence of bushes, and the distance from the mainland, had discouraged tree and meadow pipits, and the hardier rock-pipit, usually confined to rocky cliffs and sea-beaches, had spread all over the grassy slopes (today, Fisher tells me, meadow pipits have become abundant). At the summit of the great cliff of Connachair we saw a unique ecological mix-up – an oceanic fulmar on its nest, surrounded by a border of very unoceanic primroses.

Fulmars eject the oily contents of their crops at intruders, a habit which certainly deters marauding gulls. As I scrambled up a cliff I was confronted by a sitting fulmar less than a yard away, making preparatory throat movements for this unpleasant performance. I nearly fell off the ledge, but just managed to duck my head, so avoiding the nasty 'spit in the eye'.

The neighbouring island of Soay was by now the only home of free-roaming Soay sheep, a goat-like breed that must have been imported in Neolithic times; but its sheer rocky cliffs prevented us from landing.

Finally we sailed the ten miles to Boreray and landed with some difficulty on the slippery rocks. We had a stiff climb up the grassy slopes, at an angle of forty-five degrees, always in danger of stepping into puffin burrows. The whole cliff on the far side, and its two great rock pillars looking as if some giant had thrust them into the sea, were white with gannets. Our efforts at counting the nesting birds (for the world census of the species that Fisher was making) were somewhat interfered with by the members of another party, shooting across us at the domestic sheep with which the island was stocked. However, we managed to reach an estimate of 12,000 pairs of gannets, while they brought down a fat sheep. I helped one of the 'sportsmen' to roll it down to the cliff, over which we pitched it, having been assured by our old skipper that it would float. Float it did, and provided all of us with an excellent mutton supper that night.

Leaving the archipelago next day, we sailed north, past the

remote rocks of Sula Sgeir and Sule Skerry, the habited island of Rona, it too now abandoned by its original crofters. Here we found Frank Darling and his wife studying the mating habits of seals: an easy job, for the great beasts hauled themselves up to the Darlings' cottage, grunting and occasionally fighting, but a potentially dangerous one too, for the old males resent any invasion of their territory and can inflict severe wounds with their powerful canines.

Both on Sula Sgeir and Sule Skerry there were large colonies of gannets, regularly raided by the local mainlanders for food.

It was a strange voyage into a neolithic world. As one result of our trip, the St Kilda archipelago was later gazetted a National Nature Reserve by Nicholson, and so this primitive and exciting area, with all its avian inhabitants, was safeguarded, I hope for ever.

At the Zoo we had just acquired our first giant panda. It was still held in quarantine in a large cage inside the Lion House and its public exhibition was eagerly awaited. We were invited by John Spencer Churchill, Winston's brother, who lived in Regent's Park, to meet Winston at lunch and take him privately to see the extraordinary creature. Winston, not then in the Cabinet, entertained a curious interest in the animal. His daughter Mary, who was at the lunch, told us that he possessed a cherished hot-water bottle with a panda cover!

During this interesting meal Churchill suggested that I might join the 'Other Club'. He had founded it when he was refused admission to the Athenaeum, whose stuffy council could not tolerate his changes of political allegiance. I wish I could remember the list of names with which he tempted me. All I recall now were his comments, after mentioning various members' names: 'Ah, but he is dead'. 'He died a year ago!' 'No, he too is dead' – all said with the tremendous gusto of a man who was very much alive. As I already belonged to three clubs, and was also exceedingly busy, I declined the honour of joining the 'Other Club' –

and now wish I hadn't, for it contained many interesting and sometimes eccentric members.

He then asked me what, in case of the imminent war, the Zoo was arranging to do. When I told him that, *inter alia*, we planned to shoot any dangerous animals that might escape during a raid, he brooded silently and suddenly said, 'What a pity'. I was baffled and could only mutter, 'A pity, Mr Churchill?' There was a longer silence, as if wheels were revolving inside that splendid head, and then he burst out in a blaze of Churchillian rhetoric: 'Imagine a great air-raid over this great city of ours – squadrons of enemy planes dropping their bombs on London, houses smashed into ruins, fires breaking out everywhere – corpses lying in the smoking ashes – and lions and tigers roaming the desolation in search of the corpses – and you're going to shoot them! What a pity! . . .' He must have been thinking what a splendid chapter it would make in the book he was already planning about the war that had not yet broken out.

I then took him to the panda: he gazed long at the animal, lying supine and unaware of the honour done to it. Churchill shook his head approvingly, saying: 'It has exceeded all my expectations . . . and they were *very* high!'

CHAPTER XVII

War

IN late August I was at the British Association in Dundee when the news came over the radio that the storm had burst. I returned to London by the night train, my first experience of the blackout. Juliette and the boys had been in Northumberland, staying with the Charles Trevelyans; she motored back through the night, arriving at the Zoo for breakfast. I sent them all to Whipsnade for the rest of the boys' holidays, and arranged to join them at week-ends.

The first thing I did on my return was to see that the black widow spiders and the poisonous snakes were killed, sad though it was, for some snakes were very rare as well as beautiful. I closed the aquarium and had its tanks emptied; and arranged that the elephants, who might well have run amok if frightened by the expected bombing (elephants are very nervous creatures) be moved to Whipsnade. I had previously set up an air-raid squad of keepers, allowed by special dispensation to carry rifles, to be on guard during the night to deal with bombs and, as I had told Winston, to shoot any dangerous animals that might escape. There were, of course, all sorts of minor but necessary details to attend to: for instance, we had now to breed our own mealworms for feeding insectivorous birds and mammals, instead of importing them from Germany.

I also organized an Animals Adoption scheme, under which organizations or individuals could pay for the keep of any animal they fancied; in return, their names were announced on the animals' cages. This helped materially in the lean years ahead, when so many potential zoo visitors had left London for country safety.

Children everywhere were being evacuated, and we had several generous offers from North America to take our boys, but decided

249

against it. Anthony was to begin his university career at Trinity College, Cambridge in September, and Francis' school, Gordonstoun, was itself evacuated to Wales. We all hoped that the war would not last long, yet foresaw with anxiety the time when both boys would be liable for war service. They were of course called up eventually. Anthony did useful work in the plotting room at Air Force H.Q. (his eyesight prevented him from more active service), and was much in demand as writer of reports because of his command of lucid English.

Francis spent four years in the Navy, and went all over the world. He was in HMS *Ramillies* during the Normandy landings, and as the great armada was gathering towards its epic beachhead, he was called by one of his shipmates to come and listen to 'your pop's' voice. A Brains' Trust session was being broadcast live from London!

Soon after the war broke out I helped to organize a War Aims group under the auspices of PEP, to study the question of what Britain hoped to achieve if we won the war. It usually met at PEP's offices in Queen Anne's Gate, though we sometimes held meetings at Whipsnade, where our accommodation was stretched to its limits. The group included Max Nicholson, soon to be head of the Bureau of Shipping Control; Zvegintzov, an authority on international affairs; my old friend, the liberal-minded William Temple, the Archbishop of York; Betty Wallace, later Mrs Collard, who had great experience of international youth groups; Dennis Routh, of the Ministry of Education; Israel Sieff, head of Marks and Spencer, who knew everything about commercial planning; Leonard Elmhirst, with his international contacts and his successful planning at Dartington; and a few others. I also made contact with Harold Nicolson, who had stood up bravely against Neville Chamberlain at the time of Munich, but as an M.P. he thought he ought not to join the group.

We all felt that winning the war was not an end in itself: after it, there would be a fundamental confrontation of problems old and new, and in those early days, when combatants and diplomats were sparring for position, we felt the restlessness of not knowing where in fact we were going. It became for me a personal problem, to which I could not help giving much attention. The Zoo was ticking over, *au ralenti*; there was really nothing much that I, as Secretary, could do except watch over its continuance. I got myself put on a half-salary basis, for I felt strongly that running the Zoo in war-time was only a half-time job, and that I must be free to devote time and energy to other and more important problems. The Council accepted this position without demur, for the time being.

The meetings of this study group and its committees went on all through the war: I shall refer later to their outcome and to my deepening commitment.

Just after war broke out I was visited at the Zoo by Howard Thomas, then at the BBC. He invited me to take part in a weekly general knowledge programme on the radio, not a mere quiz, when a group of three or four people would be asked to discuss various questions submitted by the public, but not previously shown to the team. I was interested and said I would gladly do so; but I thought that such a programme was not likely to last very long, as the public would get tired of it. I also thought that the membership of the team might need to be changed from time to time.

We started late in 1939 at the BBC's old place at Savoy Hill, with myself, Professor Joad and Commander Campbell as guinea-pigs (Campbell had really been a ship's purser, but the BBC granted him the title of Commander, much to the Admiralty's annoyance!), and Donald McCullough as question-master.

My first prophecy was speedily proved false – the combination of an argumentative philosopher with an equally argumentative biologist, and an endearing buffoon as foil to the two intellectuals, proved irresistible. Campbell had travelled widely (one of his typical answers began, 'When I was in Patagonia . . .') and had an immense fund of miscellaneous information, not always accurate.

My other prophecy *was* correct; many distinguished (and

undistinguished!) people clamoured to be invited; quite soon we had guest-members, among whom I recall Kenneth Clark, Robert Boothby, Malcolm Sargent, Arthur Bliss, Gilbert Murray, William Beveridge and Professor Bronowski.

By the time the 'phony' war ended, we had moved to Broadcasting House in Portland Place and continued the programme there. One question, I remember, completely stumped us. It came from a young girl, who asked how a fly managed to land upside-down on the ceiling. The answer was provided much later by high-speed cinematography – the fly does not reverse and turn a back-somersault, but executes a sideways roll.

I got some amusing comments from listeners, including a post-card from Bernard Shaw (who believed in the inheritance of acquired characteristics):

'I listened in on Tuesday and thought you got mixed up between evolution and education. Education goes on for a lifetime: but the evolution of perhaps thousands of years is recapitulated and compressed into as many minutes by the foetus. My ancients who got through their childhood in four years were strictly according to Cocker[1] biologically, though of course their oviparity was a stage necessity, mammalian birth on the boards being permissible only in China.

Biology is in a bad way. The Laboratory mind is more degenerative than malaria. The descent from Huxley, Darwin and Spencer – broken by Butler, Bergson and Back to Methuselah – to the simpleton Pavlov is a precipitous *dégringolade* (Mrs Huxley will translate).

. . . our friendly recollections remain.

15.5.42.   *G.B.S.*'

He also wrote to the Editor of the *Listener* (who sent his letter on to me).

'29th Oct. 1942. *To the Editor of the Listener.*

My friend Dr. Huxley, in his broadcast on Charles Darwin, dismissed me from consideration as a biologist on the ground that I am "emotional", offering as a sample a passage from one of my prefaces, which was recited by the actor who impersonated me in such a manner as to make it sound like the raving of a sentimental drunkard.

[1] Slang for 'all correct'.

War

I am not the author of this passage. It is a quotation from the Canticle in the order for Morning Prayer entitled *Benedicite, Omnia Opera*. Dr. Huxley is unacquainted with the Book of Common Prayer, having been brought up as a Natural Selectionist; but I shall be happy to lend him my copy if he desires to verify the quotation.

Faithfully

G. Bernard Shaw.

P.S. Darwin did not exclude the emotions from the biological field. He wrote a whole book about them which I read before Dr. Huxley was born.'

The Editor of the *Listener* added that the passage *was* actually taken from G.B.S.'s *Back to Methuselah*, and of course, I knew all about Darwin's splendid book on *The Expression of the Emotions in Animals and Man*. But Shaw's approach to evolution *was* definitely emotional – he adhered passionately to his own peculiar brand of Lamarckian vitalism, and hit out violently at the 'materialist' believers in natural selection.

It was amusing for us, but also turned out to be valuable for the country's morale and reputation. After the war, when I was at UNESCO in Paris, I learned that among the most encouraging British broadcasts that the war-darkened world of France secretly listened to were the news, which they knew was unbiased; ITMA, with Tommy Handley and his comic charlady, showing that Britain could still make fun of itself; and the Brains' Trust, which demonstrated that we could continue to discuss interesting subjects dispassionately in spite of all the horrors of war.

At the Zoo life went on, though very few of the public came to see the animals. Every time there was an air-raid warning we descended to the office basement, spent the evening listening to the radio, reading and writing, and slept in camp beds. Friends often shared our shelter, including Max Fry and Jane Drew (who became engaged there), and Jack Haldane, who had suffered a direct hit in a public shelter and felt that our basement was perhaps a little safer than the cement pill-boxes offered to the public, or even the platforms of the Underground. We were in fact lucky that the building never had a direct hit, as we should certainly not have survived it.

We motored down to Whipsnade for the week-ends, coasting wherever possible to make our petrol ration last, and these little moments of peace in the country made an enormous difference. One Saturday night the Germans dropped a cluster of incendiary bombs in and near the London Zoo. A church and a number of houses were badly damaged, but thanks to our well-trained air-raid protection squad the fires in the Zoo itself were quickly extinguished before any harm was done. When I returned on Monday, I asked the head of the air-raid squad to report. He made light of the danger but had been struck by the macabre loveliness of the scene. 'Oh, it was beautiful,' he said, 'really beautiful – only wanted a spot of music to make it just like Fairyland.' His name, I may add, was Shelley . . .

We were at Whipsnade, too, when the first terrible raid on the City took place. We could see the ominous glare of the flames from our windows thirty miles away. Back in London I took an hour off to see the damaged area. It was fantastic. All round St Paul's one looked through gaping shop-fronts, where ARP squads and firemen were still quenching the smouldering debris, and broken glass lay in the gutters like snow-drifts: yet along the pavements there was a stream of businessmen, girl secretaries and office-workers going about their daily affairs as if everything was normal. Though the shock had gone deep, the people strode along in silent pride: 'Britain can take it.' This courage of the British under heavy bombing is a matter of history; but the post-war generation is apt to forget it, and I want to record this outstanding example.

One night, about eleven o'clock we heard a stick of bombs exploding nearer and nearer to our shelter, until the last bomb shook the foundations of the building. I put on my tin hat and went across into the Zoo to find that five bombs had hit the grounds, the Zoo's water-main had been cut and the restaurant was burning. Curiously enough, I felt no fear, but rather a sense of exhilaration. This, I later discovered, was normal in those engaged in salvage work.

Firemen soon turned up and I conducted them to the sea-lion pond, the only source of water left, which they nearly drained before the flames were under control. The camel house, the only original building remaining from the first Zoo in 1830, had been badly damaged, yet the camels were sitting in their now open cage as if nothing untoward had happened!

The Zebra House also had been smashed, luckily without damaging any of the animals. As I returned to the office, the night watchman reported that he had seen an adult zebra cantering through the tunnel out on to the Outer Circle road. The air-raid squad and I set off in pursuit, and with much manoeuvring managed to shepherd the animal back before he reached Camden Town. We headed him into the stores yard, and then tried to persuade him to enter the shed, where he could be locked in for the night. He was a Grevy zebra stallion, almost as large as a horse, and his nerves were naturally on edge. Every time the AA guns went off on Primrose Hill he backed violently – towards me, as it happened: I was frankly alarmed that he would kick me in the stomach. We did eventually coax him into the shed, and went thankfully to bed, at about four o'clock.

It had been quite a night, but I was a little disillusioned when the zebra keeper came to see me. When I told him of last night's affair, and my fear that his charge would disembowel me, he looked at me rather pityingly, surprised that his boss should be so ignorant: 'Cor, bless you, Sir, you needn't have been frightened, 'e's a biter, not a kicker . . .'

Kenneth Clark, in charge of the war artists, commissioned Carel Weight to record the zebra's escape and recapture, as one of the less usual incidents of the blitz.

During all this time, in the meetings of PEP's War Aims group, my mind was working towards whatever future we should be planning for. I wrote a memo deploring the fact that the Ministry of Information were not making any use of scientists or scientific method in their propaganda, either at home or abroad; also a few general articles for the *Spectator* and the *Fortnightly Review*, which Francis -Williams later used in a volume called *The Democratic Order*. My booklet, *Reconstruction and Peace,* was published under the pseudonym Balbus (for he was proverbially a builder, and we wanted to build better for the future), and because I did not want to compromise the Zoological Society by using my own name. It set forth the need for a sane peace without too heavy war indemnities, stressing the necessity for aid not only to the countries conquered by Hitler but also to a defeated Germany, to prevent discontent and avoid the rise of another dictatorship; to promote new industries in place of those that had been destroyed by bombing or by our own blockade, and to provide for more democratic planning in all countries.

I sent a copy to Archbishop Temple, whose reply gave me great encouragement:

August 10. 1941

My dear Julian,

I was delighted to get your book as a present from you, and also to find how closely I agreed with you. Isn't it odd how talking to Americans makes one aware of the excellence of the British Empire?

I think I go all the way with all you say. Of course the real *crux* comes in the last chapter. All the schemes which call out 'service and sacrifice' in war are almost impracticable in peace. We must find the way to let reasonable self-interest play its part in alliance with 'service' as the incentive to enterprise and effort – more to effort than to enterprise, because, to the only temperament that will indulge in it anyhow, enterprise is rather fun. But steady effort takes some real incentive to keep it up. And this self-interest need not be in the least bad: it is less good than 'service', but it is all right in second place.

What is vital is to transform the structure of society and the spirit of education *together*. Is R. A. Butler up to that?

Yours affectionately
William Ebor

In the autumn of 1941 I was invited by the Rockefeller Foundation, who had heard of our work on war aims, to lecture in the USA. The lectures were to be on general subjects, as well as on war aims, and would be useful propaganda to demonstrate how Britain was carrying on with the everyday business of life. I was also to visit various universities all over the country, to find out anything I could about American plans for the future. Though the

USA was not yet in the war, and though there was a large volume of American public opinon in favour of non-intervention, shrewder men like the Rockefeller trustees realized that the country would eventually be drawn into the conflict. They couldn't avow it publicly, but got me, as a citizen of a nation already at war, and a person who knew the USA well, to talk on post-war planning.

I asked the Zoo Council to give me leave of absence for what I thought would be only a few weeks. As I have already mentioned, I had already voluntarily relinquished half my salary, for there was virtually nothing to do at the Zoo except keep the animals fit, and this could perfectly well be done by Dr Vevers, the able superintendent. Now I said I would relinquish my salary entirely while I was away. On this the Council finally gave me a qualified authorization, adding that the decision was 'on my own head'. I felt very restless and insufficiently occupied and I longed to do more to help the war effort; so I decided to go. I sailed on a cold November day.

I didn't want any prominent Americans to be involved, so refused an invitation to stay with the Lamonts and took rooms in a mid-town hotel. Here, of course, I was confronted with a battery of reporters and photographers, who bombarded me with questions. The man from the *Evening Telegram* was particularly insistent, and took me into another room for more photographs. In answer to one of his framed questions: 'Did I hope that America would come into the fighting?' I said, rather incautiously: 'Yes, under certain conditions', and named them. He went on snapping away, once asking me to hold up my hand.

I then went on to see Warren Weaver, Secretary of the Rockefeller Foundation, to discuss my itinerary. On returning to my hotel, I suddenly found myself looking at my own picture – for there, on the front page of the *Telegram* was the photograph of me with upraised hand, with the caption, HE WANTS WAR in block lettering – nothing, of course, about my conditional phrase.

This was bad; a question was asked about me in Parliament; but worse was to come. I was deluged with offensive letters from Americans, some even containing human excrement. To escape from this persecution, I took advantage of the Elmhirsts' invitation to stay at Applegreen, the Straights' big house on Long Island (Dorothy Elmhirst had previously married Willard Straight), with lovely gardens to walk in. One day as I came down to tea the radio gave the news that the Japs had just attacked Pearl Harbour and sunk several warships of the US Fleet. The President had proclaimed a state of emergency; the US was now at war with Japan, and therefore an ally of Britain. I got no more abusive communications, and was well received wherever I lectured.

I revisited the Tennessee Valley Authority, whose beginnings I had seen in 1932. I was more than ever impressed by the imaginative development of the first nationally financed scheme to go in for multi-planning over a whole region. Its programme included such diverse projects as electric power, soil-erosion, flood-control, health, agriculture, reforestation, and liaison with the general public through schools and colleges and broadsheets. Provision had also been made for recreation – swimming, canoeing and camping on the shores of the many miles of lakes produced by the great Norris Dam and its subsidiaries.

The title of a little book I wrote on this enterprise was *T.V.A. Adventure in Planning*, which was published in 1943, and, to my pleasure, was later used by the US Information Services in their propaganda.

I obtained an indirect contact with the President through his wife, Eleanor, though she was (typically) so busy that it had to take place in the Presidential car on the way from the White House to the airport. She was a very intelligent and liberal-minded person, and I suspect that she was able to influence her husband in many ways.

I also had an introduction to Felix Frankfurter, one of the most liberal of the Supreme Court judges, often consulted by Roosevelt. I told him of our work on war aims, in which he was much interested, saying that he would speak to the President on the subject. This too was the beginning of a long friendship and I kept up a correspondence with him till his death.

I also had the good fortune to meet Mr Justice Holmes, the legendary doyen of the Court. At ninety he was still extremely good-looking, with well-curled moustaches and a white slip under his waistcoat; it was he who got all the admiring glances from the women as we walked across to his club.

I remember his saying that he spent all his spare time reading the great classics of literature, 'in preparation for the Last Judgment'. Somewhat startled, I asked whether he believed that the Last Judgment would involve intellectual and artistic values as well as moral ones. 'Of course, dear boy,' he said. 'How could I face the Almighty if he asked me whether I had read Shakespeare and Goethe and Dante, and I had to confess that I hadn't. I'm sure I wouldn't be admitted to Heaven, though (with a twinkle) I don't know where he would send me. . . .'

I managed to get out to California, where I saw Aldous and Maria. He was busy writing film scripts, which he found much more lucrative than essays and novels. And I met their charming friend Anita Loos, already famous for her *Gentlemen Prefer Blondes*. She herself was a brunette, very tiny (Aldous once said he would like to keep her as a pet) and full of witty talk and interesting memories. We remained good friends, and only last summer she came to see us at Hampstead, as vivacious as ever, with a copy of her autobiography, *A Girl Like I*. It was not only very amusing but recorded the astonishing fact that she had been the main support of her family since the age of thirteen.

Aldous took me to Hollywood where they were filming *The Island of Dr Moreau*, H. G. Wells' horror story. Charles Laughton was the doctor who turned men into animals by grafting bits of animal skin on to their faces, and the stage was crowded with ghastly semi-human monsters. Indeed, the whole thing was so horrible that the film never went into circulation.

From the studios to Forest Lawn, the vast cemetery of Los Angeles, specially recommended to me by my taxi driver as a wonderful place for meditation. I didn't find it so, except on human brashness.

I gave a lecture at Leland Stanford University, where the Geology professor showed me the earth-movement – a twelve-yard lateral displacement – which had caused the great San

Francisco earthquake and subsequent fire in 1906, whereby the city was virtually destroyed. He was very gloomy about the likely repetition of the disaster – as the new city is sitting well in the centre of an earthquake belt – and marvelled that people should choose to live there.

In San Francisco itself I saw the results of the human folly which had imposed a rectangular grid on the rebuilding of the city. This meant that roads went up slopes so steep that cable-cars had to be introduced instead of ordinary trams and buses, while a really excellent scheme for roads gently winding round the hills was rejected. But intellectually, the city was liberal-minded, and the view over the bay was superb. One can only devoutly hope that the threat of further earthquakes will never materialize.[1]

Up in the sierras I was deeply struck when I beheld the giant sequoia trees, which may live three or four thousand years and are so huge that one had a road tunnelled through its trunk. These glorious monsters are the largest and longest-lived of all creatures, animal or vegetable.

The rest of my tour remains rather blurred in my memory. I went on with my chores of lecturing and inquiries about war aims – simple enough to make now that America had joined the allies. My six weeks' leave from the Zoo had long run out, and I was anxious to return to England.

I got back to New York in April, and left my report with the Rockefeller Foundation: I expect it is still in the vaults! I now felt free to accept the Lamonts' invitation to stay, and renewed my acquaintance with Marion Greenwood, who painted a portrait of me which now hangs over my study door.

It makes me look a little sad. Perhaps this was prophetic, for on April 21, 1942, I was woken (after midnight) by a reporter and informed that I had just got the sack from the London Zoo – and had I any comment? (I had not!) Next day there was a cable from Juliette with the news that my post as Secretary had been suppressed, ending with the words, 'Come back and fight it out'.

---

[1] This year (1969) I read in the papers that minor tremors are beginning and a major quake is quite likely in the near future.

But now I found a terrible difficulty in securing a passage back. Planes were all booked up, and the few allied ships travelling in convoys had no berths to spare and also had to face all sorts of hazards. It was another month before I managed to get a berth on a Portuguese ship which, sailing under a neutral flag with all its lights on at night, landed me safely in Lisbon, only to find that there were no places available on any flight for London.

However, this was my first acquaintance with that wonderful city, and I spent my enforced leisure pleasantly enough, in spite of my anxieties about the Zoo, looking at the splendid Hierony-mus Bosch and the anonymous portrait of Henry the Navigator in the art gallery, drinking coffee in the great piazza with its wavy black and white marble pavement, and admiring the unique baroque architecture of San Geronimo and other churches, where carvings of anchors and sea-creatures writhing round the pillars remind one that Portugal was once the world's premier maritime nation.

But it was unpleasant to hear Germans talking everywhere. Some perhaps were tourists; others were certainly spies, and still others were buying uranium for atomic bombs. The British Consul told me that they were offering fabulous prices, and that peasants with uranium on their land were going about in Mercedes-Benz cars, with gold fountain-pens in their pockets.

When, at long last, I got a plane back to London I found that Juliette had been summoned down from our flat, that day in April, and brusquely told by Lord Onslow, the new President, that the Council had decided to make the post of Secretary an honorary one, and to appoint a new resident Scientific Director to look after the Society's internal affairs. The Council had taken advantage of my absence to kick me out: it was as brutal as that.

Juliette, under the guidance of our friend Francis Hemming, got together a group of Fellows to protest against the Council's arbitrary decision, including Cyril Diver, James Fisher, Lord Horder, Gavin de Beer, Max Nicholson and many others. Thanks to Hemming, who was a very knowledgeable Civil Servant, as

well as a distinguished entomologist, they found that the Council
had acted out of turn in suppressing the post of paid Secretary,
which was an integral part of the Society's statutes. The
Privy Council was brought in and pronounced the decision
invalid.

Thus I was still nominally Secretary. But our group were sure
that the old Council would make things increasingly difficult for
me, and accordingly called an Extraordinary Meeting of all
Fellows, to which they proposed a new Council, more sympathetic
to me, to be headed by Lord Horder as President, with me as
Secretary and Francis Hemming as Treasurer, and R. A. Fisher,
the geneticist; Professor Goodrich; my good friend James Gray,
now Professor of Zoology at Cambridge; and Norman, the
liberal-minded Deputy Keeper of Zoology at the Natural History
Museum, as members.

The lecture hall was packed and, as the matter had attracted a
good deal of publicity, many reporters were present. *Picture Post*
had an illustrated article about the affair. I defended myself by
reminding the meeting that I had voluntarily relinquished half my
salary at the outbreak of war, and had received nothing while
speaking on behalf of Britain on my trip to America. But the
influence of the grim-faced Council was too strong, and the
meeting voted against the informal committee's proposals by
three to two. There was nothing left for me to do but resign.

As Francis Hemming wrote to me the day after the meeting:

'. . . If I thought that as Secretary you could still help the Society and,
through the Society, help the advancement of science, I would strongly
urge you to retain the post, even though the new Council includes not
one of your supporters among its members, and despite the fact that
your personal position would be extremely difficult. I am convinced,
however, that at the present moment there is nothing you can do to
help the Society, and that to remain on as Secretary would be to expose
yourself to vexations and possible humiliations to no point.

The fact that on resigning the Secretaryship you will be entirely free
will throw the door open for you for new forms of usefulness in fields
even more important than biology. I should like very much to see you

taking an important part in preparing plans for reconstruction in the social and scientific spheres, for this is a task for which you are peculiarly fitted, both by your special gifts and by your past achievements.

Yours ever
Francis.'

I received a great many letters from friends and supporters, and also from zoo keepers, deploring my resignation. The affair had certainly been mismanaged by the Council. Their attack on me while I was in America helping the cause of Britain was ill-timed and ill-natured, though I must admit that the Council had warned me that I went at my own risk, and also that, through no fault of mine, my six weeks' leave of absence had extended to five months.

It was a bitter pill to swallow but, looking back, I agree with Hemming that it was really a good thing for me. At any rate, I was now free to do as I liked. The only problem was money, not to mention somewhere to live.

The Council permitted us to retain our flat in the Zoo's office building until we found a new abode, and I worked frantically at finishing my *Evolution, the Modern Synthesis*, which was sent to the publishers at the end of the year (p. 237). It was, I think, my most influential work, and I am proud that the demand for it continued until I had to bring out a revised edition twenty years later.

Finding a fresh home was difficult. At last, as we were exploring Hampstead one early autumn day, we saw the sign 'Pond Street'. 'Let's go down it,' said Juliette. 'I remember an enchanting house I saw there once, with the door opening right through into a garden.' This turned out to be an extraordinary intuition; the very same house was marked 'To Let'. We went round the corner to the agent, inspected the house, and took it on the spot. It was in late Regency style, with no basement but a large kitchen on the ground floor, a library above, and a charming small garden with a fine ash tree in the corner. It was also within a few minutes of Hampstead Heath, where I still take my daily walks.

There were many repairs and alterations to be made, which our architect, Ernst Freud, son of the famous Sigmund, told us were going to be difficult and expensive. Seasoned wood was almost unobtainable, and we had over 4,000 books to make shelves for. However, we managed somehow and it is in my spacious library that I write these words. Juliette soon had the garden blooming and found it an endless comfort and joy. We hope to end our days in this house.

I went on with my writing and planning, as well as attending meetings of the Colonial Office education committee, and the New Naturalist Board, which Collins, the publishers, had set up to publish a comprehensive set of books on British natural history.

There are now over fifty volumes in the series, and we are continuing to bring out new ones – a tribute not only to Collins' insight, but also to the British public's interest in Nature in all her manifestations.

CHAPTER XVIII

West Africa

IN the early months of 1943, I was busy earning money from lectures and talks on the BBC; sitting on various PEP groups and committees on higher education and planning, which involved discussions with Gerald Barry, William Holford, Max Fry, his wife Jane Drew, and Pevsner, the architectural historian; acting as one of the editors of a new set of illustrated popular encyclopedias for Aldus Books; attendance at Colonial Office education committee meetings, with liberal Creech Jones, then PPS at the Colonial Office, in the chair. Here we took evidence from authorities on primitive or under-developed peoples, like Meyrowitz, Margaret Meade, Margery Perham and Gordon Childe, the brilliant but far from handsome anthropologist who eventually died during a fit of depression by falling over a cliff – perhaps deliberately? – in Australia.

I also saw that delightful man Winant, then US Ambassador to Britain, about PEP's ideas on post-war reconstruction. He too died by suicide later – was it disillusion or the effect of some terrible disease? His death was a great shock.

I also spoke to my old friend Solly Zuckerman about war aims (by a strange chance the two chief scientific advisers to the War cabinet were Solly, whose main work had been on the sexual behaviour in baboons, and Desmond Bernal, an expert on bio-chemistry and bio-physics); I attended meetings on international and colonial affairs at Chatham House, discussed post-war policies with Sir William Beveridge, the economist and social reformer; with Keen, an agricultural expert who with Max Nicholson was advising on trade contacts and our aid to the Middle East; and Watson Watt, who had been largely responsible for our radar screen against enemy aircraft; and Pearsall the botanist about plant conservation in National Parks, etc. etc. I shudder to think of all the rushing about and consultation.

For a holiday we went to Ronald Lockley's farm on Dinas Head, where soldiers were helping in pulling his flax, and where I supplemented our rations by lugging heavy sacks of fresh mussels over the hill from the next bay. We saw a tame peregrine falcon which had been trained to catch pigeons and bring them back to its trainer – many were carrier pigeons carrying messages from spies in this country to the enemy. We also visited the desolate range of hills from which the inner circle of blue stones at Stonehenge had been constructed.

Later in the year, the Colonial Office asked me to go out to West Africa as member of the Commission on Higher Education in the British Colonies there. Walter Elliot was chairman and other members included James Duff, Vice-Chancellor of Durham University, Harold Channon, cheerful biochemist from Unilever (a very enlightened firm which had many connections in West Africa), and a woman don. There were also three West African members; a doctor from Sierra Leone; a distinguished lawyer called Korsah from Ghana, who later became Chief Justice and chairman of the University College Council; and a Nigerian headmaster called Kuti, who was rather a buffoon.

Before we left in mid-January 1944, Elliot invited me and the three Africans to spend a week-end at his home in Roxburghshire. It was bitterly cold, and for the Africans their first sight of snow; yet Elliot, who prided himself on his hardiness, persisted in going out in his ordinary clothes, while the poor Africans shivered in their overcoats. As we tramped round the estate I heard an unfamiliar song: I went off with my binoculars and discovered that it was a common chaffinch, singing in what may be called a local dialect. (These local song-forms are handed down by tradition, the young birds remembering their parents' song-type when they start singing next spring.) The Africans were delighted to find that British birds, like African tribes, have their own dialects.

The flight was memorable for my first sight of West African

rain-forests, so much larger in extent and more various in composition than those in the east.

We landed in Lagos – not, at least in those days, a city with much to get excited about – and were put up in Government House, where beneficent geckos crept over the walls and ceiling, ridding the place of surplus flies and mosquitoes. Lagos was a dirty, over-crowded place, only redeemed from squalor by its magnificently clad inhabitants. The men wore indigo-coloured robes which fell in great folds to their feet, and the women brilliantly patterned gowns draped on their opulent hips, with aggressive knotted turbans. We later discovered that the British had set up a group of West African women to advise our factories in the Midlands on the sort of florid designs they preferred. I remember seeing a woman in the Gold Coast wearing a blue gown with a striking pattern of yellow cricket motifs – bat, ball and stumps; while another was covered with green hand-telephones on an orange background. What splendid bravura!

I made the acquaintance of Duckworth, a tall eccentric man with a passionate dedication to West Africa, and an unceasing flow of words. He was then helping to start a Nigerian museum, and had just taken over the editorship of *Africana*, an important new maga-zine, from K. C. Murray, the museum's chief curator. Here I first discovered the richness and variety of West African art, from Benin bronzes to masks of every description – white masks for Ibo women which had a strange Japanese look, with slit eyes and frozen features; antelope masks from the north; household and tribal idols and fetishes, and grotesquely carved stools and thrones supported by crouched human figures.

This exuberance of West African art, of which we were to see more in Ghana and Dakar, was in striking contrast to its paucity in East Africa, where there is little but plain stools and neck-rests and decorated calabashes, with a few musical instruments and bangles. This is doubtless due to the invasions of mainland East Africa by a succession of half-naked nomads from the north, who concen-trated their artistic efforts on their own bodies, with ritual scarifi-cation and mutilation, feathers in their hair and bright armlets of colobus fur, with leopard skins for major chiefs. While West Africa grew rich through trade, including slaves, in East Africa almost the only rich area was Zanzibar, the centre of the East African slave trade.

Yorubaland, the heart of Nigeria, was then a confederacy, originally of six states. Each of the 'kings' or chiefs possessed a piece of a complicated wooden jigsaw, and important decisions could not be taken until their owners had met and fitted all the pieces together. Each king had his special mouth-filling title: the three most important were the Alake of Abeokuta, the Alafin of Oyo, and the Oni of Ife, the sacred city of the confederacy.

The Alake of Abeokuta had visited us at Whipsnade when he came over for the coronation of George VI, and now received the Commission in his rather dilapidated 'palace', furnished in what I can only call Tottenham Court Road style. To entertain us he clapped his hands, gave his servant girl the key of his tea-caddy (shades of Victorian England!) and served us with an exceedingly strong syrupy mixture. Under British guidance, he had started a good school system and was interested in offering his people further opportunities at college level.

So was the Alafin of Oyo who, however, still enjoyed an almost mediaeval way of life. There was a stockade round his palace, and as the inner gates were thrown open to our delegation, a court jester made three double somersaults back and forth, then ushering us into the royal presence. The Alafin was on a high dais surrounded by his court officials. In older days, before Lugard had imposed peace and federation on Nigeria, there were nearly a hundred of these, and even today there were plenty. The Master of the Horse, looking like a burly executioner, was alarmingly close to me. I remembered Frazer in his *Golden Bough* describing the method of despatching an unpopular Alafin who refused to take the hint of a dish of parrots' eggs and clear out: he was promptly decapitated by just such a grim figure of a man. Why parrots' eggs were used to convey the message, I never discovered.

We then partook in a ceremony of friendship. We and the Alafin were given kola nuts on the back of our outstretched hands, a gesture which proved we were not holding concealed weapons; the nuts were then exchanged, and had to be chewed. They are very bitter, and contain a depressant and soothing alkaloid, which both promotes and symbolizes non-aggression. I was fascinated to be plunged into this world of barbaric ritual, so much in contrast with our ensuing discussion on higher education.

The Commission now moved to Ibadan, then the largest town in black Africa. It was not the seat of a king, but had grown in less than a century from a local market into a city with nearly 100,000 inhabitants – though alas, as so often in Africa, the houses were mostly roofed with galvanized iron. After a discussion with leading notables, all clad in splendid robes, we decided to recommend it as a site for a university college.

Here again we were on the fringe of a changing way of life, for Ibadan was still a cult-centre for the thunder god. I was taken through a maze of little streets to his 'temple' – a dark little tin-roofed shack, inhabited by an aged priestess in white robes, amidst various cult-objects, including a trident. Tridents I had already seen in East Africa, but it was easier to understand how this symbol of Poseidon the sea-god (or perhaps of Zeus, lord of thunder and lightning) had made its way from the Mediterranean to the coast of Kenya, than across the Sahara to this land-locked market town.[1]

The priestess consented to my taking her photograph, trident in hand. But she made her assistant bring out a piece of corrugated iron for her to stand it on, so that the power of the trident to prevent thunderstorms should not leak away into the unsanctified earth. We later found that young chiefs and 'kings' were, for the same reason, not allowed to let their bare feet come in contact with the ground.

Our next port of call was the little town of Ife, whose king or Oni was now the station-master – a fallen monarch, for Ife had originally been the capital of all Yorubaland. Duckworth had told

[1] Today, however, archaeological research has shown that the climate of the Sahara was much milder after the end of the last glacial epoch, and that it was crossable by horse-chariot well after 1000 B.C.

me of the strange bronze and terracotta heads which had been excavated here by the German archaeologist Frobenius, in the early years of the century. He had taken the best of them to Berlin (we had similarly stolen many splendid bronzes from Benin and sacred objects from Ashanti), but many were left at Ife. When I asked to see them, I was taken to the so-called Town Hall, a ramshackle building in pseudo-Yoruba style with crudely painted walls, and found the heads lying on and under a deal table in one of the public rooms, at the mercy of careless or thieving hands.

I was shocked: one glance was enough to convince me of their unique importance. They were in what I can only describe as a classical style, handsome and realistic portraits of sacred kings and their wives, with regular features, totally unlike the fetishes and masks of the rest of West Africa.

This type of realistic sculpture, involving the *cire perdue* method of bronze-casting, must also, it seems to me, have been brought across the desert from the Mediterranean. This impression was strengthened by the repetition of the trident motif on the huge, curved pillar representing a sacred elephant's tusk, which stood in a grove just outside the town. The male Ife heads had a hole in the top of the cranium, apparently designed for the insertion of a real elephant's tusk: the elephant was, after all, the chief symbol of royalty in West Africa, as was the lion in the East. This characteristic hole for the insertion of a tusk is also found in some of the royal bronze heads in Benin, whose art was certainly derived from that of Ife, though much Africanized in the process, and with traces of Portuguese influence.[1]

I sat up half the night writing to the Governor in Lagos, pleading that a safe place should be found for these magnificent relics. In due course a museum was built in Ife and the collection was housed there, together with more sculptures unearthed by systematic excavation – though I fear that many precious objects disappeared

---

[1] The latest study of the Ife heads maintains that they wore crowns instead of tusks, and that their style was autochthonous. However, I still feel that some Mediterranean influence was at work, notably in the method of casting. *Cire perdue* is a very complicated business, and I find it hard to believe that it was independently developed by African Negroes, however cultured.

in the years before the secretariat made up its mind to spend government money on a mere art project.

Shortly after leaving Ife I crossed the Benue River, accompanied by the local D.C., to talk with the chief on the opposite bank about schools in his area. As at Oyo, all had to be done in accordance with ancient ritual. I could not address the chief directly, but only through my herald-interpreter, the District Commissioner; he addressed the chief's herald, who transmitted the conversation to the chief, and answered in a queer pidgin English. He escorted us back to the river, and when I asked him if there were any Christians in the area, replied with a grin, 'Too many – *too* many.' This it appeared signified very many, not an excess.

We had a long paddle downstream in the evening, through beautiful scenery, but scenery swarming with mosquitoes. They must have infected me, for on my return I had a severe attack of malaria – or perhaps yellow fever, for it was accompanied by depressing jaundice – and, as the rest of the Commission were leaving, I had to be put in Mrs Kuti's bed at Abeokuta and later taken to Lagos hospital.

When I recovered, I was flown to Zaria to inspect the Agricultural College, and later catch up with the Commission, who had already reached Kano. Kano, with a mainly Mohammedan population, was then the largest market in black Africa, drawing trade from north, east, west and south. There were jewellers and leather-workers, potters and carpenters, weavers and basket-makers. Raw cotton was being dyed in indigo pits, and bright textiles piled up in little booths, all jumbled together in alleys with stinking drains between them. It was a fascinating microcosm of human activities, of patient and skilful handiwork, answering the needs of a swarming population.

Here too were groups of pastoralists with their handsome cattle; for lack of processing plants, the poor beasts had to be driven hundreds of miles along hot dusty roads to southern markets, where they arrived in a terribly emaciated condition. Yet the craving for animal protein in the non-pastoral south was so great that the practice is, I believe, still in existence. The dry desert heat (over 100°F. in the shade) was almost unbearable to me: and opening the car windows made it worse. But the market folk, in their turbans and long gowns, did not seem to mind.

Higher education seemed indeed a far cry from this bustling and trade-obsessed crowd, ruled by feudal sultans and with only Koranic schools, where the scholars were taught to recite passages from the Holy Book by rote, like so many parrots. They were living in a present threatened on all sides by the mechanized forces of the century, and by the cleverer and better-educated Ibos from the south-east who were taking all the best jobs.

I went to see Fagg, the archaeologist, who in the spoil-heaps of the tin-mines at Nok, some sixty miles away to the east, had discovered palaeolithic tools, and small clay figures with prominent eyelids, open mouths and flaring nostrils of a type unknown elsewhere. They are much earlier than anything to be found in the south, perhaps dating back to the Mousterian epoch, when the climate was much more humid. Were they the humble predecessors of Ife's courtly style? We simply do not know, any more than we know why Ibo female masks have a far-Eastern look.

Then a hot train journey to Enugu, where the Commission spent some time visiting the forest areas. We were taken to see a ritual fertility dance with drummers and dancers armed with swords, ushering in an extraordinary figure rather like a Jack-in-the-Green, but with an enormous mask topped with a beribboned hat like that of Lear's Quangle-Wangle, and a bright quilted suit. This strange symbol of vegetative fertility rotated to the centre of the clearing and then, still spinning, retreated into the secret gloom of the trees.

I also saw an African wood-carver at work. As he was making sacred objects, he had to operate in the hidden depths of the forest. Small idols lay about, destined for household shrines. For a few shillings I bought the effigy of a nude man with elongated neck and a small black hat on his head; it now stands on a shelf in my library, still a tutelary deity, though in a very different kind of household.

Another form of ritual art took the shape of shrines for the secret societies called M'bari, in the form of miniature houses, usually with human figures of painted plaster or wood. These didn't seem to have any sacred character, for some were Negroes with muskets (Portuguese influence here!), others laughable caricatures of moustachioed Englishmen; while in Enugu itself, where Africans had first made acquaintance with the railway, the main juju object was a painted clay locomotive with passengers looking out of its boiler.

All this we saw after being ferried across the mile-wide Niger, into Ibo country. As I write this, the Ibo, having incurred the hostility of other, especially Muslim, tribes for their superior talents and success, and after many had been massacred in the north, have seceded and called their country Biafra. And now many more thousands are being killed and the survivors are starving. What a sad contrast to the happy and busy life we saw in Iboland in 1943, and what a blow to the unity and prosperity of Nigeria, one of the largest countries in black Africa, which now obtains much of its income from the oil wells that can only be reached through Ibo country.

After Enugu we visited Onitsha, a big market town close to the great river. We inspected the local school, and proceeded up country to Awka. Here again there were schools to see, but also much else. There was a tree-orchid in our host's garden; there was a big village with separate compounds for blacksmiths and carvers (both sacred professions); social houses full of ancestral skulls, and a powerful women's society whose members performed a slow ritual dance for us.

Close by we saw some terrible erosion: the road passed the edge of a sandy cliff, which the little stream below had cut to a depth of 800 feet, leaving pyramids of earth standing on its barren sides. The village women had to descend this steep half-mile for water and toil up again with their heavy jars. What was needed here was not only education, but soil-conservation and piped water.

We recrossed the great river to Benin, where we saw the Obah's dilapidated palace (the original, much grander, had been destroyed by the British in the anti-slavery wars a century and a half earlier). There was little left of the best sculptures, for we had pinched most of them for the British Museum, but enough to remind one of their aesthetic value and the elaborate techniques used. The warriors were shown in chain mail, with metal collars up to their chins, and some carrying muskets – here again Portuguese influence had been at work.

From Benin we flew back to Lagos, and then by plane to Accra, capital of the Gold Coast, as Ghana was called before independence.

Accra was terribly steamy and hot, but the moist heat was relaxing, not fierce and sterile like that of the Saharan fringe. Walter Elliot and I were lodged in Government House, an old Portuguese castle, from whose dungeons batches of wretched slaves were ejected into boats which took them to be battened down in the stinking holds of slave-ships bound for American and West Indian plantations. In blaming ourselves for our own share in the slave-trade, we must also remember that the Portuguese started it, in combination with the Arabs, and also that, throughout tropical Africa, chieftains regularly raided their neighbours' and even their own villages for victims to be sold to the slave-traders. But it was certainly one of the most iniquitous human crimes, and one whose repercussions are still continuing, notably in the USA, but also in the UN, where the newly independent African nations cannot forget their humiliation and that of their relatives, the ex-slaves in the Americas.

We went every morning to swim in the sheltered bay, and were surprised to see women picking scraps of charcoal off the surface. They were among many of the local people too poor to buy coal or even wood, for the plains round Accra were so denuded that timber had to be brought from up-country.

The market at Accra was even more colourful than those in Nigeria. The fat market-women were dressed in the most gaudy and magnificent clothes, exchanging saucy remarks with the men, who wore a robe leaving one shoulder bare like a Roman toga, but bright-coloured instead of white, or indigo as in Nigeria. The market-mammies dominated their husbands, held the purse-strings and conducted most of the retail trade. In spite of being illiterate, they had an uncanny memory for their accounts and carried on a very profitable business.

Our first official visit was to Achimota College, which was really a glorified high school. It was presided over by an Englishman who thought in terms of his own Oxford past, and had erected a number of separate 'colleges' with their own dormitories, hall, library and classrooms, so that the students were always tramping from one place to another. However, the standards were reasonably high and we recommended it as the site for a future university, which is now flourishing.

From there we went to Cape Coast, with another Portuguese castle, this time on top of a tall crag. I suddenly realized what was lacking in African scenery – the sight of handsome buildings set in beautiful landscape, so common, and so splendid, in Europe.

Then, with Duff, to Tamale in the arid north. Centuries ago, some local chief had constructed remarkable underground reservoirs, roofed by the hard laterite rock of the surface. The present Ghanaian Government has recently designated this area a National Park to preserve the few remaining lions and antelopes, and allow them to multiply.

After watching an extraordinary performance by robed stilt-dancers, and inspecting the local school, we drove to Navrongo on the border of French Guinea. The agricultural school here was rather primitive, but showed one sign of progress: the wooden wagon wheels, though solid and spokeless, were fitted with rubber tyres, an immense boon in rough country. This was a pastoral area, semi-desert, full of sheep and goats. But the sheep were very small, with large horns, rather like the primitive Soay sheep on St Kilda. Duff remarked that even the Almighty would find it difficult to separate these sheep from the goats!

Next day we pushed down to Kumasi, just within the forest zone, capital of the cruel Ashanti kingdom. (Other West African kingdoms, like Dahomey and Benin, had been equally cruel, but in Ashanti barbarism had survived longer.) The Commission took some evidence from the Asantihene, the hereditary king of Ashantiland, and visited a high school run by the Wesleyans.

Eventually, as a result of our recommendations, it became an Agricultural College attached to the University of Ghana at Achimota.

In the afternoon the Governor, who had come up from Accra, gave a garden party at the residence. It was a wonderful spectacle. H.E. stood on the steps, in full British panoply of gold-braided frock-coat and plumed cocked hat. But the Ashanti chiefs were equally resplendent: borne in litters in their bright togas, with necklaces and bangles and huge rings, all of gold, fanned by their personal attendants, they were the arrogant equivalents of Roman senators.

Ashantiland was still the home of many barbarous practices, including the sacrifice of human victims on the accession of a new king or chief. A member of the Governor's staff told me that when the present Asantihene acceded to his gorgeous throne, there was a mass exodus of 'pagan slaves' from the north, fleeing from possible decapitation. And a very pleasant and well-educated African in Accra, from whom we took evidence, told us that after he had been elected to his chieftainship by the Council of Women (as was the custom in this matriarchal country), he received a deputation of elders bringing thank-offerings of fruit. After the first formalities, they asked that the doors should be locked, and proudly disclosed a human head among the fruit, as earnest of their loyalty...

In Accra, I had been asked by Mrs Meyrovitz, widow of the well-known anthropologist, to look into the question of the gold ornaments of the Ashanti chiefs. She suspected that many of these were being illegally smuggled out of the country, to be melted down and sold by weight. Accordingly, in Kumasi I arranged an interview with an intelligent Lebanese pawnbroker (the Lebanese are the Jews of West Africa), and asked if he had any gold ornaments for sale. After the customary cup of coffee, he produced a big sack bulging with them. I put a few on one side for myself, including a huge and quite fantastic gold ring, representing the sacred bird of war, with miniature culverins on wings and tail, and another charming one of a frog among lotus leaves, a sign of humility, indicating that the owner's home was as humble as the frog's. When I asked their price, he stretched out his hands and said: 'I give them to you, sir.' My British guide whispered that I should offer something in return – and the trader suggested a copy of the *Life and Letters of T. H. Huxley*! I must say that this, from the lips of a Lebanese pawnbroker in a barbarous part of Africa, astonished me. However, my wife secured and sent off a second-hand copy of the work, and I brought home the gold ornaments, fascinating reminders of an old and cruel civilization which is rapidly being westernized. Meanwhile Mrs Meyrovitz took steps to prevent further export.

On the way back we stopped at Bosumtwe, an eerie lake in a forested crater, where no one is allowed to fish or bathe. It doubtless harboured sacred crocodiles, once propitiated by human victims. Crocodiles are the kelpies of Africa, but very real, instead of fabulous.

From Accra we flew on to Freetown, capital of the diminutive colony of Sierra Leone, and seat of a theological college affiliated to Durham University. We didn't think very highly of it, but clearly it could become a full university if funds were available, and we recommended this development.

We had no time to go up-country, but I learnt the interesting geographical fact that a bare 150 miles away were the head-waters of the Niger, which we had seen at the other end of its immense semicircular course of two thousand miles, through Timbuctu and down to Onitsha and the sea.

It was hot, and we went bathing on the sandy beach, a great refreshment for our tired and sweaty bodies. Stranded on the sand were a number of Portuguese men-of-war, those remarkable colonial jellyfish provided with sail-like pneumatic floats and vicious stinging cells on their immensely long tentacles, which contract to bring their poisoned prey to the collective mouth of the creature – a cluster of food-grabbing polyps below the floats. I took one up to examine it, but was so badly stung by the tentacles that a painful red weal was left on my hand, and I developed a temperature which lasted a couple of days.

The Commission was divided on the question of siting: should there be a single university for all British West Africa, or one in each of the three colonies? The majority favoured the latter course, but Channon and I thought that higher standards could be reached, despite the difficulties of travel, by concentrating on a single institution. The majority view prevailed and universities were set up at Freetown, Accra and Ibadan. I was soon proved wrong – so great was the demand for higher education that not only did these three main territorial universities flourish, but several others have since been set up, including those at Kumasi, Zaria, Lagos and Nsukka beyond Enugu (today, I fear, destroyed in the Biafran war).

Looking back, I think the British Government were exceedingly courageous and far-sighted over colonial higher education. During the worst part of the war they sent out four commissions on the subject – not only ours, but others to East Africa, the Caribbean and Malaysia.

My own impression of West Africa was one of great vitality, especially among the women, who (except in the Moslem north) enjoyed much greater freedom than those in East Africa, and exercised considerable commercial and political power.

This vitality also extended to its culture; as I have already pointed out, the variety and abundance of their sculpture and painted plaster and wood decoration was prodigious, far beyond anything to be found in East Africa. Even the little bronze weights used in Ghana for weighing gold-dust were miniature works of art, sometimes extremely fetching.

Another fact was that, both in the south and the Moslem north, there had been a long tradition of firm government, sometimes cruel, but well organized and capable of adaptation to modern ideas and conditions, if only tribal rivalries could be overcome.

Finally (and here in agreement with East Africa) there was a growing demand for more and better education and more opportunities for travel, especially as the 'Been-to's' – Ghanaian pidgin for men who had 'been to' Europe or America – had a better chance of securing a rich wife and interesting employment than the stay-at-homes.

Now it was time for us to return. But first we stopped at Dakar to see what the French were doing. They too were setting up university colleges in their various colonies, and at Dakar they had also built a splendid museum of West African art attached to the local university: it contained huge masks crowned with antelope horns, more extravagant than any in British territory. It was under the charge of Professor Theodore Monod, who, it was said, enjoyed nothing better than travelling across the Sahara on camelback, with plenty of books in his saddle-bags. He was a real polymath, who had studied African geology, archaeology, biology, art and linguistics. Much later, in 1965, he was chosen, on my and Worthington's suggestion, as a member of the UNESCO mission to report on nature conservation in Ethiopia.

At Dakar, too, we went for a swim. Here the sandy shore was alive with long-legged racing-crabs, *Ocypoda*: they rushed in and out of the surf like tiny shore-birds, brandishing their huge claws, their eyes held up on long protruding stalks. They could run sideways faster than a man, and it was only by a combined operation that two of us managed to catch one.

Our final stop was at Rabat, from whose port Robinson Crusoe set off when he escaped from his slavery. It was beautiful weather: there were storks' nests on the buildings, with the birds clapping their beaks at each other in greeting, and old mosques and mysterious *souks* to see. But I felt miserable as a result of my attack of fever, and also perhaps because of my forced resignation from the Zoo, having now to face earning my living as a free-lance. I got home yellow with jaundice and deeply depressed. I was put to bed and couldn't attend the final meeting of the Commission, which reported in favour of three separate universities.

My illness became a real ordeal, and on the advice of my old friend and pupil, Dr Russell Brain, now a leading neurologist, I was moved to the London Hospital. However, the blitz was at its worst, and one large flying bomb fell on a corner of the building. The inmates had to be evacuated, and I was taken in an ambulance to a private nursing home near Harrow Weald. It became clear that I was in for a serious breakdown, aggravated by the hepatitis which I had contracted in West Africa. Sir Philip Manson-Barr was called in, and cured me of that, but the breakdown was more difficult. Electric shock through the brain had been recommended by Russell Brain, but it was before the days when patients were first anaesthetized, and the shock produced violent epileptiform convulsions. So Juliette had to sign a form accepting possible broken bones and dislocations. She was deeply anxious, and only signed at Brain's insistence.

I shall never forget the doctor's eyes peering into mine as he fixed the electrodes on my skull, nor the horrible moment of threshing about before I fell into unconsciousness. However, the treatment did me good, though to this day nobody really understands why electro-shocks should help in depressions; probably they wipe out memory-traces of the predisposing incidents. In any case they do affect memory – it takes over a month before it is fully restored. After three weeks or so I was able to go for little walks, accompanied by a nurse, or by Juliette, who came out regularly to see me; and in the evenings I was able to join the doctor and his wife and other patients for bridge.

At last the weary time was over, and I went home in January 1945 to convalesce. We stayed for a month at Dartington, where the Elmhirsts put a small set of rooms in the peaceful courtyard at our disposal; then another three weeks at Northallerton, staying with a kind, understanding friend, Mrs Philippa Pease.

I had bought a number of books on West Africa before I went out, and intended to write a book on the subject, as a companion volume to my *Africa View*, which dealt with East Africa. I enjoyed reading them, but to plan and write a book of my own was more than my energy could cope with: the project had to be abandoned.

It was a long time before I felt fully fit again. What really cured me was an extraordinary and stimulating visit to the USSR.

CHAPTER XIX

Russia 1945

To celebrate the Academy of Sciences' bicentenary, which coincided with the end of the war in Europe, the Soviet Government had invited a party of scientists in which I was included.

We flew direct to Leningrad, there to be taken on the usual round of visits to galleries and museums, and also to a big steel works where sentries were posted to prevent the escape of political prisoners working there – something we had never seen in 1931.

And, of course, there was a banquet, again with over-abundance of food and drink in spite of war's aftermath of famine. Once more the half-starved interpreters collected the abundant left-overs to take back to their hungry homes.

The train journey to Moscow was lovely. It was April, and all the spring flowers were out. Wherever we stopped, delegations of notables greeted us with addresses of welcome and bouquets.

In Moscow there was still a black market (as in England and in France, but worse). There was also a great deal of overcrowding, after the terrible destruction of the war; but the Russians had managed to do a great deal of building, and were starting on an enormous (and hideous) prefabricated erection which became the new University of Moscow.

We were duly taken to see the house where Lenin died, out in the forest, now preserved as a national monument. I was astonished by its resemblance to the planters' houses I had seen in Louisiana, made of white-painted timber with covered verandas and galleries extending right round the building. I don't know if the Russians had copied the American model or if the style was independently evolved to cope with the summer heat.

We visited the Volga canal, where more political prisoners were working, and were taken to see another national monument, Tolstoy's country house at Yasnaya Polyana. It was just like a scene from *War and Peace*: the great meadows with peasants hay-making, and the big manor built in the old Russian style. Among the exhibits I found a letter from my great-uncle Matthew Arnold, then Chief Inspector of Schools in Britain, inviting Tolstoy to come over and see something of our educational system. I don't know if the invitation was accepted, but the letter was a strange link between the exuberant Tolstoy and my critical and poetical Victorian relative.

We were flown south to Georgia to see new sanatoria and medical clinics, and the free provision made for workers on their annual holiday at the seaside. It was a striking example of socialized medicine and recreation: but I must confess that what impressed me most was the sight of a tribesman from the Caucasus, outlandishly dressed, dismounting from an electric tram with a lance in his hand! – proof that the Government were still tolerant of local custom and variety in the congeries of separate communities that made up the vast Soviet Union.

I much wanted to meet Lysenko, the agricultural inspector who followed Michurin in claiming that the effects of grafting were inherited and that other treatments of individual crop-plants were permanently impressed on later generations (see page 201). This, of course, was biological nonsense: many experiments had shown that new characteristics acquired during the life-time of an organism, whether plant or animal, are not passed on by heredity. Lysenko, however, was a deluded fanatic. He proclaimed that he and Michurin were the protagonists of a new 'Soviet' science of heredity, and that the well-tested neo-Mendelism of all other civilized countries was 'bourgeois genetics', and therefore wrong. He had pushed his case so forcibly at a couple of National Congresses of the Academy of Agricultural Science, and later at a general Congress of the Communist Party, that Michurinism became the accepted genetic creed of Russian biology and agriculture.

It was he who had engineered the downfall of Vavilov, in spite of all that that great and practical scientist had done for Russian agriculture by introducing new strains of cereals, produced by Mendelian methods of crossing and subsequent selection. He had then stepped into Vavilov's shoes as President of the Academy of Agricultural Science and Director of the All-Union Institute of Plant Industry, was decorated with the Order of Lenin, and even for a time became a Vice-President of the Supreme Soviet.

I had pressed for an interview with Lysenko, at first without success, when I was suddenly informed that he would give a public lecture next morning at the Academy (a typical example of Russian muddle). I went to listen, accompanied by Eric Ashby, a distinguished plant geneticist who was British scientific attaché in Moscow, and later Master of Clare College, Cambridge. He had seen Lysenko previously, and was convinced that his 'improved' types of tomatoes, allegedly produced by cross-grafting, had been carefully selected from a number of less valuable strains to demonstrate the success of Michurin's methods, especially as they were only exhibited in the form of wax models. He also pointed out that Lysenko had omitted to make adequate control experiments, or test the validity of his results by statistical methods.

At the lecture we were given a very good woman interpreter, trained in biology. The same tomato wax models, and others of improved potatoes, all allegedly built up by the inheritance of beneficial treatment, were duly produced, with much gesticulation, and also samples of improved winter wheat which Lysenko claimed to have produced by exposing the parent strain to low temperatures over several years.

Then he launched forth into a bitter tirade against 'bourgeois' theories of heredity, talking nonsense about plants and animals 'assimilating' new characters into their make-up, by a process analogous to digestion, when given new kinds of fertilizer, or when grafted on to a superior stock, and denying that there were any special organs of heredity such as chromosomes.

At one point our interpreter's translation was interrupted by a burst of laughter from the large and distinguished audience. When we asked her what this was all about, she told us that Lysenko had been mocking at the fact (or hypothesis, as he called it) of dominant and recessive Mendelian characters and their segregation after crossing. Dominance, he said, was due to the 'digestion' of one 'heredity' by another, and as for segregation of recessive characters in the second generation after a cross between two varieties, he explained that in terms of his former metaphor: 'We know in our own persons that digestion is not always complete. What happens then? We belch. So-called Mendelian segregation is nature's belching!'

From this, and from his remarks during our private discussion with him later, it was clear that he was scientifically illiterate, and had not even troubled to look at the scientific papers by the rest of the world's geneticists, but was merely asserting his own extraordinary beliefs. It was interesting, though maddening, to see a real fanatic, a Savonarola of science, in operation. It seemed that Stalin believed in him absolutely because he promised quick results, granting him all he asked for and supporting his persecution of dissident biologists.

Lysenko was indeed a strange and disturbing phenomenon in the twentieth-century world of science. In 1948 the Praesidium of the USSR gave a pledge 'to root out unpatriotic, idealist, Weismann-Morganistic ideology', claiming that 'Michurin's materialistic direction in biology is the only acceptable form of science, because it is based on dialectical materialism and on the principle of changing nature for the benefit of the people'. I wrote a letter to Britain's chief scientific journal, *Nature*, saying that these announcements 'demonstrate that science is no longer regarded in the USSR as an international activity of free workers whose prime interest it is to discover new truths and facts, but as an activity subordinated to a particular ideology and designed only to secure practical results in the interests of a particular national and political system'. In a further letter to *Nature*, A. V. Hill, the noted physiologist and Nobel prizeman, wrote that 'Russian geneticists are torn by faction about the application of dialectical materialism to genetics'. He added that while solid achievement had no doubt been made by Russian scientists, 'it would be easier to recognise it and give credit if it were not overlaid by fraud and propaganda'.

J. B. S. Haldane, eminent in the application of mathematics to evaluate genetical results, was deeply involved in the controversy.

Finally, after valiant efforts to justify Lysenko's science by Lysenko's practical aims, he resigned his Communist Party ticket in 1950. Lysenko's repudiation of all statistical control was the final straw that broke his allegiance.[1]

In 1949 I wrote a book on *Soviet Genetics and World Science* in defence of 'that freedom of the intellect which we fondly imagined had been laboriously won during the past three or four centuries'. 'Michurinism,' I wrote in my Preface, 'as their form of genetics is called, is largely based on ancient superstitions which the advance of scientific knowledge has left behind: in any event, it is less a branch of science comprising a basis of facts, than a branch of ideology, a doctrine which it is sought to impose upon facts.'

It was not till well on in the fifties that we learnt that Lysenko had been demoted and his theories no longer accepted, though, so great had been his power, he retained the directorship of the Agricultural Institute. But only for a short time: the latest rumour was that he had been taken to a lunatic asylum.

The dead hand of the past, the denial of freedom of expression and the socialist ideal of immediate appeal to the common people, combined with dislike of Western nations and the novelties they were producing, were also evident in music and other arts. Shostakovich was abused, and writers like Sholotov and Zoschenko were treated as criminals.

The return to the past was apparent even in opera and ballet. When our delegation were treated to a night at the opera, we found that there was nothing on its programme except well-tried three-act ballets from the nineteenth century, nothing modern either in choreography or music. We saw *Swan Lake*: it was technically a splendid performance, and I was enthusing over it to my neighbour, Henri Laugier, a left-wing French delegate, who was a great connoisseur in such matters. 'Yes, of course,' he said, 'but I am getting rather tired of fossil ballet.'

[1] Michurinism attempted to justify the belief that a few generations of improved material and educational conditions would lead to a *genetical* improvement in the Russian people's physical and mental make-up, whereas Haldane was well aware of human genetic inequality, and that only by some form of eugenic selection could man's innate capabilities be slowly raised.

Not long afterwards, the Moscow Opera daringly commissioned Prokofiev to produce a modern ballet. This was too much for the authorities (Stalin, in the old Imperial box, asked angrily where all the tunes had gone), and Prokofiev and other 'modern' musicians and writers were disciplined by the Party: they were 'out'.

Meanwhile the time for our departure drew near. We had heard rumours of another banquet but, typically of Russian bureaucracy (and possibly for security reasons), it was not announced till the afternoon of our last day.

It was as lavish as the one in Leningrad – even more so, because the hors d'oeuvres and toasts lasted for an hour and a half instead of a mere hour: never have I seen so much caviare and vodka, and there was even a boar's head among the appetizers. I took advantage of the admirable Russian custom of changing places during dinner, to cut in at the Maiskys' table. He had been recalled from his ambassadorship in London and had so far miraculously escaped the occupational dangers of those with Western contacts. While I was talking to him, a Russian scientist came over to present Madame Maisky with a large bouquet he had simply taken from his own table!

When I got back to my own place my neighbour, R. H. Tawney, the economist, was laboriously spelling out the next item on the programme. 'What *does* it mean,' he said, 'something about beautiful soldiers?' I happened to know that *beautiful* in Russian is synonymous with *red* – the Red Square really means the Beautiful Piazza – and suggested that it meant a performance by a Red Army troupe. And so it was. An army band came on stage, with singers and tumblers, turning somersaults, doing the splits and bouncing about on bent knees in traditional Cossack fashion.

It was a tremendous spectacle; but Stalin sat immobile in his chair just below the stage, never even turning his head to look at the performance. This immobility was characteristic of the man; but I was surprised by his physique. He had thin sloping shoulders, instead of the robust, broad-chested look he acquired by putting on his military greatcoat.

Even on this festive occasion he was jealously guarded. I wanted a word with Ashby, whose seat was nearer Stalin than mine. As soon as I began to walk towards him, I was courteously but firmly escorted back by a 'waiter', doubtless a member of the security police.

The banquet, with its innumerable toasts, dragged on till after midnight. We were rushed back to our hotel, and put on the plane at four o'clock. On the approach to London Airport I looked down to see my own house. I can boast of having been one of the few people to have dined with Stalin in the Kremlin one night, and had tea with my wife in Hampstead next afternoon.

We had read about the terrible purges of old Party members carried out by Stalin, including the torture and forced 'confessions' of fine men like my old acquaintance Bukharin, and the still more terrible persecution of the kulaks, the rich 'bourgeois' farmers and landowners, in which many million people had died in labour camps or as exiles in the Arctic climate of Siberia. But little of this was apparent to foreign visitors. The only evidences of tyranny were the stricter security precautions surrounding Stalin, the armed guards at the prisons and factories, the way in which we were kept away from all contacts with the common people (whereas in 1932 I had wandered freely all over Moscow without hindrance) and of course the ideological tyranny exercised by men like Lysenko, not to mention the stiffening of the Soviet attitude to so-called bourgeois art and literature.

I had realized on our first visit that Russia was an empire: now it had become imperialist, with a ruthless coterie at its head, determined to stamp out all dissent, whether political or ideological. Marxist-Leninism had become a dogmatic religion, with 'Socialist Realism' as its theological basis, and, like all dogmatic religions, had turned from reform to persecution.

Later in that summer of 1945, I was put on the Hobhouse Committee on National Parks for England and Wales. Max Nicholson, permanent secretary in the Lord President's office, was responsible for setting it up and had chosen an excellent team, including Sir Arthur Hobhouse as chairman, a wise and witty county magistrate with much experience in local administration; Leonard Elmhirst, with his knowledge of Dartmoor, of his own planned estate, and of the problems of access to wild country; Pauline Dower, the strong-minded daughter of Sir Charles Trevelyan in Northumberland; Professor Tansley of Cambridge, the leading plant ecologist in Britain; myself, with general biological knowledge and experience of national parks in Africa; Clough Williams-Ellis, and one or two others, with Max himself as secretary. Hobhouse was responsible for the National Parks side, while I was made chairman of the Ecological Committee, which dealt with the problems of nature reserves and general ecological damage—and its prevention.

After formal meetings in London we set out on a round of visits to possible sites for parks and reserves. We went to the Yorkshire dales and Pennine moors and saw the wonders of Malham Cove, with its underground stream issuing from the bottom of a great cliff (very like the source of the Adonis River in Lebanon), and Cauldron Snout, with its waterfall tumbling down a wild gorge, almost as precipitous as the narrow defile I later saw at Petra, debouching into a charming area of greensward where picnickers were enjoying themselves. From the Roman Wall we descended, via the Brecon Beacons, to Pembrokeshire, where I stayed with Lockley, and poor Hobhouse and the rest had to be put up in the house of an old lady who kept a pack of smelly Corgi dogs.

I remember a triumphal moment. Just after mentioning that I had earlier seen a Montagu's harrier in the district, one of this same rare species flapped away from our car – emphasizing the need for preserving this wild area and its wonderful bird life.

I never got round to Snowdonia, nor to the Lake District, because of my work on the UNESCO Preparatory Commission; but I already knew these areas well.

This experience introduced me to new aspects of Britain's scenery, more varied than that of any country of comparable size. The Committee eventually recommended the creation of six large National Parks, including the unique coastal park in south Pembrokeshire, and the creation of nearly a hundred nature reserves of biological interest, besides so-called areas of natural beauty, where access and commercial development were restricted. The success

of the commission encouraged me to go ahead with a similar scheme
on a multi-national basis when I was at UNESCO – the International
Union for the Conservation of Nature—IUCN for short.

In August, Juliette was able to go to Neuchâtel to see her mother,
her first visit after six years of anxious wartime; and I accompanied
her. Switzerland was like paradise after our war experience –
economically and industrially flourishing, a glittering island of peace,
saved from aggression or invasion by her well-armed neutrality.

During our stay we heard of the dropping of the first atomic
bomb on Hiroshima, which marked the end of the war in the Far
East. It was, to us personally, a great relief, as our son Francis was
then in Australia on a warship preparing for the invasion of Japan.
The bomb itself, however, deeply jolted our moral conscience, and
when, shortly afterwards, I was invited to an enormous meeting at
Madison Square Garden in New York, to speak on the future of
this terrifying weapon, I accepted at once.

The dangers were obvious enough – indeed, later developments
have become so appallingly destructive that we have reached an
uneasy truce of mutual terror. But I had discussed its possible peaceful uses with Professor Bernal, the eminent physicist who lived
close to us in Hampstead; and we had agreed on various points:
excavation for dams; moving of earth to create new reservoirs for
irrigation; melting the polar ice-caps to free new land and ameliorate
the climate (though this would have the disadvantage of raising the
sea-level by over a hundred feet, and flooding areas like north-east
India and Holland, as well as eroding many coasts); and above all its
employment to generate electric power, which has now passed
from theoretical possibility to established fact. So I had plenty of
ammunition for my speech.

Behind the scenes I met other participants, notably Danny Kaye,
the charming comedian, always ready to support a good cause;
and also that phenomenal creature, Helen Keller, who was struck
with complete blindness and deafness at a few years of age. She had
been brought out of this total immurement by a gifted woman who
enabled her to communicate by spelling out sign language on her
hand – and even taught her to speak, though the complete deafness

to the sound of her own voice made her utterance harsh and difficult to understand. Helen Keller was a very intelligent woman, with indomitable courage; she had won a college degree, and travelled all over the world in unending efforts to improve the condition of people deprived as she was.

She still relied largely on touch: when she asked if she might stroke my face I felt slightly embarrassed, but was delighted when she said: 'I am so glad to know you, you *feel* just as I thought you would!' I later met her in Florence, where I was attending a UNESCO conference, and heard how she was taken by Joe Davidson, the American sculptor who had done a fine bust of her, to 'see' the famous Michelangelo group in the Medici chapel. She climbed on to an improvised scaffolding, and caressed the statues in such an appreciative way that it brought tears to the eyes of the attendants; Joe told us later that he had never understood so well the beauty of great sculpture as when he saw her discovering it for herself through her sensitive fingers.

I must say that making a speech in Madison Square Garden with a spotlight focused on oneself, and 10,000 people listening in the semi-dark, was a nerve-racking ordeal. But after a few sentences, I somehow *felt* that my audience was with me, and everything went off well.

As one result of the meeting, the Committee of Atomic Scientists was formed, which has since done much valuable work in publicizing both the dangers of atomic bombs in war, and the useful harnessing of atomic energy for peaceful purposes.

Late in the previous year, 1944, I had attended a meeting in London which decided to transform the League of Nations' Institute for Intellectual Co-operation into a more elaborate agency of the new UN, to deal with the international aspects of education and culture, UNECO for short.

This, though I never guessed it at the time, was destined to affect drastic changes in my life. But I must leave to my next volume the story of the addition of science to the new organization's field of action, so giving it the abbreviated title UNESCO, and of my association with it.

Index

Index

Index

Hughes, A. L. 99
Humanity (nude torso by E. Gill) 239
Hutchinson, Mary 148
Huxley, Aldous 30, 31, 32, 33, 38, 43, 47, 50, 54, 55, 58, 65, 66, 67, 70, 107, 114, 120, 121, 147, 149, 160, 212, 213, 217, 259
Huxley, Anthony Julian 126, 139, 142, 223, 224, 229, 244, 250
Huxley, Francis John Heathorn 139, 141, 229, 244, 250, 289
Huxley, Gervas, 75
Huxley, Harry 15, 97; family of 74, 75
Huxley, Henrietta Anne (Gran'moo-Moo) 23, 26
Huxley, Julia (*née* Arnold) 17–22, 215; death of 70
Huxley, Julian, childhood 20–8; relationship with brother Trev 20–1; early interest in nature 27; early boyhood 29–40; at Hillside School 32–4, 41; birdwatching 33, 56, 84, 103, 131, 217; at Eton 41–59; relationship with K. 46, 68, 69, 70, 74, 102; Zoology scholarship to Balliol (1905) 52, 61, 84; first love affairs 54; at Oxford 60–75; studying biology in Germany 60–1, 96; interest in poetry 65; study of protozea 66, 80; the Newdigate Prize (1908) 67, 68; visits to Switzerland 69, 227–9, 243–4; B.A. First Class 73; awarded the Naples Scholarship 76; in Naples 76–83; experimentation with cells 79–80; work on zooids 81–2; study of sea-urchins 81–2; publishing first paper on bird courtship 85; formally engaged to K. 85; offered Chair of Biology at Rice Institute 85; vists to America 90–5, 211; working with Hertwig 97; breaking engagement with K. 97; nervous breakdowns 97–8, 124, 153, 279–80; at Rice Institute (1913) 98–100, 103; at Houston 103–19; during World War I 115–17; learning Italian 115; marriage 120–1; Fellowship at New College (1918) 121; on honeymoon 122–3; scientific studies of bird display 123; axolotl experiments 126, 137; first son born (1920) 126; awarded the Kalinga Prize 127; with Oxford University Expedition to Spitsbergen 128–34; Professor of Zoology at King's College, London 147; advocating birth-control 150–2; the Lasker Award (1956) 151; compiling *Science of Life* with H. G. Wells and G. P. Wells 155–78; break with H. G. Wells 173; joining the Society for Psychical Research 174; experiences with spiritualism 175–7; in East Africa 179–96; educational mission in East Africa 181–2; pleading for game reserves in East Africa 196; first President of the Association of Scientific Workers 197; lecture tours in the USA (1930) 197, 211; first visit to Russia 199–213; with PEP (Political and Economic Planning) 210–11; research on Sabella 221–2; experiences with zoos 227–9; Secretary of the Zoological Society 230–1, 233, 262; at Whipsnade and

London Zoo 230–48, 249–57, 261–4; preparation for a book on evolution 236–7; furthering the cause of the Arts 240–3; as head of UNESCO 242–3, 253, 288, 289; trip to the Hebrides 245–7; organizing a War Aims group 250–1, 255; publishing under the pseudonym Balbus 255–6; teaching in America (1941) 256; in West Africa 266–80; visit to Russia, 281–90; on the Hobhouse Committee 287–9
Huxley, Juliette 117, 122, 123, 124, 126, 134, 138, 139, 140, 141, 143, 145, 159, 160, 165, 167, 171, 173, 174, 176, 179, 192, 195, 199, 206, 209, 211, 221, 223, 224, 227, 231, 234, 243, 249, 260, 261, 263, 264, 280, 289
Huxley, Leonard, career of 13–15; death of (1933) 214; friendship with George Eliot 14–15
Huxley, Margaret 30, 32, 37, 71
Huxley, Maria (*née* Nys) 147, 160, 212
Huxley, Mathew 160, 212, 213
Huxley, T. H. 13, 15, 22, 26, 28, 74, 76, 92–3, 98, 155; influence of Darwin on 13, 14; unveiling the statue of (1901) 47
Huxley, Trevenen 19, 20, 21–23, 26, 30, 34, 39, 40, 43, 64, 69, 70, 85, 89, 122; breakdown of 101; suicide of 102

Individuality (J. Huxley) 170
Irwin, Will 171

James, Philip 241
Jekyll, Miss 43
Jekyll, Timmy 43
Jenkinson, J. W. 66
Joad, Professor 251
John, Pope 151
Jones, Sir Roderick 149
Jourdain, Rev. F. C. R. 128, 129, 130
Jowett, B. 215
Joynson-Hicks, Sir William 166–7

K., relationship with Julian Huxley 46, 68, 69, 70, 74, 75, 97, 102
Kaye, Danny 289
Keeble, Lady 140, 171, 172
Keller, Helen 289, 290
Kellogg, Norman 113
Kennington, Eric 239
Keun, Odette (H. G. Wells's mistress) 165–6, 168
Kingsley, Charles 22, 30, 218
Knatchbull-Hugessen 42, 60
Knox, Ronnie 44, 45, 53, 64, 65
Koch, Ludwig 236
Korda, Alexander 219
Korsah, K. A. 266
Kotelianski 148
Kuti, Mrs 271

Lady Chatterley's Lover (D. H. Lawrence) 160
Lamarckism 201, 202, 253
Lamb, Charles 35

Index

Index

Index

Ward, Dorothy 38
Ward, Humphrey 17
Ward, Janet 20–4, 38–9, 117
Ward, Mrs Mary Humphrey 16, 18, 19, 37, 38, 83, 85, 153, 168
Warde-Fowler (ornithologist) 138, 139
Warre, Edmund (Headmaster of Eton) 48, 53
Warre-Cornish (vice-Provost of Eton) 48
Water Babies, The (C. Kingsley) 22–30, 218
Watt, Watson 265
Weaver, Warren 257
Webb, Sydney 196
We Europeans 216
Wegener, A. 133, 134
Weight, Carel 255
Well of Loneliness, The (R. Hall) 166
Wells, Frank 171
Wells, G. P. 171; compiling *Science of Life* with H. G. Wells and Julian Huxley 155
Wells, H. G. 149, 151, 259; compiling *Science of Life* with J. Huxley 155–78; illness and death of 173–4
Wells, Jane 159
White, Gilbert 138

Whitridge, Arnold 92
Wiener, Norbert 100
Wilberforce, Bishop 73
Wild Lives of Africa (Juliette Huxley) 179, 192
Williams, Mrs Hanbury 166
Williams-Ellis, Clough 288
Williams-Freeman, Agnes 58
Wilson, E. B. 91
Wilson, H. V. 79
Wilson, President 114
Winant (US Ambassador) 265
Wood, Anthony 125
Woolf, Virginia 148

Yacovlev (Head of Agriculture in Russia) 202
Yeats, W. B. 148
Ylla 236
Young, Geoffrey 117
Young, Hubert 51, 212
Young, Stark 100

Zoschenko, M. 285
Zuckerman, Solly 265
Zvegintzov 210, 250